AAT

Technician Level 4

Unit 10
Managing Accounting Systems

Textbook

1035/J01

FOULKS*lynch*

British Library Cataloguing-in-Publication Data

A catalogue record for this book is available from the British Library.

Published by Foulks Lynch Ltd
Number 4
The Griffin Centre
Staines Road
Feltham
Middlesex
TW14 0HS

ISBN 0 7483 5103 5

Printed and Bound in Great Britain by Ashford Colour Press, Gosport, Hants.

Acknowledgements

CONTENTS

PREFACE – USING THIS TEXTBOOK

This is the new edition of the AAT NVQ textbook for the Revised Standards for Unit 10 – Managing Accounting Systems.

It has been written to cover the Revised Standards in great detail and adopts a brick-building style, building up the knowledge or practical skills required in a carefully constructed manner. At the start of each chapter we identify the underpinning information and performance criteria covered and then list the main topics covered to show how the subject matter is built up.

These textbooks are written in a way that will help you assimilate information easily and give you plenty of practice at the various techniques involved. A practical approach has been taken with the inclusion of many simulations and examples to illustrate clearly and precisely how the various techniques work.

Particular attention has been paid to producing an interactive text that will maintain your interest with a series of carefully designed features, which may include:

- **Introduction.** Each chapter starts by outlining the relevant part of the Standards of Competence covered within that chapter. The chapter structure and coverage of key learning areas are also outlined and, where appropriate, we show you how the chapter builds on the content of earlier chapters.

- **Definitions.** The text clearly defines key words or concepts. The purpose of including these definitions is not that you should learn them by rote, but to help focus your attention on the point being covered.

- **Brick-building approach.** Each topic is developed slowly and carefully, with clear explanations and illustrations to build your understanding.

- **Activities.** This text involves you in the learning process with a series of activities designed to capture your attention and enable you to concentrate and respond.

- **Step-by-step illustrations.** Where appropriate, we illustrate topics using a step-by-step technique that explains how each part of an operation or answer is performed in a logical way.

- **Conclusions.** Where helpful, the text includes conclusions throughout the chapter that summarise important points as you read, rather than leaving the conclusion to the chapter end. The purpose of this is to summarise concisely the key material that has just been covered to enable you to continually monitor your understanding of the material as you read it.

- **Self-test questions.** At the end of each chapter there is a series of self-test questions. These have been included to help you revise some of the key elements of the chapter. The answer to each is a paragraph reference, encouraging you to go back and re-read and revise that point.

Complementary workbook

The complementary workbook contains numerous practice questions and simulations that reflect and simulate the workplace environment. It also includes practice assessments which will prepare you for the assessment procedures that are part of your course.

SYLLABUS

UNIT 10: MANAGING ACCOUNTING SYSTEMS

UNIT COMMENTARY

What is the unit about?

This unit relates to the co-ordination of work activities within the accounting environment. The unit focuses on responsibility for the planning and monitoring of work activities as well as dealing with contingencies and any problems and queries. The monitoring and review of accounting systems and the prevention of fraud within the system are contained within the unit.

Elements:

10.1 Co-ordinate work activities within the accounting environment

10.2 Identify opportunities to improve the effectiveness of an accounting system

10.3 Prevent fraud in an accounting system

Content	*Chapter where covered*
KNOWLEDGE AND UNDERSTANDING	
The Business Environment	
• The range of external regulations affecting accounting practice (Elements 10.2 & 10.3)	Throughout
• Common types of fraud (Element 10.3)	13
• Implications of fraud (Element 10.3)	13
Management Techniques	
• Scheduling and planning methods (Element 10.1)	5, 6
• Time management (Element 10.1)	5, 6
• Methods of measuring cost effectiveness and systems reliability (Element 10.2)	9, 10
• Quality management, quality circles (Element 10.2)	9
• Methods of detecting fraud (Element 10.3)	13
Management Principles and Theory	
• Principles of supervision (Element 10.1)	4, 8
• Principles of human relations, team building, staff motivation (Element 10.1)	4, 8
The Organisation	
• Understanding that the accounting systems of an organisation are affected by its organisational structure, its MIS, its administrative systems and procedures and the nature of its business transactions (Elements10.1, 10.2 & 10.3)	1, 9, 10, 11, 12
• Overview of the organisation's business and the critical external relationships (customer/clients, suppliers, etc.) (Elements 10.2 & 10.3)	2, 3, 11
• Purpose of the work activity and its relationship with other related work activities (Element 10.1)	2, 6
• Organisation of the accounting function; relationship between the accounting function and other departments; structure of the accounting function (Elements 10.2 & 10.3)	1, 11, 12

Element 10.1 Co-ordinate work activities within the accounting environment

	Performance Criteria	***Chapter where covered***
i.	Work activities are planned in order to optimise the use of resources and ensure completion of work within agreed timescales	1, 3, 4, 5, 6
ii.	The competence of individuals undertaking work activities is reviewed and the necessary training is provided	4, 8
iii.	Contingency plans to meet possible emergencies are prepared with management and, if necessary, implemented within agreed timescales	5
iv.	Work methods and schedules are clearly communicated to all individuals in a way which assists their understanding of what is expected of them	4, 5, 8
v.	Work activities are closely monitored in order to ensure quality standards are being met	3, 7, 9
vi.	Work activities are effectively co-ordinated in accordance with work plans and any contingencies that may occur	6
vii.	Problems or queries concerning work activities are identified and either resolved or referred to the appropriate person	8

Range Statement

1. **Work activities**: within the accounting function
2. **Plan includes**: computer security routines; absence cover; contingency plans for changes in work patterns and demands

Evidence Requirements

- Competence must be demonstrated consistently over an appropriate timescale, with evidence of performance being provided of candidates co-ordinating work activities within the accounting function

Sources of evidence (these are examples of sources of evidence, but candidates and assessors may be able to identify other, appropriate sources)

- **Observed performance, eg,**
  - Meetings / discussions with colleagues
  - Ongoing working relationships with colleagues
  - Training sessions designed and delivered
- **Work produced by candidate, eg,**
  - Schedule and plans of accounting staff activities and accounting functions work activity
  - Contingency plans
  - Staff work briefings
  - Training materials designed
- **Authenticated testimonies from relevant witnesses**
- **Personal accounts of competence, eg,**
  - Report of performance
- **Other sources of evidence to prove competence or knowledge and understanding where it is not apparent from performance, eg,**
  - Reports and working papers
  - Performance in simulation
  - Responses to verbal questioning

Element 10.2 Identify opportunities to improve the effectiveness of an accounting system — *Chapter where covered*

Performance Criteria

		Chapter where covered
i.	Weaknesses and potential for improvements to the accounting system are identified and considered for their impact on the operation of the organisation	3, 8, 9, 10
ii.	Methods of operating are regularly reviewed in respect of their cost-effectiveness, reliability and speed	7, 9
iii.	Recommendations are made to the appropriate people in a clear, easily understood format	1, 4, 8
iv.	Recommendations are supported by a clear rationale which includes explanation of any assumptions made	1, 4, 8
iii.	The system is updated as in accordance with changes in internal and external regulations, policies and procedures	3, 7, 9

Range Statement

1. **Recommendations** : verbal; written

2. **Accounting system** : one section of an accounting system

---

Evidence Requirements

- Competence must be demonstrated consistently, over an appropriate timescale with evidence of performance being provided of candidates making recommendations to improve the effectiveness of the accounting functions

---

Sources of evidence (these are examples of sources of evidence, but candidates and assessors may be able to identify other, appropriate sources)

- **Observed performance, eg,**
  - Meetings / discussions with colleagues
  - Meetings / discussions with external specialists
  - Presentations relating to improvements in the accounting system

- **Work produced by the candidate, eg,**
  - Schedule and plans for implementing changes
  - Specifications for accounting system
  - Reports containing details of the likely impact of changes on cost, reliability and speed of the system

- **Authenticated testimonies from relevant witnesses**

- **Personal accounts of competence, eg,**
  - Report of performance

- **Other sources of evidence to prove competence or knowledge and understanding where it is not apparent from performance, eg,**
  - Reports and working papers
  - Performance in simulation
  - Responses to verbal questioning

Element 10.3	**Prevent fraud in an accounting system**	***Chapter where covered***

Performance Criteria

i.	Existing systems for preventing fraud are evaluated and compared with examples of best practice	13
ii.	Past examples of control avoidance are analysed and used to inform evaluations of the controls within the system	13
iii.	Areas of potential fraud within the control avoidance accounting system are identified and the risk graded	13
iv.	Areas of concern and weakness within the system are reported to management	1, 13
v.	Possible methods of avoiding the risks and safeguarding the system are identified	13
vi.	Recommendations for the prevention of fraud are made to the appropriate people	13

Range Statement

1. **Examples of best practice** : within the organisation; outside the organisation
2. **Recommendations** : verbal; written
3. **Accounting System** : one section of an accounting system

Evidence Requirements

- Competence must be demonstrated consistently over an appropriate timescale, with evidence of performance being provided of candidates identifying potential areas of risk within an accounting system and suggesting potential solutions

Sources of evidence (these are examples of sources of evidence, but candidates and assessors may be able to identify other, appropriate sources)

- **Observed performance, eg,**
  - Meetings / discussions with colleagues relating to fraud prevention
  - Meetings / discussions with external specialists relating to fraud prevention
  - Presentations relating to improvements in the accounting system to prevent fraud
- **Work produced by the candidate, eg,**
  - Schedule and plans for implementing changes
  - Specifications for accounting system
  - Report containing details of the ways to prevent fraud
- **Authenticated testimonies from relevant witnesses**
- **Personal accounts of competence, eg,**
  - Report of performance
- **Other sources of evidence to prove competence or knowledge and understanding where it is not apparent from performance, eg,**
  - Reports and working papers
  - Performance in simulation
  - Responses to verbal questioning

Chapter 1
WRITING REPORTS

PATHFINDER INTRODUCTION

This chapter covers the following performance criteria and knowledge and understanding

- Understanding that the accounting systems of an organisation are affected by its organisational structure, its MIS, its administrative systems and procedures and the nature of its business transactions (Elements 10.1, 10.2 & 10.3)
- Organisation of the accounting function; relationship between the accounting function and other departments; structure of the accounting function (Elements 10.2 & 10.3)
- Work activities are planned in order to optimise the use of resources and ensure completion of work within agreed timescales (Element 10.1)
- Recommendations are made to the appropriate people in a clear, easily understood format (Element 10.2)
- Recommendations are supported by a clear rationale which includes explanation of any assumptions made (Element 10.2)
- Areas of concern and weakness within the system are reported to management. (Element 10.3)

Putting the chapter in context – learning objectives.

Unit 10 Managing Accounting Systems requires that you write a report, detailing how you will manage a given accounting system to improve its efficiency, both in terms of its own efficient operation, and in terms of how it impacts on other areas of your organisation.

It is therefore essential that you know precisely how to lay out such a report and present it to management. This is a valuable skill to have, as no doubt you will be writing many more reports throughout your career.

At the end of this chapter you should have learned the following topics.

- The key features of a report
- The format of the body of the report
- The format of the conclusion of the report
- The format of a summary of the report
- The use of tabulation, graphs and diagrams to clarify and emphasise the report's content

1 EFFECTIVE BUSINESS COMMUNICATION

1.1 Introduction

A report can range from a verbal explanation through to a many-paged complex document. In this chapter the basic skills of writing a report are to be considered and these can then be applied to whatever the situation that is given, and specifically your management report.

Definition A report is a form of business communication, written in the third person, designed to convey efficiently information requested, in the terms of reference.

1.2 Object of the report

The object of the report is communication. The reason for writing the report may be to:
Inform – by simply gathering the information and packaging it into a report.

Analyse - by gathering the information and presenting that analysis in a report.

Evaluate - by evaluating the information so that the reader can make a decision as a direct result of reading the report.

Recommend – the report writer might be charged with the task of making a recommendation for a future course of action.

Describe - the writer might have witnessed an accident or have been asked to investigate how a specific job of work was progressing and to produce a report noting his or her observations.

1.3 Types of report

A report can take on a variety of different forms:

Formal or informal reports – a report to the board of a company analysing the potential profitability for a new product might be in the form of a large formal document incorporating large amounts of detail such as marketing information and competitor product detail. However, a report to a manager explaining how an employee dealt with a problem customer yesterday may well be a simple memorandum on a single sheet of paper.

Routine and special reports – routine reports may be produced on a regular basis eg, weekly sales reports and annual labour turnover and, because they are often statistical in nature, may require diagrammatic, tabulated or graphical data. Other reports may be one-off or special reports and commissioned on an ad-hoc basis eg, the effect of computerisation or the level of employee wage rates.

Reports for an individual or a group – the report might be commissioned by an individual such as the sales manager (effectiveness of advertising report) or it could be requested by the board of directors (balance sheet and profit and loss accounts).

Internal or external – most reports are for use within the organisation but there may be situations where a report for an outside organisation is required eg, a grant awarding agency.

Confidential – these are usually of a more formal nature, following a formal layout and must be clearly labelled as confidential.

1.4 Activity

From the following examples of reports decide whether they would be classed as general reports or reports addressed to either the manager of the production department or the marketing and sales department managers.

Financial reports (eg, Balance sheets and profit and loss accounts)
Idle time reports
Machine downtime reports
Advertising reports (eg, costs, effectiveness)
Shift reports (eg, units produced, materials used, hours worked)
Sales order reports
Material usage reports
Maintenance reports
Customer complaints reports
Cash reports (ranging from daily to monthly)
Rejection/scrap reports

1.5 Activity solution

Production reports – addressed to the manager of the production function responsible:

- idle time reports;
- machine downtime reports;
- shift reports;
- material usage reports;
- maintenance reports;
- rejection/scrap reports;

Marketing and sales reports - addressed to the managers of marketing and sales:

- advertising reports;
- sales order reports;
- customer complaints reports.

General reports:

- financial reports;
- cash reports.

Conclusion

Reports vary in length and status from simple printed forms, such as accident reports, to the major investigative reports commissioned by government. Five different functions that reports can serve have been identified. They are:

- informing
- analysing
- evaluating
- recommending
- describing

2 PLANNING A REPORT

2.1 Introduction

Like any piece of written work it is essential that any report is properly planned. When planning a report there are a number of factors that should be considered.

2.2 Aim of the report

In order to make a report effective, it is obviously important that the aim of the report is clearly understood by the report writer. One way of ensuring that the aim is clear is to set out the following statement and then complete it:

'As the result of reading this report, the reader will...'

There are a number of possible aims that could be established such as:

- '... agree to authorise the project.'
- '... take the necessary action.'
- '... make a decision.'

2.3 Checklist for planning

The following additional points are the sort that should be considered when planning a report:

- who commissioned the report and who is to use the report? It may be that there are a number of different users of the report with different needs, levels of knowledge and levels of understanding;

- what information does the user of the report require?

- what background information does the user of the report already have?

- what type of report would best suit the subject matter and the user?

- what is required in the report: information only or judgement, opinions and recommendations?

- what is the time scale of the report?

- what is the cost budget for preparation of the report?

- what is the format to be used ie, should there be appendices, graphs, diagrams etc.?
- what detailed points will need to be made in the body of the report?
- is the report confidential?

2.4 Principles of report writing

Once the bare bones of a report have been sketched in the planning stage, the report will need to be written in detail. When writing any type of report it is worth bearing in mind a few stylistic points:

Layout of the report – information is not only conveyed by the contents but also by its design and presentation. The overall impression is important.

Size of the report – diagrammatic, tabulated or graphical illustrations might make the data clearer and emphasise key facts and figures but will obviously add to the bulk of the report. Care should be taken not to waste managers' time by making a report overly long.

Logic of argument – the report should be clearly structured into sections under relevant headings so that the main topic of the report is clearly set out, developed and explained, and the subsequent conclusions fully supported.

Writing style – a formal report is written in the third person eg, 'you will be able to see that..' becomes 'it should now be clear that..' but simple reports in memo, letter or report format concerning day to day problems tend to be from and to people who address each other informally. The writing style tends to be more personal, using I, we and you.

Language – a report should communicate as quickly, as easily and as precisely as language will permit. There are a number of points to note:

- avoid abbreviations, slang, jargon, acronyms, foreign phrases and colloquialisms (a Scot may use 'wee' in speech but should use 'little' in writing);
- never use a long word where a short one will do;
- prefer the active to the passive voice (more important for informal reports) eg, 'a receipt was issued by the shopkeeper' (passive) should be written 'the shopkeeper issued a receipt';
- shorter sentences can improve clarity;
- use words economically eg, 'in short supply' can be replaced by 'scarce';
- avoid clichés ('explore any avenue'), ambiguity (For sale – bull dog. Eats anything. Very fond of children) and split infinitives (I want to fully understand you);
- choose the right word – some words are eagerly seized, such as blueprint, escalation, ceiling and target, while their predecessors – plan, growth, limit and objective, remain discarded;
- replace longer words with shorter. Can you think of short words for *perception*, *initiate* and *utilise*? It might be easier to use *view*, *start* or *use*.

Objectivity – Even if the report is to inform rather than reach any conclusions it is important that it appears to be written from an objective point of view ie, is unbiased and impartial. Any emotive or loaded wording should be avoided at all costs.

2.5 Activity

Our language is cluttered with phrases that are best replaced by shorter expressions. Try to replace the following with one word.

In the near future
Along the lines of
In short supply
At this moment in time
Prior to
In very few cases
With regard to / in connection with
A number of

2.6 Activity solution

In the near future - soon
Along the lines of - like
In short supply - scarce
At this moment in time - now
Prior to - before
In very few cases - seldom
With regard to / in connection with - about
A number of - several

Conclusion

Unless your aim is to confuse, you have an obligation to be clear.

When writing reports try to replace long words with shorter, simpler ones. Avoid jargon, acronyms, slang and ambiguity.

Jargon, as described in the Penguin dictionary of troublesome words, may be defined as 'the practice of never calling a spade a spade when you might instead call it a manual earth-restructuring implement'.

3 KEY FEATURES OF A REPORT

3.1 Introduction

Reports can take many forms and can vary in length and status from:

- simple reports in memo, letter or short report form;
- fixed format reports such as accident reports;
- reports on internal matters within a company which may be formal or informal
- formal reports such as the findings of public enquiries

Knowing what to leave out of a report is as important as knowing what to put in. You must consider the user of the report and ask yourself the following questions:

- Who is the user?
- How much background information does the user have?
- Why did the user commission the report?
- How much technical or business knowledge does the user have?
- What does the user wish to get out of the report?

3.2 General structure of a report

All reports, whether short or long, formal or informal, need the basic structure of beginning, middle and end:

The **beginning** should determine:

- what the document is about
- the relevance for the reader

The **middle** should contain:

- the main analysis
- the detailed argument supporting your conclusions, recommendations or proposed action.

The **end** should tell the reader:

- what will happen or what you want them to do
- conclusions and recommendations

3.3 Structure of a formal report

Structure is very important. The report will be used for reference so readers need to be able to find the information they need quickly and easily. Formal written reports usually contain the basic sections listed below, though there are slight variations, and sometimes differences of heading.

Title page:

- Addressee or circulation list– the person or persons receiving the report should be identified. At this stage it would be worth stating clearly if the report is to be treated as confidential.

- Date - the date of issue of the report should be stated.

- Name of author(s).

- Title –should give a good idea of the subject of the report, without being too long. It should be easy to find in a filing system.

- Author's position and department.

- Name and address of organisation.

Index - many reports will be quite extensive and will include not only the main report but also appendices. The contents page should provide an overview with a list of headings and sub-headings and their page numbers.

Summary or Synopsis - the major uses of summaries are to:

- help readers decide whether to read the whole report
- enable readers to see the key points
- focus attention on the aim of the report

Write the summary after the report is finished. As a rough guide it should be about 10% of the length of the report and should only contain material found in the main report. It will include:

- a brief statement of the problem investigated;
- a summary of relevant main points, but mainly concentrating on the conclusion;
- an outline of any recommendations.

Conclusions and recommendations – a brief summary of any conclusions reached and any recommendations made regarding further actions.

Main Body of the report – the content and length will depend on the type of report. It should have informative headings for each section and sub-section. The sections include:

- Introduction – will state the main topic of the report and give background factual information explaining any limitations on the report eg, confidentiality or time. You may also be required to give terms of reference.

- A fuller statement of the problem.

- How it was investigated and what was discovered – there is usually a paragraph that explains or identifies the methods of investigation or research used. When other sources of information have been used in writing the report, they can be acknowledged here.

- The results or findings

- An analysis, discussion and interpretation of the results.

Conclusion to the report - a summary of the points made in the main body and of the findings, showing briefly but clearly how they are logically derived from the reasons and supporting evidence presented in the main part of the report. The recommendations, if required, can be included with the conclusions or treated separately and should recommend a certain line of action in accordance with the conclusions reached.

Appendices – are used to present detailed information (numerical, graphical or tabular) that supports the arguments, findings or conclusions of the report and which is of interest but either too technical or too peripheral for most readers of the report. They may also include documentation (letters) or computer programs for facts presented in the report. The contents of the appendices will be referred to in the main body of the report.
NB. Your project word count allocation of 3000-4000 words does not include the index or appendices.

References - must contain a list of books or articles that have been consulted, if the report has required it. When referring to information from these sources in the body of the report, they must be acknowledged by means of a referencing system. The list of references needs the following details:

- Books: - Author, Title, Publisher, Edition (unless 1st), Place of publication, Date, Chapter, and page number if relevant.

- Journals: - Author, Title, Journal, Volume, Number, date and page number if relevant.

Conclusion

All reports will have the basic structure of a beginning, a middle and an end. The possible elements of a report are as follows:

- Title page with addressee, date, title and author
- Index
- Summary
- Conclusions and recommendations
- Main body of the report
- Conclusion to the report
- Appendices
- References

4 WRITING A REPORT - EXAMPLE

4.1 Introduction

In this paragraph the process of writing a report will be considered step by step using an example. The information required for the report will be given and then each of the main elements of the report will be produced.

4.2 Example information

Given below is a five year summary of the financial results of a division of your organisation. You are required to write a report explaining, analysing and highlighting these results. The report is to the Employee Representatives Committee of that division and should make particular reference to the part played by wages costs over the period.

Information is also supplied showing the organisation's overall summarised profit and loss account for 2000.

Five year summary - Division

	2000 £'000	*1999* £'000	*1998* £'000	*1997* £'000	*1996* £'000
Turnover	1,000	1,200	900	750	700
Production materials	440	500	400	350	300
Wages	310	300	220	170	150
Selling costs	100	100	80	70	60
Administrative costs	40	50	46	44	20
Profit	110	250	154	116	170

2000 Summarised profit and loss account - organisation

	£'000
Turnover	9,400
Production materials	4,500
Wages	2,000
Selling costs	700
Administration costs	600
Profit	1,600

4.3 Steps to report writing

Step 1 Headings - the first step is to show the addressee of the report, its date, who it is from and its title.

REPORT

To: Employee Representatives Committee
From: Accounts Clerk
Date: 12 March 2001
Subject: Divisional financial performance 1996 to 2000

Step 2 Main body of the report - it is now necessary to write the main body of the report, although this will appear after the summary and conclusion. However the summary and conclusion cannot be written until after the main body of the report.

In order to write the report it will often be necessary to further analyse the data given and prepare tabulations. Such analysis and tabulations will be presented in an appendix to the report.

(1) **Purpose of report**

This report has been commissioned to provide analysis and explanation of the division's profits from 1996 to 2000 for the division's Employee Representatives Committee.

(2) **Information**

The explanation and analysis provided in the report is based upon summarised profit and loss information for the five years from 1996 to 2000 together with the overall organisation's results for the year 2000. This information has been summarised and tabulated in Appendix 1 to this report.

(3) **Annual turnover**

Over the last five years annual turnover has increased from £700,000 to £1,000,000, an increase of 43% over the period. There was however a peak of £1,200,000 in 1999 but this fell to £1,000,000 in 2000.

(4) **Annual profit**

The annual profit has however decreased over the period both in absolute terms and as a percentage of annual turnover. The 2000 profit of £110,000 is only 11% as a percentage of turnover. This compares particularly unfavourably to a 21% profit in 1999 and 24% in 1996.

(5) **Annual costs**

The percentage of turnover represented by each of the major cost classifications is given in Appendix 1. This illustrates the areas of cost that have altered significantly during the five year period. Most of the costs have remained reasonably constant as a percentage of turnover over the period with the exception of the wages cost that has risen significantly.

(6) **Wages costs**

The wages costs, as a percentage of turnover, have increased from 21% in 1996 to 31% in 2000. The increase was fairly steady from 1996 to 1999 but then jumped from 25% in 1999 to 31% in 2000. This increase seems to have played a major part in the reduced profit percentage over the period discussed above.

(7) **Divisional and organisation wage costs**

The final table in Appendix 1 compares the costs classifications for the division and the organisation as a whole for 2000 in terms of their percentage of turnover. This shows that all of the cost categories for the division, with the exception of wages, have been reasonably in line with the overall organisational cost. However whereas wages for the organisation as a whole totalled 21% of turnover (2000 ÷ 9400 x 100%) in 2000, for the division the relevant percentage was 31%.

APPENDIX 1

Five year summary - division - costs as a percentage of turnover

	2000	*1999*	*1998*	*1997*	*1996*
	%	%	%	%	%
Turnover	100	100	100	100	100
Production materials	44	42	44	47	43
Wages	31	25	24	23	21
Selling costs	10	8	9	9	9
Administration costs	4	4	5	6	3

Five year summary - division - profit as a percentage of turnover

Profit £'000	110	250	154	116	170
Profit	11%	21%	17%	15%	24%

2000 - division and organisation - costs and profits as a percentage of turnover

	Division		*Organisation*	
	£'000	%	£'000	%
Turnover	1,000	100	9,400	100
Production materials	440	44	4,500	48
Wages	310	31	2,000	21
Selling costs	100	10	700	8
Administration costs	40	4	600	6
Profit	110	11	1,600	17

Step 3 Write the report conclusion - the conclusion of this explanatory report is that the divisional profits have significantly decreased over the last five years and that this is largely due to a disproportionate increase in wages costs.

Step 4 Write a report summary - this report has summarised, in Appendix l, the profit and loss account information for the division for the years 1996 to 2000. This has shown a significant decrease in divisional profit over the period and the figures indicate that a major cause of this loss of profitability is a disproportionate rise in the level of wage costs. The wage costs for the division, as a percentage of turnover, were also compared to those of the organisation as a whole and again the wage costs for the division seem to be disproportionately high.

Step 5 Prepare any necessary graphs or diagrams - at this stage it is necessary to consider whether there are any alternative ways in which the information in the report might be usefully presented, for example by using graphs or other types of diagrams.

In this instance it might be interesting to plot a graph, for example, showing total turnover, wage costs and profit for each of the five years for the division. Another useful diagram might be a pie chart illustrating the differing proportions of cost classifications in the division and organisation as a whole. This information would be shown in Appendix 2.

Step 6 Produce the full report - the final step is to put all of the elements of the report together as one package. This might also include an index to indicate the contents of the report.

REPORT

To: Employee Representatives Committee
From: Accounts Clerk
Date: 12 March 2001
Subject: Divisional financial performance 1996 to 2000

Index

Summary
Conclusion
Report
Appendix 1
Appendix 2

SUMMARY

This report has summarised, in Appendix 1, the profit and loss account information for the division for the years 1996 to 2000. This has shown a significant decrease in divisional profit over the period and the figures indicate that a major cause of this loss of profitability is a disproportionate rise in the level of wage costs. The wage costs for the division, as a percentage of turnover, were also compared to those of the organisation as a whole and again the wage costs for the division seem to be disproportionately high.

CONCLUSION

The conclusion of this explanatory report is that the divisional profits have significantly decreased over the last five years and that this is largely due to a disproportionate increase in wages costs.

REPORT

(1) **Purpose of report**

This report has been commissioned to provide analysis and explanation of the division's profits from 1996 to 2000 for the division's Employee Representatives Committee.

(2) **Information**

The explanation and analysis provided in the report is based upon summarised profit and loss information for the five years from 1996 to 2000 together with the overall organisation's results for the year 2000. This information has been summarised and tabulated in Appendix 1 to this report.

(3) **Annual turnover**

Over the last five years annual turnover has increased from £700,000 to £1,000,000, an increase of 43% over the period. There was however a peak of £1,200,000 in 1999 but this fell to £1,000,000 in 2000.

(4) **Annual profit**

The annual profit has however decreased over the period both in absolute terms and as a percentage of annual turnover. The 2000 profit of £110,000 is only 11% as a percentage of turnover. This compares particularly unfavourably to a 21% profit in 1999 and 24% in 1996.

(5) **Annual costs**

The percentage of turnover represented by each of the major cost classifications is given in Appendix 1. This illustrates the areas of cost that have altered significantly during the five year period. Most of the costs have remained reasonably constant as a percentage of turnover over the period with the exception of the wages cost that has risen significantly.

(6) **Wages costs**

The wages costs, as a percentage of turnover, have increased from 21% in 1996 to 31% in 2000. The increase was fairly steady from 1996 to 1999 but then jumped from 25% in 1999 to 31% in 2000. This increase seems to have played a major part in the reduced profit percentage over the period discussed above.

(7) **Divisional and organisation wage costs**

The final table in Appendix 1 compares the costs classifications for the division and the organisation as a whole for 2000 in terms of their percentage of turnover. This shows that all of the cost categories for the division, with the exception of wages, have been reasonably in line with the overall organisational cost. However whereas wages for the organisation as a whole totalled 21% of turnover in 2000, for the division the relevant percentage was 31%.

APPENDIX 1

Five year summary - division - costs as a percentage of turnover

	2000	*1999*	*1998*	*1997*	*1996*
	%	*%*	*%*	*%*	*%*
Turnover	100	100	100	100	100

Production materials	44	42	44	47	43
Wages	31	25	24	23	21
Selling costs	10	8	9	9	9
Administration costs	4	4	5	6	3

Five year summary - division - profit as a percentage of turnover

Profit £'000	110	250	154	116	170
Profit	11%	21%	17%	15%	24%

2000 - division and organisation - costs and profits as a percentage of turnover

	Division		*Organisation*	
	£'000	%	£'000	%
Turnover	1,000	100	9,400	100
Production materials	440	44	4,500	48
Wages	310	31	2,000	21
Selling costs	100	10	700	8
Administration costs	40	4	600	6
Profit	110	11	1,600	17

APPENDIX 2

At this point appropriate graphs and charts would be included.

5 WRITING A REPORT - ACTIVITY

5.1 Introduction

In this final session of the chapter you will be required to write a report step by step. Firstly the information required will be given and then you will be required to produce each of the main elements of a report.

5.2 Activity information

You are an accounts clerk in a division of a manufacturing organisation which makes and sells three products. The marketing department has commissioned some market research indicating the mix of sales that could be achieved by changing the selling prices and/or quality of the products.

There are two scenarios that have been proposed:

(1) to increase the price and quality (therefore also cost) of product C. This however will mean a drop in sales quantity.

(2) to cut the price but not the quality of product B in order to increase the number of units sold.

The results of this market research are summarised below.

You are required to prepare a report for the marketing manager summarising the financial implications of the findings of the market research.

MARKET RESEARCH FINDINGS

	Selling price per unit	*Cost per unit*	*Number of units sold*
Current year (2000) sales and costs			
Product A	£20	£15	10,000
Product B	£50	£34	2,000
Product C	£5	£3	40,000
Proposal 1 - Estimated sales 2001			
Product A	£20	£15	10,000
Product B	£50	£34	2,000
Product C	£8	£5	30,000
Proposal 1 - Estimated sales 2002			
Product A	£20	£15	12,000
Product B	£50	£34	3,000
Product C	£8	£5	32,000
Proposal 2 - Estimated sales 2001			
Product A	£20	£15	10,000
Product B	£44	£34	4,000
Product C	£5	£3	40,000
Proposal 2 - Estimated sales 2002			
Product A	£20	£15	12,000
Product B	£44	£34	6,000
Product C	£5	£3	44,000

5.3 Activity solution

Step 1 Prepare the headings for the report.

Step 2 Write the main body of the report

Step 3 Write the conclusion to the report.

Step 4 Write the summary to the report.

Step 5 Prepare any graphs or diagrams that might help to illustrate the data.

In this case perhaps a compound bar chart might be used to show the number of units of each product to be sold under current conditions and each of the two proposals. These bar charts would shown in Appendix 2.

Step 6 Put the entire report together in its correct order, possibly with an index.

REPORT

To: Marketing Manager
From: Accounts Clerk
Date: 24 January 2001
Subject: Market research into sales price and mix

Index

Summary
Conclusion
Report
Appendix 1

Appendix 2

SUMMARY

This report summarises the financial effects of the two alternative marketing proposals regarding selling price and cost per unit of each of the three products. The estimated profit to be achieved under each of the proposals is shown in Appendix l. Each of the proposals shows an estimated profit in 2001 and 2002 that is greater than the current 2000 profit. The effect of each proposal on the number of units of each product sold is indicated in Appendix 2.

There are however a number of limitations to the market research information that makes a full analysis impossible to perform.

CONCLUSION

From the information given in the market research there would appear to be little difference in the financial effects of the two proposals. Both proposals show an increase in profit over 2000 although there is no indication to indicate the 2001 and 2002 profit level if neither of the proposals were adopted.

REPORT

(1) **Purpose of the report**

This report has been commissioned by the marketing manager in order to assess the financial implications of the market research that has been undertaken. The market research concerned the selling price, cost and number of units of each of our products estimated to be sold in 2001 and 2002 under two possible alternative proposals.

(2) **Information**

The information provided by the market research indicates the estimated selling price, cost per unit and number of units to be sold of each of the three products in 2001 and 2002. These estimates are given for two independent proposals as follows:

Proposal 1

- to increase the price and quality (therefore also cost) of product C. This however will mean a drop in sales quantity.

Proposal 2

- to cut the price but not the quality of product B in order to increase the number of units sold.

The information provided also gives the current year (2000) details for the selling price, cost per unit and number of units sold. This is before any alternative marketing strategies are considered.

(3) **Annual profit**

In Appendix 1 the market research has been tabulated to show the estimated profit for 2001 and 2002 under each of the two proposals. The actual profit for 2000 has also been shown.

(4) **Effect on profit**

The overall effect on the profit for 2001 and 2002 under both proposals is that there will be an increase over the current 2000 profit figure. Proposal 1 gives a marginally higher profit in 2001 and Proposal 2 a marginally higher profit in 2002.

(5) **Effect on market share**

The effect on changes in market share for each product beyond 2002 cannot be established from the information given. However it would appear that if Proposal 1 were adopted there would be a dramatic decrease in the number of Product C units sold in 2001 followed by a small increase in 2002.

If Proposal 2 were chosen then the figures would indicate a remarkable strengthening of demand for Product B in both 2001 and 2002. However there is no indication whether this increase in sales could be sustained.

An illustration of the effect on the unit sales is given in Appendix 2.

(6) **Limitations of the information**

As well as the limitations mentioned above regarding unit sales beyond 2002 there is one further limitation of the market research that should be highlighted at this stage.

There would appear to be no information available regarding the unit sales for 2001 and 2002 if neither proposal were adopted. In order to fully assess the proposals suggested it would be necessary to compare the profits under each proposal to the profits that could be achieved if the current situation were to remain.

APPENDIX 1

Current year (2000) profit

	£
Product A (£20 - £15) × 10,000 units	50,000
Product B (£50 - £34) × 2,000 units	32,000
Product C (£5 - £3) × 40,000 units	80,000
	162,000

Proposal 1 - Estimated Profit

		2001 £	*2002* £
Product A	(£20 - £15) × 10,000 units	50,000	
	(£20 - £15) × 12,000 units		60,000
Product B	(£50 - £34) × 2,000 units	32,000	
	(£50 - £34) × 3,000 units		48,000
Product C	(£8 - £5) × 30,000 units	90,000	
	(£8 - £5) × 32,000 units		96,000
		172,000	204,000

Proposal 2 - Estimated Profit

		2001 £	*2002* £
Product A	(£20 - £15) × 10,000 units	50,000	
	(£20 - £15) × 12,000 units		60,000
Product B	(£44 - £34) × 4,000 units	40,000	
	(£44 - £34) × 6,000 units		60,000
Product C	(£5 - £3) × 40,000 units	80,000	
	(£5 - £3) × 44,000 units		88,000
		170,000	208,000

APPENDIX 2

At this point appropriate graphs and charts would be included.

Chapter 2
ORGANISATION

PATHFINDER INTRODUCTION

This chapter covers the following knowledge and understanding.

- Understanding that the accounting systems of an organisation are affected by its organisational structure, its MIS, its administrative systems and procedures and the nature of its business transactions. (Elements 10.1, 10.2 & 10.3)
- Overview of the organisation's business and the critical external relationships (customer/clients, suppliers, etc.) (Element 10.2 & 10.3)
- Purpose of the work activity and its relationship with other related work activitires (Element 10.1)

Putting the chapter in context – learning objectives.

When an organisation has grown too big for control by a single individual it needs a clearly defined structure with specified lines of authority and responsibility if it is to run efficiently. This chapter considers the various types of structure, the factors influencing choice and structure, and the advantages and disadvantages of the alternatives.

At the end of this chapter you should be able to:

- distinguish between differing types of structure;
- understand how organisational structures develop;
- appreciate the significance of the inter-relationships between responsibility, authority, delegation and control;
- design appropriate charts depicting the structures of a number of differing types of organisation;
- understand why and how a periodic review of the structure of an organisation should be undertaken.

1 THE ORGANISATION

1.1 Introduction

The word 'organisation' can broadly be used in two ways. Firstly, it can refer to a group or institution arranged for efficient work (factories, offices and schools). These entities have three characteristics:

- they have people;
- they exist to achieve a given purpose or objectives; and
- they have some form of structure that defines and regulates the behaviour of the people.

Secondly, organisation can also refer to a process ie, structuring and arranging the activities of the enterprise or institution to achieve the stated objectives. A generally acceptable definition of an organisation is:

Definition A social and technical arrangement resulting from a number of people being brought together in various relationships in which the actions of some are planned, monitored and directed by others in the achievement of certain tasks

A football team can be described as an organisation because it has a number of players who have come together to play a game. The team has an objective (score more goals than its opponent) and, to do their job properly, the members have to maintain an internal system of control to get the team to work together. In training they work out tactics so that in play they can rely on the ball being passed to those who are more skilled and can score goals. Each member of the team is part of the organisational structure and is skilled in a different task: - the goalkeeper has had more experience in stopping goals being scored than those in the forward line of the team. In addition, there must be team spirit, so that everyone works together. Players are encouraged to do their best, both on and off the field.

1.2 Classifying organisations

Classifications that highlight similarities and differences among organisations can be based on legal form, ownership, control, size, technology, activity, and many other features.

Legal form - the choices are sole trader, partnership or registered company. Registered companies may be classified according to whether they are limited or unlimited or according to whether they are public or private,

Ownership - may be public (government owned) or private (shareholders).

Control - a sole trader has full control of his/her own business, a multinational has employees controlling on its behalf and publicly owned organisations have regulators sponsored by the government.

Size - the concept of size is problematic. It can be viewed in terms of:

- numbers employed
- volume of output
- volume of sales
- assets employed
- profits earned
- net worth in real terms.

Technology – is the machinery or equipment, along with the associated technique, which is used for carrying out certain tasks. Some organisations eg, mobile telephone manufacturers, have a high technology usage compared to others eg, a window cleaning company.

Activity – the Standard Industrial Classification categorises organisations according to the work they do:

1 Agriculture, forestry and fishing
2 Mining and quarrying
3-19 Manufacturing industries
20 Construction
21 Gas, water and electricity
22 Transport and distribution
23 Distributive trades
24 Insurance, banking and finance
25 Professional and scientific services
26 Miscellaneous services
27 Public administration

Social aspects - historically, it was expected that, no matter who managed an organisation, they had economic responsibilities to operate an efficient and profitable organisation. More recently, however, the trend is to emphasise the social, ecological and ethical responsibilities. This involves considering:

- relations with customers and suppliers;
- attitudes to employees;
- attitudes to both the local and world communities;
- attitudes to the environment;
- the type and quality of product and/or service.

1.3 Classification according to needs

Organisations can be classified according to the particular needs of their members:

(a) Government organisations that satisfy the need for order and continuity - national and local government.

(b) Protective organisations that protect persons from harm - the armed forces, the police, fire and ambulance services.

(c) Economic organisations that provide goods and services in return for some form of payment - sole traders, partnerships, companies and public corporations.

(d) Social service organisations that stand ready to help persons without requiring payment for the service offered - schools, hospitals, parks etc.

(e) Social organisations that serve the social needs for contact with others - sporting clubs for activities such as golf, cricket etc.

(f) Voluntary organisations that satisfy social and welfare needs. However, there are differences between these type of organisation eg, the anti-smoking body ASH advances a cause, and trade unions and employer associations are primarily concerned to advance the material interests of their members.

1.4 Activity

Write a short informal report for a colleague, Mr Brown, classifying the organisation you work for.

1.5 Activity solution

A short informal report generally has only two or three sections. The main areas are:

- the name of the person requesting the report;
- the title;
- an introduction, which might include the background;
- the procedure, information, findings and 'overview' of the problem;
- the name and position within the company of the writer; and
- the date

To: Mr Brown

Classification of Eastern Electricity

Introduction

This report classifies the organisation in terms of its Standard Industrial Classification, legal form, ownership, control, size, technology, activity,

Procedure

The majority of the information was found on the Internet.

Findings

(a) The Standard Industrial Classification, which categorises organisations according to the work they do, is 21: Gas, water and electricity

(b) Legal form - Eastern Electricity is a public limited company and is a subsidiary of the Eastern Group which is one of Great Britain's leading energy companies, and a nation-wide supplier of gas and electricity. The group is part of The Energy Group plc which was formed by the de-merger of Hanson plc in February 1997. The Energy Group plc also includes Peabody Coal, the largest private producer of coal in the world and Citizens Power, one of the leading power marketers in the USA.

(c) Ownership - Eastern Electricity is owned by shareholders. The shares are publicly quoted on the Stock Exchange.

(d) Control - as well as control procedures that are normal within a large company, the privatisation of electricity distribution has been accompanied by the setting up of a regulatory body to oversee pricing and performance, providing a framework of control over their commercial objectives.

(e) Size - Eastern Electricity's area covers, Suffolk, Norfolk, Essex, Bedfordshire, Hertfordshire, Cambridgeshire, part of Buckinghamshire and a large part of North London. It distributes approximately 30 TWh of electricity to over 3 million customers, operating and maintaining the largest electricity network in Great Britain with approximately 89,000km of cable, of which around 53,000km are underground, and approximately 62,000 transforming points.

(f) Technology - Eastern Electricity would be classified as a high technology user. It owns and operates its distribution network system and is continually investing in network improvements and developing a number of innovative techniques for the day-to-day maintenance of the network.

(g) Needs - as a public limited company it is an economic organisation that provides services in return for payment.

Conclusion

Eastern Electricity is a large publicly owned company, which distributes electricity to many customers for profit.

Jo Soper
Trainee accountant
Accounts department

Conclusion Similarities and differences among organisations can be based on legal form, ownership, control, size, technology, activity, needs and many other features.

2 ORGANISATIONAL OBJECTIVES

2.1 Establishing an organisation

The basic steps in establishing an organisation are expressed in general terms:

- deciding on the aims, goals and objectives of the organisation as a whole;
- determine the policies and procedures necessary to attain the aims, goals and objectives of the organisation as a whole;
- outline the responsibility for each policy and procedure area, and the subsequent allocation via the establishment of functional areas;
- allocate responsibilities within each functional area to individuals, and groups of individuals;
- establish formal relationships between functions, and between individuals within those functional areas;
- recognise that, whilst formal relationships exist, there are also informal relationships.

2.2 The aims, goals and objectives

The primary purpose of an organisation is to satisfy the needs of its market or clients. A business will have a hierarchy of aims that will be achieved at different times. If it is to survive it ought to optimise its performance whilst, at the same time, making sure it maintains a system of control to look after the people in the organisation and the environment of which they are part.

The terms 'objectives', 'aims' and 'goals' in everyday language tend to be used interchangeably. The aim of an organisation is sometimes outlined in its mission statement, which could be called the topmost statement in a hierarchy of organisational objectives.

Definition The **mission statement** describes the basic purpose of an organisation, ie, what it is trying to achieve.

The statement can be quite lengthy or short and punchy. Federal Express Corporation's US operation has a short, but powerful mission statement 'Absolutely, Positively Overnight!' Everyone in the company knows what the statement means. Almost nothing more has to be said to ensure that every action of every person is aimed at total customer satisfaction. Goals are derived from the mission.

Definition **Goals** are long-run, open-ended attributes or ends a person or organisation seeks and are sufficient for the satisfaction of the organisation's mission.

Generally, more than one goal statement is required to satisfy the organisation's mission. They are open-ended which means that they are not stated in quantifiable terms, and they have no time-assigned basis.

Definition **Objectives** are time-assigned targets derived from the goals and are set in advance of strategy.

In this unit we will stick with the notion that an organisation's goals are the intentions behind its decisions or actions, and objectives are goals expressed in a form in which they can be measured. An example of a goal is that of Avis:

We want to become the fastest growing company with the highest profit margin in the business of renting and leasing vehicles.

One of the objectives Avis could set to achieve this goal could be: 'To increase our market share for family saloon rentals world wide to 20% within three years'.

For objectives to be of use in practice, they must have three components:

- A characteristic chosen to be measured eg, profit, return on capital, output.
- A scale by which it is to be measured eg, £, %, tonnes.
- A target ie, the level on a scale which it is hoped to achieve £2m, 15%, 60,000 tonnes, 6 months.

2.3 Activity

Write down the three components of the Avis objective identified above.

2.4 Activity solution

- market share
- 20%
- within three years.

Conclusion The organisation's mission statement could be called the topmost statement in a hierarchy of organisational objectives. Goals are derived from the mission and are open-ended, which means that they are not stated in quantifiable terms, and they have no time-assigned basis. Objectives are goals expressed in a form in which they can be measured.

2.5 Range of objectives

Companies have a whole range of objectives. Some are short term, some longer term. Some may be the objectives of a small department, while others may cover the whole organisation. A business will have a hierarchy of aims to be achieved at different times. At the top of the list is survival and, in attaining that, strategic objectives may be defined by the business in the following areas:

- Marketing and market share
- Sales volume
- Production
- Inventory levels
- Financial and human resources
- Profitability
- Research and development
- Social and environmental

2.6 Constraints

Definition A constraint is a factor that restricts the capacity of the system to achieve its objectives.

There are, for example, many constraints that restrict private sector organisations in their quest for profit, including the following:

- scarcity of resources (eg, raw materials, skilled labour, cash);
- technological ability;
- timescale;
- legal constraints;
- the actions of competitors.

Some people regard social objectives - to be responsible employers, to acknowledge social responsibilities and to protect the environment - as constraints rather than objectives. Being responsible employers is seen as a moral constraint, operating above the legal requirements which protects employees' welfare at the expense of profit. However, it is short sighted to regard these social objectives as constraints. Caring for employees or for the environment may reduce short-term profits, but in the long run these approaches help to build a motivated workforce and a loyal customer-base which will improve longer-term profitability.

2.7 Activity

Establish your own hierarchy of objectives. You probably have a career mission, a means of getting there and, by the availability of this course, a means of measuring your progress towards the goal.

3 ORGANISATIONAL STRUCTURE

3.1 Introduction

Whilst many writers refer to the process of organisation and to the organisation of a company, the expression 'organisation' is very much over used, and should be avoided in this context. **Structure** is a far better term, and can be defined as:

Definition **the established pattern** or relationships among the components or parts of the organisation.'

Organisations of many different kinds serve the great variety of our needs in society. Every day you come into contact with organisations, some small, some large, in both the private and the public sectors. You have direct involvement with organisations as a consumer, as an employee or as a student.

Organisations exist because they are more efficient at fulfilling needs than individuals attempting to cater for all their requirements in isolation and without assistance from others. The primary reason for this can be attributed to the ability that organisations have of being able to employ the techniques of specialisation and the division of labour.

3.2 Specialisation and division of labour

Specialisation is perhaps the oldest organisational device. It occurs when organisations or individual workers concentrate on a limited type of activity making it possible to become much more efficient.

Definition Specialisation means that tasks are grouped into jobs or offices where each office has a clearly defined sphere of competence.

By concentrating its expertise into a limited range of activities, the organisation arranges its production to achieve the most efficient use of resources. As organisations grow, there is inevitably pressure towards specialisation. To an extent this pressure comes from the cost advantages which arise. These can include lower training costs, higher performance standards and increased subordinate suitability. At one level this specialisation can be merely individual, but as businesses grow this specialisation extends to groups of employees. Eventually it may become cost-effective to concentrate specialised functions in their own locations.

The key to specialisation involves what is called the 'division of labour'. It is important to note, however, that the excessive use of labour specialisation techniques means that each worker may be restricted to a boring and repetitive job that provides very little satisfaction. The side effect of mass production processes, such as car production, is cited by industrial psychologists as a major cause of industrial unrest, such as absenteeism and unofficial strikes.

3.3 Hierarchy

Modern industrialised economies make great use of specialisation and the division of labour, but for organisations to gain the full benefits of these techniques they also employ another organisational device known as the hierarchy.

Definition A hierarchy in an organisation means there is a firm order in relationships between offices whereby the lower offices are supervised by the higher.

The term hierarchy refers to the distribution of authority, responsibility and accountability within the organisation.

- *Authority*: - the right to exercise powers such as hiring and firing or buying and selling on behalf of the organisation. The authority is with the post holder and not with an individual eg, a cheque signatory who has authority to sign cheques on behalf of the organisation.
- *Responsibility*: - the allocation of tasks to individuals and groups within the organisation.
- *Accountability*: - the need for individuals to explain and justify any failure to fulfil their responsibilities to their superiors in the hierarchy.

The hierarchy is generally outlined in an organisation chart.

Definition Organisation charts are diagrammatic illustrations of the formal relationships and communication flow between positions within an organisation.

The organisation chart shows the formal relationships that exist between positions or offices (levels of responsibility and authority). It indicates positional authority ie the authority to direct the activities of the persons below in the line relationship (who reports to whom). The chart also shows the lines of essential communication.

3.4 Scalar chain and span of control

An essential feature of the hierarchy is that, within the organisation, authority passes downwards, and accountability upwards. The vertical arrangement of direct authority and responsibility is called a 'scalar chain'. Some contemporary writers call this the 'job task pyramid'. The length of the chain is the number of levels of authority and responsibility that constitute the hierarchy.

Another feature of the hierarchy is the number of people who report to any single individual - the span of control. If the job is relatively simple, and most employees in the department are doing the same job, then large numbers can be controlled by one manager or supervisor quite easily. However, if the jobs are complex, fewer people can be supervised effectively. The organisation chart below shows a scalar chain of three - top management, middle management and operatives. It also shows a small span of control - supervisor A and a large span of control - supervisor C.

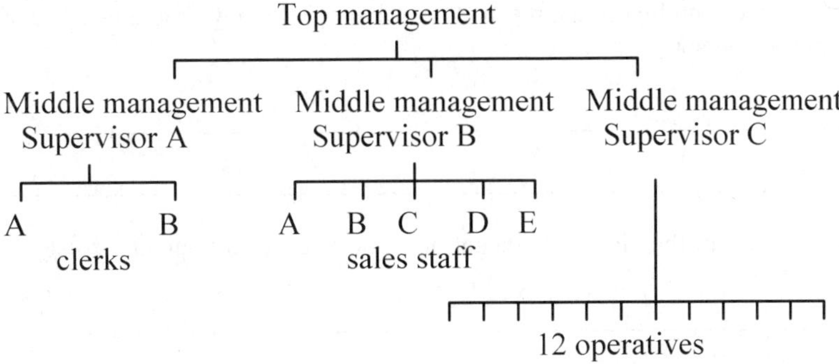
Top management
Middle management Supervisor A
Middle management Supervisor B
Middle management Supervisor C
A B
clerks
A B C D E
sales staff
12 operatives

3.5 Activity

What does the term hierarchy refer to?

3.6 Activity solution

The term hierarchy refers to the distribution of authority, responsibility and accountability within the organisation. For example, a bishop has authority over a diocese, while the range of authority of a local clergyman is confined to his or her local parish.

3.7 Delegation and organisational structure

Definition Delegation is giving someone else the freedom and authority to do a job for which you are accountable.

Delegation is associated with the organisation structure, authority and responsibility. At the top of a typical organisation chart is generally the managing director but we must realise that in most situations, he or she cannot take all the decisions and do all the work. However, subordinates cannot do the work without the necessary authority and power. The chain of delegation in an organisation begins with the shareholders and ends with the operatives who are responsible for the performance of various tasks. This chain is illustrated below with the arrows down showing the delegation:

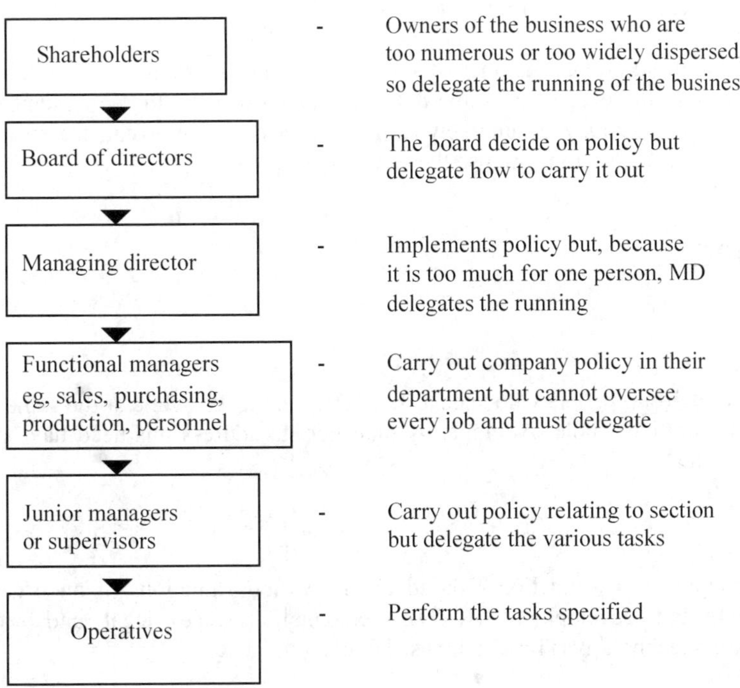
Shareholders
- Owners of the business who are too numerous or too widely dispersed, so delegate the running of the business
Board of directors
- The board decide on policy but delegate how to carry it out
Managing director
- Implements policy but, because it is too much for one person, MD delegates the running
Functional managers eg, sales, purchasing, production, personnel
- Carry out company policy in their department but cannot oversee every job and must delegate
Junior managers or supervisors
- Carry out policy relating to section but delegate the various tasks
Operatives
- Perform the tasks specified

The chain of delegation gives employees the means to resolve or refer any problems or queries regarding work activities to the appropriate person.

3.8 Activity

Do you know where you are in the chain of delegation? Can you go to your immediate superior and ask for help regarding your work?

Conclusion — Authority is the power to carry out a task or duty. Delegation is the passing of authority and/or responsibility to carry out that particular task or duty.

3.9 Centralisation and decentralisation

Another method of analysing structures is by reference to the level at which decisions are made.

- A *centralised* structure is a condition where the upper levels of an organisation's hierarchy retain the authority to take decisions.
- A *decentralised* structure is a condition where the authority to take decisions is passed down to units and people at lower levels in the organisation's hierarchy.

The choice will depend to a certain extent on the preferences of the organisation's top management, but the size of the organisation and the scale of its activities is equally important.

3.10 The development of structure

Even the smallest business has an organisation structure. As soon as a sole trader employs one person, he or she establishes a structure.

- The employee is given certain duties and thereby **a division of activity**, and **a delegation of responsibility** take place.
- As the employee is answerable to his employer a relationship of **accountability** is created.
- As the owner allocates duties there is an element of **direction**.

If it becomes necessary to appoint an additional member of staff the structure is changed. The duties of the original employee may be reduced, to the extent that some duties are taken over by the new member; or the duties may be shared; or the new member may assume new responsibilities. In any event, the structure will change and at some stage, it may be necessary to formalise these relationships.

4 CHOICE OF STRUCTURE

4.1 Introduction

In an organisation there is a need to group people who specialise in different tasks, while at the same time co-ordinating all the activities into a unified whole. Attempts by managers to address this need have produced various forms of organisation structure.

4.2 Grouping by function

The most common form of grouping is by function - based on the various functions of an organisation: production; marketing; research and development (R&D); personnel; finance; legal and secretarial; information processing; information technology (IT); and industrial relations.

Oil companies are sometimes divided in this way with exploration, production, refining, marketing, and finance departments. In a technically complex organisation there is more specialisation of function, as shown in the following hierarchy:

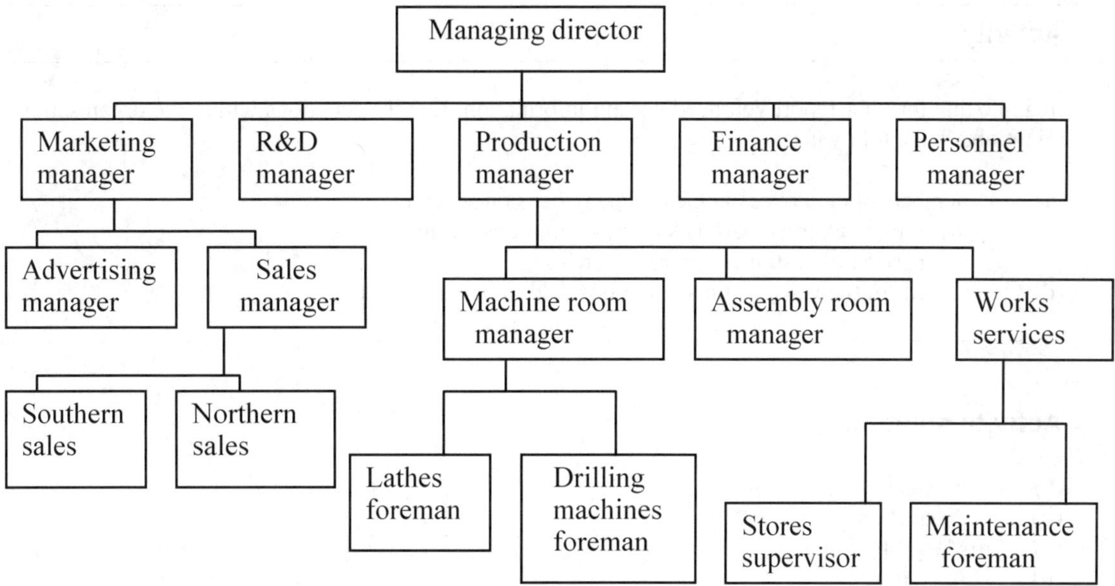

4.3 Grouping by product or type of service

Product or service specialisation is a very popular way of organising activities within departments, especially with large companies that have a wide diversity of products or services. For example, Proctor and Gamble, the manufacturer of household goods, divides its organisational structure between each of the P&G divisions - food products, toilet goods, paper products, packaged soap and detergents, coffee and industrial food.

4.4 Other types of grouping

The way in which the organisation is structured depends on the nature of the business, the number of sites or departments, the number of employees, etc. Most will be grouped by function, product, area or division but other types include:

(a) **Time** - the use of shifts under day and night supervisors or managers.

(b) **Customers or clients** - a solicitor may have departments for conveyancing, criminal work, divorce and probate.

(c) **Geographic location** (territorial)- it may be necessary to site units to provide for the needs or convenience of customers eg the sub-division of banks or estate agents.

(d) **Combination** - many businesses consist of a combination of functional and divisional organisation.

4.5 Grouping by matrix

A matrix can combine functional, product or project grouping. For example, a sales and servicing company could be organised in the matrix of:

	North region	*South region*	*East region*	*West region*
Sales Manager	4 sales staff	6 sales staff	3 sales staff	3 sales staff
Chief service Engineer	14 service engineers	10 service engineers	7 service engineers	8 service engineers

The Sales Manager and Chief Service engineer may be based at Head Office and each region headed by a Regional Manager. The Regional Manager of the North is responsible for sales and service performance in his region. However, the Sales manager is responsible for sales performance throughout the UK. Therefore, neither has sole responsibility and they must co-operate and agree on matters affecting the four sales staff.

4.6 Activity

Imagine that for your report you need certain information. List the functions within the organisation where you might obtain the following:

(a) numbers of employees in the company pension scheme;
(b) levels of stock (raw materials held) - volume not value;
(c) comparison of customer orders by territory;
(d) records of the value of finished goods sold in the last month.

4.7 Activity solution

(a) Personnel.
(b) Production.
(c) Marketing/Sales.
(d) Accounts.

Conclusion Specialisation is the basis on which all structure is founded. The basis for the structure may be by:

- function;
- product or type of service;
- geographical location;
- division or group

5 ORGANISATION REVIEW

5.1 Introduction

An organisation review may be undertaken as a specific exercise or as part of a larger project. For example, many large companies often combine an organisation review with a study of management information systems, where changes in the system often require changes in the way things are organised.

Organisation reviews can be undertaken with a small section of a department, a group of units or for the company as a whole. Organisation at section level (for example, bought ledger, sales ledger, costing department) in a company might form part of an organisation and methods (O & M) review with the primary aim of work simplification or cost reduction

5.2 Influencing factors

The existing structure of any organisation may have been the result of careful planning or it may have evolved informally. Factors that may have influenced the present structure include:

- management style;
- type of products and services offered and the nature of the inputs required, for example capital or labour intensive;
- degree of centralisation and/or the location of premises;
- type of skills required and the various characteristics of the employees;
- nature of past growth, for example, by acquisition;
- past approach to organisational matters, such as manpower planning or career development;
- impact of technological developments;
- type of financial ownership.

5.3 Review

Any shortcomings in the structure are likely to be well hidden. This is not because managers deliberately hide such matters but merely that structures are not often carefully planned. It is more likely to be the result of external factors such as the markets in which the firm operates and/or the personal idiosyncrasies of top management. In addition, many so-called business problems often have underlying causes that are more closely related to organisational matters. The key question that must be answered in any organisational review is whether delegation is clear in principle and effective in practice?

5.4 Approach to the review

A general approach that might include some or all of the following steps:

(a) *An initial short survey* involving the development of a simple checklist with a series of yes/no type questions. Typical subjects to be included are:

- objectives of the present departments;
- organisation charts;
- job descriptions;
- means of communication;
- salary structure and grading;
- use of committees.

(b) *A critical review* to establish whether the present arrangements appear to be satisfactory or whether there is a case for looking at the organisation in more depth and if so in what particular main areas.

(c) *A detailed study* assuming that more in-depth work was necessary, which might include:

- collection of facts, such as department titles, names, number of staff, salary costs, ages;
- preparation of organisation charts;
- critical analysis and review of present arrangements identifying all shortcomings and/or weaknesses;
- development of outline proposals and recommendations.

(d) *Presentation of proposals* involving discussions with management and staff.

Conclusion As part of a cost-cutting exercise, management may initiate an organisation review. It may reveal weaknesses in the organisation's objectives, structure, or the chain of delegation.

6 SELF TEST QUESTIONS

6.1 Outline the different ways of classifying an organisation (1.2)

6.2 Give two examples of a protective organisation (1.3)

6.3 What areas are covered in a short informal report? (1.5)

6.4 What does a mission statement describe? (2.2)

6.5 List the three components an objective should possess (2.2)

6.6 What type of constraint restricts private sector organisations? (2.6)

6.7 What does specialisation mean? (3.2)

6.8 Explain how an organisation chart is used (3.3)

6.9 What type of job allows one person to control many subordinates? (3.4)

6.10 Outline some of the functions in an organisation (4.2)

6.11 What type of an organisation would use product grouping as its structural form? (4.3)

Chapter 3
SYSTEMS AND PROCEDURES

PATHFINDER INTRODUCTION

This chapter covers the following performance criteria and knowledge and understanding

- Overview of the organisation's business and the critical external relationships (Elements 10.2 & 10.3)
- Understanding that the accounting systems of an organisation are affected by its organisational structure, its MIS, its administrative systems and procedures and the nature of its business transactions. (Elements 10.1, 10.2 & 10.3)
- Work activities are planned in order to optimise the use of resources and ensure completion of work within agreed timescales (Element 10.1)
- Work activities are closely monitored in order to ensure quality standards are being met (Element 10.1)
- Weaknesses and potential for improvements to the accounting system are identified and considered for their impact on the operation of the organisation (Element 10.2)
- The system is updated in accordance with changes in internal and external regulations, policies and procedures (Element 10.2).

Putting the chapter in context – learning objectives.

At this stage in your studies you should be thinking about the system that you are considering for your project. The report will obviously detail the system; its procedures, personnel and costs. Further detail can cover how the success or effectiveness of the system is measured.

The project is about improving the system and, therefore, you will want to outline what is wrong with the current system in terms of costs, location, resources and the skills of the staff. To explain how you found out the system was not working as well as it might be, you must identify the sources of this information and the methods you have used to identify the weaknesses. Having identified the problem, or problems, you must then continue by looking for alternative solutions and researching the constraints that will apply when you are evaluating these options.

In this chapter we will be identifying the different systems within an organisation and in later chapters we will be exploring the ways of improving the system.

When you have studied this chapter you should be able to do the following:

- Describe systems in terms of their elements, objectives, boundary and environment.
- Apply systems theory to organisations.
- Describe the components of a control system and apply this analysis to accounting systems.

1 SYSTEMS THEORY

1.1 Introduction

There are a wide variety of different systems that are familiar to most people. The solar system, the human digestive system, the ecosystem, the political system, the judicial system, and a central heating system are all examples where we can understand immediately what is meant by the word 'system' because we have experience of the entity in question. The unit you are studying is called **managing accounting systems** and, because of the nature of your work, you may have had experience of other systems such as purchasing systems, stock control systems or payroll systems. However, there is no easy, universally accepted definition of the word 'system'. In the context of an organisation, the following will suffice:

Definition A system is a group of related elements or activities, which are organised for a specific purpose.

1.2 Organisations as systems

The systems that operate within organisations can be viewed in many ways, for example:

- Social systems - composed of people and their relationships.
- Information systems - relying on information to support decisions.
- Financial systems- emphasising the organisation's cash flows.
- Economic systems - utilising resources to produce economic welfare.

Organisations are called 'open systems' because they have a dynamic relationship with their environment. The environment may produce controllable, uncontrollable or unexpected input to the system. For example, the level of recruitment is controllable but interest rates are not. Organisations draw resources from the environment (people, finance etc) and put back into that environment the products they produce or the services that they offer. In doing so the inputs are converted into outputs, hopefully with value being added. A car manufacturer may buy parts and assemble these into finished vehicles. Depending on a wide variety of factors, not least the efficiency of the assembly, the cars will be sold for more than the cost of the labour, components and overheads, because value is added.

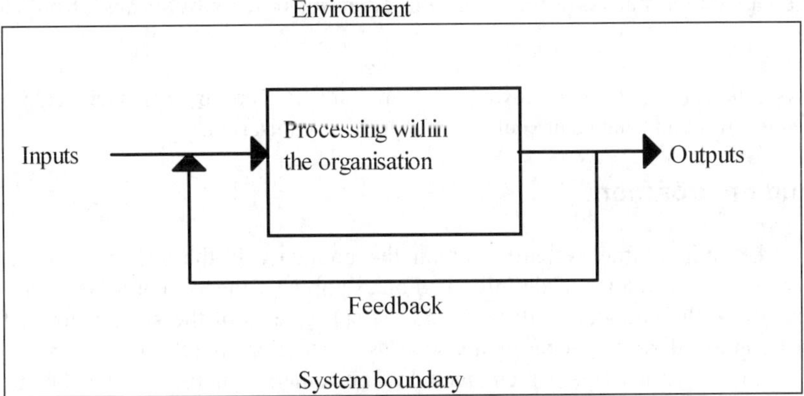

To be successful, any system must produce outputs that meet its objectives and, to ensure conformity with these objectives, a control system must be designed and operated. The control system will receive feedback in the form of information and will respond to it to achieve the system objectives.

1.3 Activity

We have already noted that 'open systems' interact with the environment. Can you think of a system that is shut off from the environment ie, a 'closed system'?

1.4 Activity solution

Closed systems do not interact with the environment. For example, the objective of a clock is to keep the correct time regardless of external influences. A self-winding clock would be a closed system. There are few examples of organisations that behave as closed systems, though it is interesting to see how the term is applied in an approximate sense.

Monasteries or ghettos come close to being closed systems and the term 'closed economy' is used for a country or region, which does not import or export significantly. An organisation, department or individual being a closed system is likely to be a disadvantage because closed systems will clearly find it difficult to adapt to changing circumstances.

Conclusion As the organisation is interacting with its environment it is viewed as an open system. This open factor has two aspects: first, inputs (factors of production) are drawn from the environment, and secondly, the outputs (the products or services) are offered to the environment. Closed systems, on the other hand, are systems that are self-supporting and do not interact with the environment outside the system.

1.5 Subsystems

Most systems can be broken down into subsystems. The departments found in organisations such as production, purchasing, sales and finance, have the characteristics of systems but are subsystems of the organisation. The activities of the subsystems are categorised as:

- **Production** - is the heart of the organisation and is where the transformation of inputs into outputs takes place. In a manufacturing organisation it would be the production department, in an insurance company it would be the underwriting department.

- **Maintenance** - keeps the organisation functioning. It may repair and service the building. Alternatively the human resource department can be seen as a maintenance subsystem in that it recruits, retires and counsels the organisation's employees.

- **Boundary spanning** - organisations must acquire inputs (raw materials, data etc.) and distribute output (the finished product or service). This subsystem can cover a variety of activities such as purchasing and marketing.

- **Adaptation** - conditions exist which means the organisation needs to adapt in order to survive. This subsystem can include research, engineering, planning and development.

- **Management** - is the subsystem that co-ordinates all the other subsystems by means of policies, plans, resolving conflict etc.

Conclusion: Most systems can be broken down into subsystems. Departments such as production, purchasing, sales and finance are subsystems of the organisation.

1.6 System boundary and environment

The **system boundary** is the limit of the system. Within the boundary is the system, outside it is the **environment.** A boundary is often a matter of definition. For example, if the system under examination is 'the whole company' then within the boundary will be found the subsystems of the system, for instance, the employees and procedures contained within departments such as production, purchasing, sales and finance. Outside the boundary is the environment, which includes customers, suppliers, the labour market, shareholders, lenders, competitors and the local community as well as more abstract and indirect influences such as the law and the economy. A diagram of the company as a system is as follows:

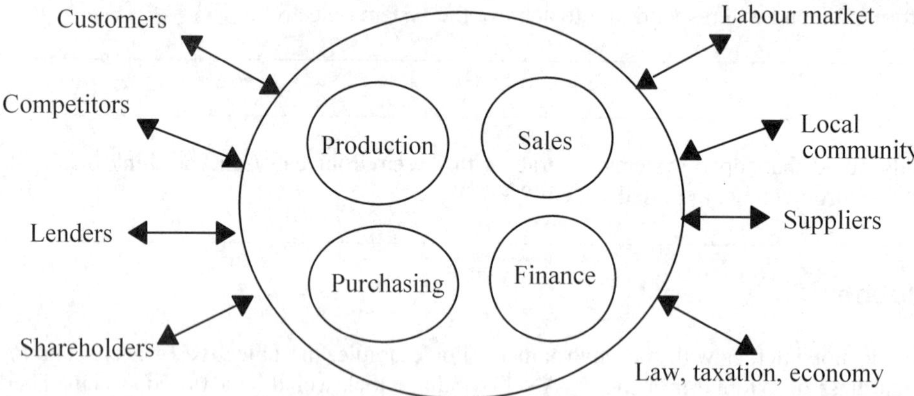

If we are concentrating on the finance system, then sales, production and purchasing become part of the environment, and within the system boundary will be found smaller subsystems such as product costing, financial accounting and treasury. The hierarchy of systems can be illustrated using a type of organisation chart.

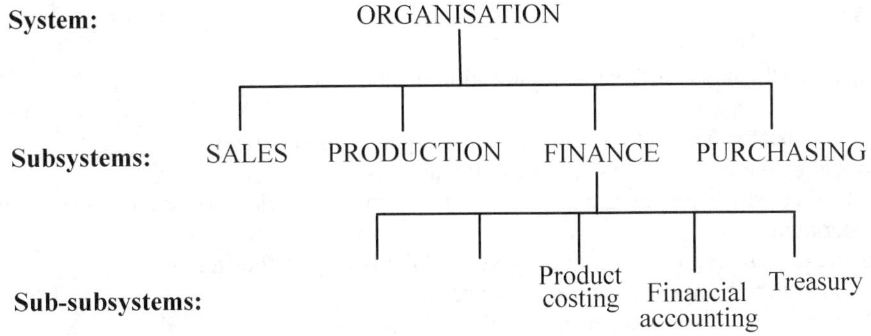

Conclusion — Everything outside the system boundary is the environment. It includes customers, suppliers, the labour market, shareholders, lenders, competitors and the local community as well as more abstract and indirect influences such as the law and the economy.

1.7 Critical external relationships

The type of organisation and its environment determines the external relationships that prevail. As well as the opportunities that these relationships offer, they will also impose some constraints on the organisation. The external relationships include those with:

- **Lenders** - providers of long- and short-term finance. They will be concerned about the security of their loan and the ability of the organisation to repay it.

- **Suppliers** - are interested in preference over other suppliers with repeat business of sufficient volume and prompt payment.

- **Employees** - management must recognise and comply with the legislation that caters for equal pay, health and safety, employment protection and discrimination. The constraints come from pressure groups or interest groups such as trade unions and employers' associations, which exist to promote the common economic interests of their members.

- **Shareholders** - a business exists to provide a return to shareholders.

- **Customers** - expect the products and services to be up to standard. The constraints come from consumer protection organisations, for example, regulatory bodies such as Ofgas, the Office of Fair Trading and the ombudsman, which encourage the adoption of codes of practice and promote competition.

- **Competitors** - the organisation will need to be aware of the actions of its competitors as this might affect it at the local, national or international level. Their actions may affect its market, its employees, its research, its suppliers and its position within the industry.

- **Government** - central government imposes legal and political constraints on organisations Examples of legal constraints include employment legislation, health and safety at work, environmental protection legislation, financial legislation (tax and the provision of financial information) and trading standards legislation (weights and measures). To some extent political constraints are tied up with legal constraints, but political changes can create indecision and uncertainty at home. Abroad it can mean the loss of markets, confiscation of assets, and freezing of funds. At the local government level constraints that may be significant include: opening hours of shops; parking regulations; construction of roads; and buildings etc.

1.8 Activity

Using the organisation you work for as an example of a system, give examples of the environmental factors that might affect it.

1.9 Activity solution

The environmental factors, which may affect the organisation, include the:

- regulatory and legislative situation within which the organisation operates;
- policies adopted by the government or ruling political body;
- economic situation which prevails and the strength of the domestic currency of the organisation's country of operation;
- number and strength of competitors in the market and the strategies they adopt;
- price and quality of the competitors' products or services;
- availability and cost of resources such as capital and labour;
- attitudes such as concern for 'green' issues.

2 CONTROL SYSTEMS

2.1 Introduction

We have many control systems such as quality control, stock control and budgetary control. The control of an organisation is exercised by managers obtaining and using information.

Definition Control is the activity that monitors changes or deviations from those originally planned.

Control has also been defined as 'nothing but the sending of messages, which effectively change the behaviour of the recipient'. Control is not an end in itself, it is a means to an end, a way to improve a system.

2.2 Thermostat example

To get a better understanding of control systems, it is useful to start with an example of one which is in everyday use - a thermostat. All central heating systems contain thermostats to regulate the temperature of the rooms they are heating. The user sets the thermostat to the required temperature on the dial. There is a thermometer in the system, which measures the temperature of the rooms. The room temperature is continually compared with the pre-set temperature on the thermostat dial. If the room temperature is above the dial temperature, the power (eg, gas) is switched off. When room temperature falls below the dial temperature, the power is switched on. This system can be represented diagrammatically as follows:

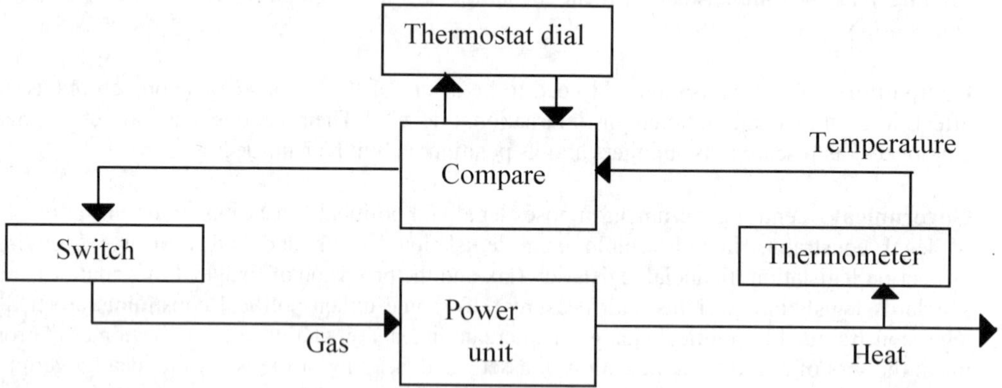

2.3 Elements of a control system

The thermostat system introduces a **controller**, which is made up of four elements, a pre-set temperature on the dial, a thermostat, a comparison unit and a switch. The general terms for the elements of a controller are:

- **Standard:** This is what the system is aiming for. In the thermostat system it is the pre-set temperature.

- **Sensor:** (or detector). This measures the output of the system. In the thermostat system it is the thermometer.

- **Comparator:** This compares the information from the standard and the sensor.

- **Effector:** (or activator). This initiates the control action. In the thermostat system it is the switch.

The information that is taken from the system output, and used to adjust the system is called **feedback.** In the thermostat example the feedback is the actual room temperature

2.4 Feedback

Definition Feedback is modification or control of a process or system by its results or effects, by measuring differences between desired and actual results.

Feedback is a central element in any control system, and is usually produced on the results of the process. In an organisational system, information about how the system actually performs is recorded and this information is available to the managers responsible for their achievement of the target performance. For effective and accurate control it is essential that timely and efficiently detailed feedback is provided so that corrective action can be taken. This may be a minor operating adjustment or it may involve a complete redesign of the system.

2.5 Control methods

There are a variety of control methods but the two that you will be concentrating on are both quantitative methods. The first type focuses on physical values such as quality control and the second focuses on monetary values such as budgets.

Definition Quality control is the control system of setting quality standards, measuring performance against those standards and taking corrective action when necessary.

The standard aimed for will depend on the nature of the product, the market the goods are produced for and the standards achieved by competitors in the same market.

Definition Budgets are statements of the desired future performance of the organisation usually expressed in financial terms and looking one year ahead.

The organisation's range of budgets needed for its control follow a typical pattern, with forecasts:

- about the probable economic climate in which the organisation will be operating;
- about the activity of the company;
- on the likely level of sales and production;
- about the capital expenditure;
- about the cash expenditure.

2.6 Application to an accounting system - budgetary control

In a budgetary control system the financial performance of a department is compared with the budget. Action is then taken to improve the department's performance if possible. The elements of the control system are:

(a) **standard:** the budget (eg, standard costs);

(b) **sensor:** the costing system, which records actual costs;

(c) **feedback:** the actual results for the period, collected by the costing system;

(d) **comparator:** the 'performance report' for the department, comparing actual with budget (eg, variance analysis);

(e) **effector:** the manager of the department, in consultation with others, takes action to minimise future adverse variances and to exploit opportunities resulting from favourable variances.

The opportunity may also be taken to adjust the standard (ie, the budget) if it is seen to be too easy or too difficult to achieve.

3 INFORMATION SYSTEMS

3.1 What is information?

Information is different from **data.** Although the two terms are often used interchangeably in everyday language, it is important to make a clear distinction between them, as follows:

The word '**data**' means facts. Data consists of numbers, letters, symbols, raw facts, events and transactions which have been recorded but not yet processed into a form which is suitable for making decisions. Data on its own is not generally useful, whereas information is very useful.

Data + meaning = information

Information is data that has been processed in such a way that it has a meaning to the person who receives it, who may then use it to improve the quality of decision making. For example, in cost accounting the accounting system records a large number of facts (data) about materials, times, expenses and other transactions. These facts are then classified and summarised to produce accounts, which are organised into reports which are designed to help management to plan and control the firm's activities.

3.2 Management information systems

Information is necessary to carry out the control function. This information can come from a number of sources and can take a variety of forms, ranging from a detailed computer-generated statistical analysis to a hand-written report based on an individual's assessment of a situation. A management information system (MIS) has been defined as

Definition 'a system in which defined data is collected, processed and communicated to assist those responsible for the use of resources'

It has also been defined as :

- a set of **formalised** procedures
- designed to provide managers **at all levels**
- with **appropriate** information
- from all **relevant sources** (internal and external)
- to enable them to make **timely** and **effective decisions**
- for **planning** and **controlling**
- the activities for which they are **responsible.**

Note that these definitions do not mention computers. However, it is clear that the increasing capabilities of computers and the development of database systems has made management information far more readily available and up-do-date. Whether this has improved the quality of the information depends on the design of the system.

3.3 Types of management information system

Within most management information systems there are four system types:

- database systems which process and store information which becomes the organisation's memory;
- direct control systems which monitor and report on activities such as output levels, sales ledger and credit accounts in arrears;
- enquiry systems based on databases which provide specific information such as the performance of a department or an employee; and
- support systems which provide computer-based methods and procedures for conducting analyses, forecasts and simulations.

Management support systems are types of MIS, which give particular support facilities to managers. There are three types of support system:

(a) **Decision support systems** are computer systems that are used by management as an aid in making decisions when presented with semi-structured or unstructured problems. The solution is chosen by setting up possible scenarios and asking the computer to predict the consequences. The manager must then use his or her judgement when making the final decisions.

(b) **Executive information systems** give the executive easy access to key internal and external data. The system works by linking the executive's personal computer with the organisation's main systems and producing information at an appropriate level of summary, yet with the ability to call for further detail when required.

(c) **Expert systems** are computer systems which hold expert (ie, specialist) knowledge and attempt to replicate the decision making procedures of a human expert. Systems of this nature are still reasonably primitive but they exist in many fields, for example: law (conveyancing); taxation; banking (granting credit); and medicine (diagnosis of symptoms)

4 THE ACCOUNTING SYSTEM

4.1 Introduction

The exact nature of an accounting system will depend on the size and nature of the organisation. The management of the organisation will rely on the accounting system to help them:

- control the organisation;
- safeguard the assets;
- prepare the financial statements;
- comply with the relevant legislation.

Such a system will be designed largely to ensure that all day-to-day transactions are accurately recorded and thus management have up-to-date information at their disposal to help them control the business and its assets. We will continue by looking at different sections of the accounting system.

4.2 Payroll system

The payroll system includes the following:

- maintenance of payroll;
- authorisation of hours worked;
- payroll preparation;
- distribution of pay;
- payroll approval;
- cheque signing (or approval of bank transfers); and
- identifying liabilities to third parties for payroll costs, and paying these when due.

Payroll costs in most businesses represent a significant expense and the administrative procedures involved can be quite complicated. As a result, a formalised system is vital if the business is to record its payroll costs accurately, pay the correct amounts to its employees and reflect the debt owed to the Inland Revenue in respect of deduction.

A typical system to deal with the processing of wages paid to weekly-paid employees is set out below.

Stage 1 Clock cards submitted and input

↓

Stage 2 Gross pay, deductions and net pay calculated

↓

Stage 3 Other amendments input eg, holiday pay

↓

Stage 4 Final payroll calculated and payslips produced

↓

Stage 5 Payment to employees and Inland Revenue

↓

Stage 6 Payroll costs and payments recorded in books

4.3 Purchases system

In its day-to-day operations, a business requires goods and/or services from outside suppliers. Management needs a reliable system to ensure that all liabilities arising from such transactions are completely and accurately recorded and, at the same time, that such items represent only valid business expenditure.

The purchases system includes the following areas of business activity:

- requisitioning of goods;
- ordering of goods;
- recording receipt of goods;
- checking goods for quantity and quality;
- claims for short deliveries or defective goods;
- putting goods into store;
- receipt of invoice and validation before entry;
- processing the invoice;
- reconciling the ledger account with the supplier's statement;
- approving invoices for payment;
- preparing the cheque, approving it and signing it;
- entry of cheque in cash book; and
- posting to purchase ledger, posting totals to control account and agreeing the control account.

Set out below is an overview of the main stages involved in the purchase system:

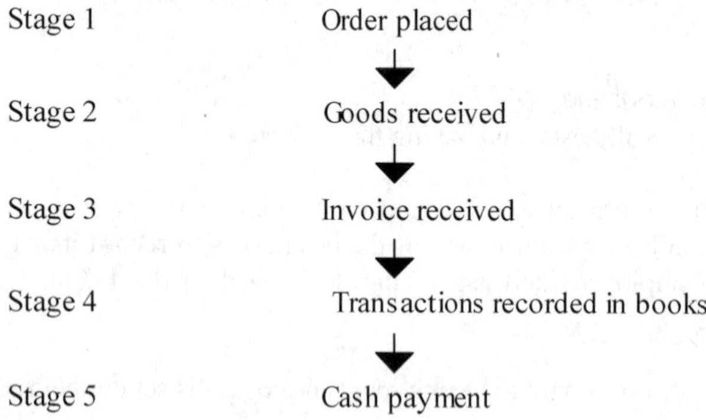

4.4 Sales system

The purpose of most business organisations is to make sales of either goods or services to its customers at a profit. In order that management may retain some degree of control over this process, a formalised system is usually developed. This system will ensure that the procedures adopted in respect of each individual sale will be the same.

The sales system covers the following areas of business activity:

- the terms of trade, the firm's policy for pricing and discounts;

- approval of sales orders and validation of credit limits;
- preparation of invoice and despatch notes;
- despatch of goods and obtaining proof of delivery;
- processing of invoices;
- validation of claims from customers and authorisation of credit notes;
- handling and processing cash received;
- monitoring sales ledger accounts, chasing overdue debts (and determining a bad debt policy); and
- recording transactions in the nominal ledger.

4.5 Activity

Using the same format as before sketch an overview of the stages involved in the sales system.

4.6 Activity solution

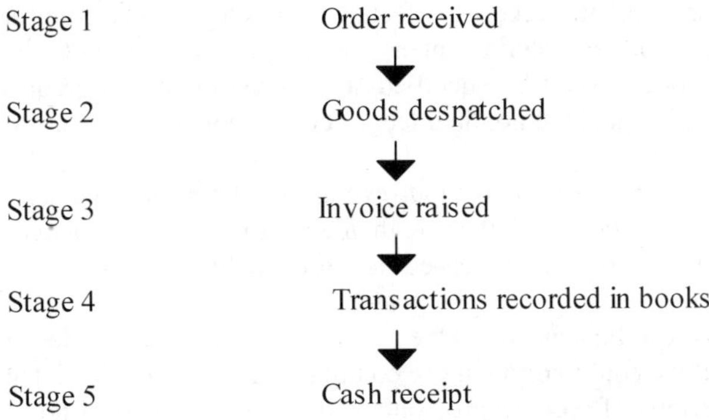

4.7 Cash system

Because cash is a significant asset for many businesses, procedures must be followed to avoid the risk of misappropriation. An overview of a typical process follows:

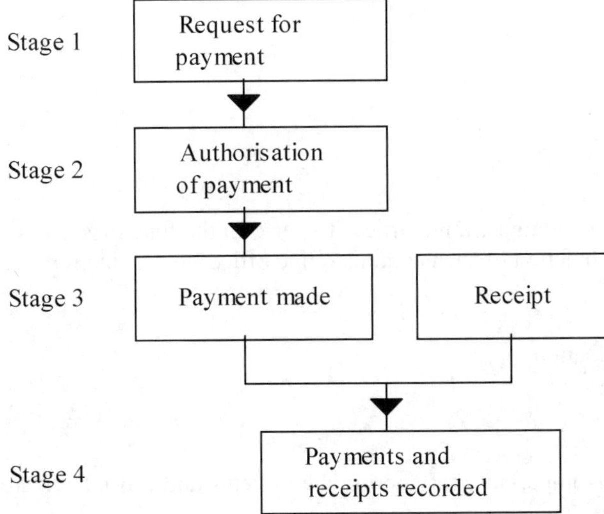

4.8 Stock system

Stock is usually one of the larger assets of a business and one, like cash, which is particularly susceptible to misappropriation. Adequate systems must be installed to control the movement of stock. An overview is shown below:

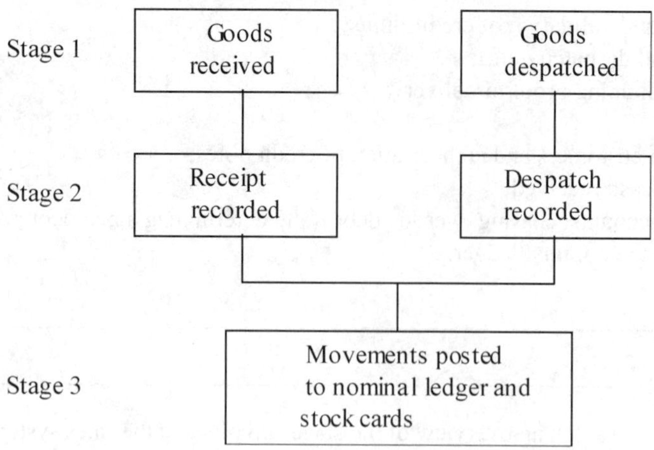

4.9 Integrated systems

This section has covered the main elements of how a typical accounting system operates in practice. However, you should remember that quite often the different elements are inter-connected or integrated. A fully integrated accounting system is one in which all the records affected by a single transaction are updated simultaneously when the transaction is input. For example, on entering a purchase invoice, both the creditor's account number and the nominal analysis codes would be specified so that the debit and credit entries are made together, the creditors ledger being credited and the nominal ledger being debited.

By contrast, in a non-integrated system there would be two input events for the same invoice. One would handle the credit to the purchase ledger and the other would handle the debits to the nominal ledger (probably carried out at quite a different time). Obviously there is an increased risk of the debits not equalling the credits.

There are various levels at which integration can be achieved. One of the most elementary is described in our example involving the purchase invoice, but we could go to a more complicated level and also integrate stock. Stock is increased as goods come in and details of receipts are contained on goods received notes and these could be used to update the stock file. It would then be normal to list the goods received note awaiting the input of the supplier's invoice.

Conclusion The organisation's accounting system will have subsystems, which may include the payroll, purchases, sales, stock and cash. Some companies combine these systems into an integrated system.

5 PROCEDURES

5.1 Administrative systems

Any organisation needs a number of different administrative offices to perform the functions necessary for the organisation to operate efficiently. It is the function of such administrative offices to provide for:

- the receipt of information;
- the recording and arrangement of information;
- the storage and security of information;
- the communication of information.

For the above to take place effectively it is important that appropriate systems and procedures are designed which facilitate these administrative services.

5.2 Office procedures

Although they are not always immediately apparent, every office has systems, which are usually referred to as 'office procedures'.

Definition Procedures represent the summation of a series of operations necessary to perform a task associated with the receipt, recording, arrangement, storage, security and communication of information.

The fact that the requirements of different organisations vary so much makes it particularly difficult to produce definitions for each individual organisation and its component sections and offices. However, included in the general definition would be systems and procedures for invoicing, paying bills, wages preparation and the other standard accounting operations.

5.3 The principles of systems and procedures

The establishment of systems and procedures will ensure that organisational objectives are attained. Data and information are constantly flowing within an organisation, some being generated internally and some stemming from external sources. All of this information must be processed and, to ensure that it is attained in the most effective, efficient and economical manner, a system needs to be established.

As with most aspects of business administration, there are certain principles that have been built up over a long period. They include the following.

- There should be a smooth flow of work with no bottlenecks.
- Movement of staff should be kept to a minimum.
- Duplication of work should be avoided.
- The best and most effective use of existing specialist attributes should be made.
- Simplicity within systems should be sought. Complications usually lead to misinterpretations and/or mistakes.
- Machines should be used to help staff where appropriate.
- Any system must be cost-effective. The benefits should be compared with the cost of implementation and subsequent supervision costs.

5.4 Formal written procedures

The implementation of procedures and systems is of immense benefit to the organisation, which will be even greater if they are formalised in writing. This is normally achieved by the preparation of 'laid-down' or written procedures in an office manual format stating the system as it should be. These written instructions should indicate clearly what is required to be done, when, where and how. There are, however, advantages and disadvantages associated with manuals. A list of the advantages would include the following:

- The preparation requires careful examination of the systems and procedures. This close attention can only be of benefit in that strengths and weaknesses are revealed.
- Supervision is easier.
- It helps the induction and training of new staff.
- It assists the organisation in pinpointing areas of responsibility.
- Once they are written down, systems and procedures are easier to adapt and/or change in response to changing circumstances.

The disadvantages include:

- The expense in preparing manuals both in the obvious financial terms and the perhaps less obvious cost of administrative time.
- To be of continuing use an office manual must be updated periodically, again incurring additional expense.
- The instructions that are laid down in the office manual may be interpreted rather strictly and implemented too rigidly. Within any organisation it is often beneficial for employees to bring a degree of flexibility to their duties to cope with particular circumstances.

Conclusion Office procedures outline the operations necessary to perform a task associated with the receipt, recording, arrangement, storage, security and communication of information.

5.5 The review of office procedures

Systems should be kept under continuous review and altered as necessary to reflect changes in the organisation, advances in technology, or indeed suggestions from the staff as to how systems can be improved. The decision to review the office procedures could stem from weaknesses which may have already been highlighted (for instance, too much paperwork). A review may be divided into two parts:

(a) an overview of the office and the role it plays within the organisation, which will consider

- the purpose of the office;
- what actually happens within the office;
- who does what within the office;
- the techniques and methods employed by staff in carrying out assigned responsibilities;
- the quality of performance.

(b) a detailed step-by-step examination of the procedures themselves.

The establishment of such information is vital as a first stage. After this a more detailed analysis of the day-to-day routine may be attempted.

5.6 Activity

Does your office incorporate the procedures into some form of office procedure manual, or in the form of a duty list issued to staff? You might like to review the current system for your project.

---

6 SELF TEST QUESTIONS

6.1 What is a system? (1.1)

6.2 What makes a system 'open'? (1.2)

6.3 List four critical external relationships of an organisation (1.7)

6.4 Draw a control system, showing the main elements (2.2/2.3)

6.5 Distinguish between information and data (3.1)

6.6 Describe a management support system (3.3)

6.7 What is the purpose of the accounting system? (4.1)

6.8 Define 'procedure' (5.2)

6.9 Outline the advantages of formal written procedures(5.4)

Chapter 4

MANAGEMENT AND SUPERVISION

PATHFINDER INTRODUCTION

This chapter covers the following performance criteria and knowledge and understanding

- Principles of supervision (Element 10.1)
- Principles of human relations, team building, staff motivation (Element 10.1)
- Work activities are planned in order to optimise the use of resources and ensure completion of work within agreed time-scales (Element 10.1)
- The competence of individuals undertaking work activities is reviewed and the necessary training is provided (Element 10.1)
- Work methods and schedules are clearly communicated to all individuals in a way that assists their understanding of what is expected of them. (Element 10.1)
- Recommendations are made to the appropriate people in a clear, easily understood format (Element 10.2)
- Recommendations are supported by a clear rationale which includes explanation of any assumptions made (Element 10.2)

Putting the chapter in context – learning objectives.

The chapters so far have been concerned with organisational systems and procedures. There comes a point, however, where employees have to fit into those systems and procedures and commence work.

After studying this chapter you should have a better understanding of the duties, responsibilities and functions of a supervisor and of how supervisors and managers can create a motivating climate for their employees.

At the end of this chapter you should have learned the following topics.

- the principles of supervision;
- the hierarchy of objectives;
- communication channels;
- the relationship between theories of motivation and work situations.

1 SUPERVISION

1.1 Introduction

Terminology can be a little confusing when one reads or talks about supervision and supervisors: 'supervising management', 'first-line management' and 'front-line management' are the most commonly used synonyms for supervision that are encountered, and 'section leader', 'chargehand', 'overseer', 'foreman', 'superintendent' are titles given to supervisors in different industries. The definition below is from the Institute of Supervisory Management.

Definition The supervisor is part of the management team, but is special in the sense that his subordinates are not managers, but operatives, clerks, fitters, etc. He is a person given authority for planning and controlling the work of his group, but all he can delegate to the group is the work itself.

A supervisor, therefore, is a type of manager whose main role is to ensure that specified tasks are performed correctly and efficiently by a defined group of people.

1.2 Duties and responsibilities

The jobs of supervisors come in all shapes and sizes. The job of the supervisor in a supermarket will be very different from that of a supervisor in a motor car manufacturing plant, for example. Nevertheless, their roles will be essentially the same and many supervisory tasks will be common to both positions. The distinctive feature of their work is, of course, their personal closeness to the job itself. The duties and responsibilities common to both might be listed as:

- allocating the tasks to, and organising the work of subordinates;
- supervising the work of subordinates and being responsible for achieving targets in the most effective way;
- introducing newly-appointed employees to their sections;
- maintaining discipline, eg, ensuring that people keep good time or that they observe regulations;
- handling personal problems and settling grievances;
- dealing with unsatisfactory performance;
- informing management;
- conveying to, and interpreting for management the feelings and views of employees.

1.3 Functions of a supervisor

These duties and responsibilities may be translated into functions (a process which, incidentally, underlines the managerial character of supervising work) in the following way:

1. *Planning* - Preparing schemes or schedules for achieving the targets that have been set by either themselves or the management.

2. *Organising* - Allocating tasks, delegating and arranging the work and resources in such a way as to enable the realisations of the plan.

3. *Controlling* - Ensuring that the workers' performance in terms of cost, quality and quantity of output matches the plan, if necessary by correcting deviations.

4. *Communication* - Keeping all concerned adequately informed and himself or herself in touch.

5. *Problem solving and decision taking* - Handling day to day difficulties and problems and deciding what needs to be done to ensure the effective performance of the supervised.

6. *Motivating and maintaining discipline* - Encouraging people to give their best within the rules that govern their employment.

Conclusion The functions of a supervisor include: planning; organising; controlling; communicating; problem solving and decision taking; and motivating and maintaining discipline.

2 THE ROLE OF THE SUPERVISOR IN RELATION TO PLANNING

2.1 What is planning?

Perhaps we can begin to answer this question by saying that planning is organising for the future, or making arrangements for something to happen. If you intend to go on holiday, for example, you decide: where you want and can afford to go; when you wish to go; how you will get there; what you need to do to get and stay there and so forth. We can see that planning entails collecting information about the action that we wish to take, or the event we wish to happen. The information collected enables us to examine and explain our desires and intentions in the context of the future.

2.2 Planning for the achievement of objectives

Planning is concerned with the arrangements that have to be made to achieve targets and objectives within given time spans or against set time horizons. A diagram showing the hierarchy of objectives is as follows:

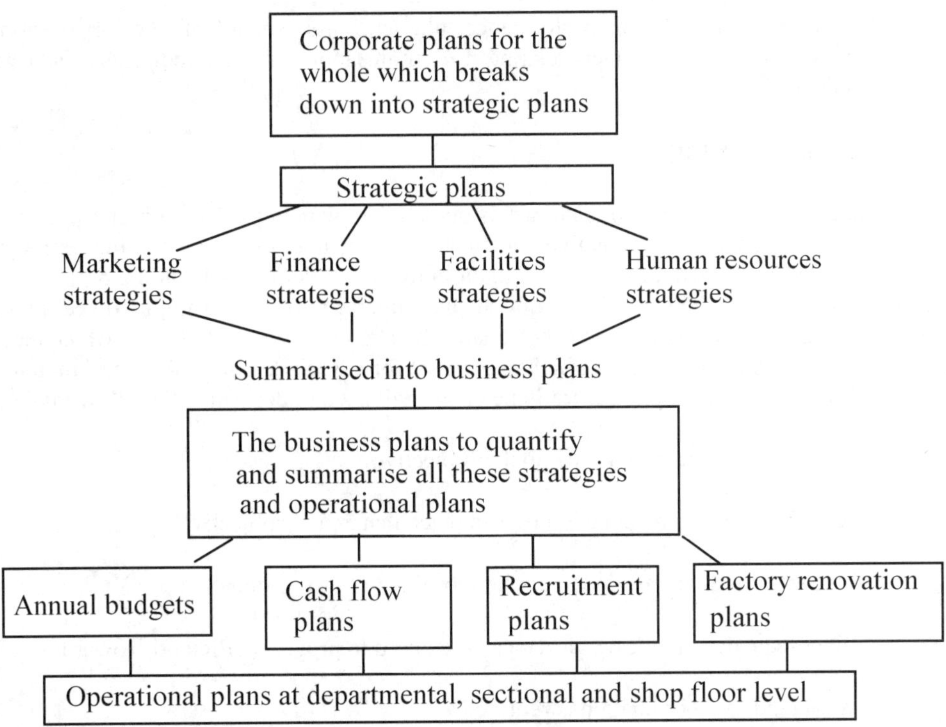

At each higher level in the hierarchy the objectives are more relevant to a greater proportion of the organisation's activities so that the objectives at the top of the hierarchy are relevant to every aspect of the organisation. Some examples of objectives are:

- in the long term (during the next 2-5 years) a corporate objective may be to become established in a new business or to dominate a market;

- as part of the business plan, a medium-term objective may be to increase market share by 8%;

- one of the short-term objectives at operational level could be to improve output from 800 units to 850 in the next month.

Objectives are a vital element within the planning process - representing as they do specific 'benchmarks' or points which indicate the direction the organisation is following - plus what it is to achieve and the time period involved.

Conclusion Planning is organising for the future, or making arrangements for something to happen.

2.3 The objectives of the supervisor

The objectives of the supervisor are the 4 M's. The aim is to make the best use of:

- Machine capacity - this includes servicing and maintenance:
- Manpower - this includes training;
- Materials - including best type of ordering/delivery schedules;
- Money - including cost reduction planning.

The setting of objectives is essential to the process of planning, since this activity:

- commits managers and their staff to the future plans and makes sure that they direct their efforts to those activities which will maximise results;

- provides direction to the planning process at all organisational levels

- directs the organisational activities as a whole and provides co-ordination in pursuing established plans; and

- provides standards of performance allowing assessment of the organisational efficiency and effectiveness (the former relating to optimisation of resource-usage and the latter relating to attainment).

2.4 Operational planning

The planning that supervisors do is known as operational planning. Generally it represents the lowest level of planning in an organisation. It involves line manager and supervisor levels in the setting of specific tasks and targets. The focus of operational plans is upon individual tasks like scheduling a particular accounting job to match some overall administrative requirement. Supervisors are mostly involved in short-term planning, covering things like the absences of subordinates, breakdowns, supply failures - which may be as short term as tomorrow - or production targets - which may be set for a week, a month or several months. Whatever it is that a supervisor intends to plan for, generally he or she will need to determine the following:

(a) What has to be achieved - the goal or objective?

(b) What jobs have to be done in order to reach that goal or objective?

(c) What resources are needed to do the jobs that have to be done?

(d) What sequence of task performance is required to progress efficiently toward the goal or objective?

(e) What kind of co-ordination is required?

(f) What has to be communicated and to whom must it be communicated?

(g) What has to be controlled and how must control be effected to ensure that the plan is realised?

2.5 Activity

If a supervisor does not make time for planning what might happen to the 4 M's?

2.6 Activity solution

- Machines - the best use might not be made of them in terms of the equipment capacity;
- Manpower - might not reach its potential; there might be idle time which could be utilised;
- Materials - because of late arrivals more expensive substitute materials may have to be used or, because of poor planning, suitable suppliers may not be considered;
- Money - all the above problems will have an effect on costs.

3 ORGANISING

3.1 Task list

We have already defined organising as:

Definition Allocating tasks, delegating and arranging the work and resources in such a way as to enable the realisations of the plan.

Organising is the next stage after planning. The tasks associated with organising include:

- Ordering the correct materials to arrive at the most appropriate time.

- Allocating jobs fairly, balancing the skills required against the labour available.
- Scheduling the work so that machinery is not idle, materials are not lying around unused and workers are not without jobs to do.
- Communicating the requirements clearly to all employees so they know exactly what to do.
- Knowing the capabilities of all the people under your control so that you can make the best use of them and develop their potential at the same time.

3.2 Activity

You are giving a small party and have planned when and where it should be held, who to invite, what food to have and what music to play. How are you going to organise it?

3.3 Activity solution

Organising it means sending or giving the invitations, buying and preparing the food, arranging the rooms suitably, having the music or tapes available and arranging for help with tasks like serving food and drink, and tidying up afterwards.

3.4 Delegation

Delegation is an important aspect of organisation and effective management, because management is the act of getting things done (accomplishing objectives) through the work of other people. Of necessity the manager or supervisor has to give some of the work to subordinates.

The main reasons for delegating are:

(a) to spread the workload;

(b) to motivate subordinates by giving them new experiences and opportunities to develop and show their potential;

(c) to train staff and prepare them for higher things.

3.5 Supervision in an accounts department

A supervisor in an accounts department will be concerned with organising the following.

Work
- Planning the work of the section, with regard to holidays, sickness, etc.
- Distributing work fairly.
- Ensuring timetables are adhered to.
- Co-ordinating work with other sections.
- Developing and introducing new methods of work to promote efficiency.

Staff
- Delegation of responsibilities.
- Ensuring understudies for relief during holidays.
- Ensuring a contented atmosphere, settling personal friction and quarrels.
- Maintaining discipline.
- Ensuring punctuality and the smooth running of any flexitime schemes.
- Fair allocation of holiday rotas.
- Training of staff as appropriate.

Superiors and other departments

- Accepting full responsibility of the work of the department.
- Co-operating with other departments.

- Receiving details of company policies.

Conclusion Organising includes allocating tasks, delegating and arranging the work and resources in such a way as to enable the realisations of the plan.

4 CONTROLLING

4.1 Control and performance

The aim of management is to succeed and this is measured by how far it achieves its broad objectives and specific targets.

Definition Controlling is the essential process of seeing that what was planned to happen actually *does* happen.

Control must be effectively and efficiently exercised over all the organisation's resources - human, financial and material. The primary method of control is to measure performance against expectations or standards with a view to taking prompt corrective action.

4.2 Control system model

Control includes the use of appropriate methods and making decisions based on information provided. The basic model of control, as we saw in the last chapter, is a **repeated cycle** to:

- establish relevant performance criteria and the standards expected to be met
- measure performance to provide information which is up to date and contains the essential detail
- compare the achieved results with expectations and investigate significant divergences
- take corrective action.

Feedback is an essential part of any control system and is usually concerned with the results of the process being controlled. For effective and accurate control it is essential that timely and efficiently detailed feedback is provided so that corrective action can be taken without delay. Corrective action may be a minor operating adjustment or it may involve completely redesigning the system. To be effective, the feedback reporting system must be designed to:

(a) provide quick, accurate reports of deviations from planned performance;
(b) be phrased in the same terms as the plan;
(c) report to the correct level within the organisation;
(d) reflect the needs of the organisation.

Conclusion The control cycle starts by establishing performance criteria, continues by measuring the performance and comparing it with what was expected and, if there are differences which do not meet the standard set, taking corrective action.

5 COMMUNICATION

5.1 Definition

We noted earlier in this textbook that the organisation chart defines the lines of essential communication.

Definition Communication is the transfer of information and may be defined as an exchange of facts, ideas, opinions or emotions by two or more persons.

5.2 Purpose of communication

The overriding purpose of an accounting system is to communicate with other people in the organisation - to give information, to signal instructions, to control and to confirm information or estimates previously given. Good communication helps to advance the aims of the organisation. Failure to impart the right information to the right person at the right time in the right manner is one of the major causes of inefficiency. The purpose of communication is to:

- convey information about what is happening, internally and externally;
- explain the nature and implications for the business of current and forecast problems;
- establish rules for dealing with different situations;
- stimulate action;
- create relationships between the members of the organisation;
- form collective decisions and render them generally acceptable.

5.3 Channels of communication

All organisations have communication channels. There will be lists of people who are to attend briefings or meetings, and distribution lists for minutes of meetings or memos. There will be procedures for telling people of decisions or changes, and for circulating information received from outside the organisation. In addition, an informal 'grapevine' exists in all organisations; people talk about their work, their colleagues and about the state of the company whenever they meet. In corridors, over lunch, after work, they swap rumour, gossip, half-truths and wild speculation.

Communication can flow in three main directions, downwards, upwards and horizontally:

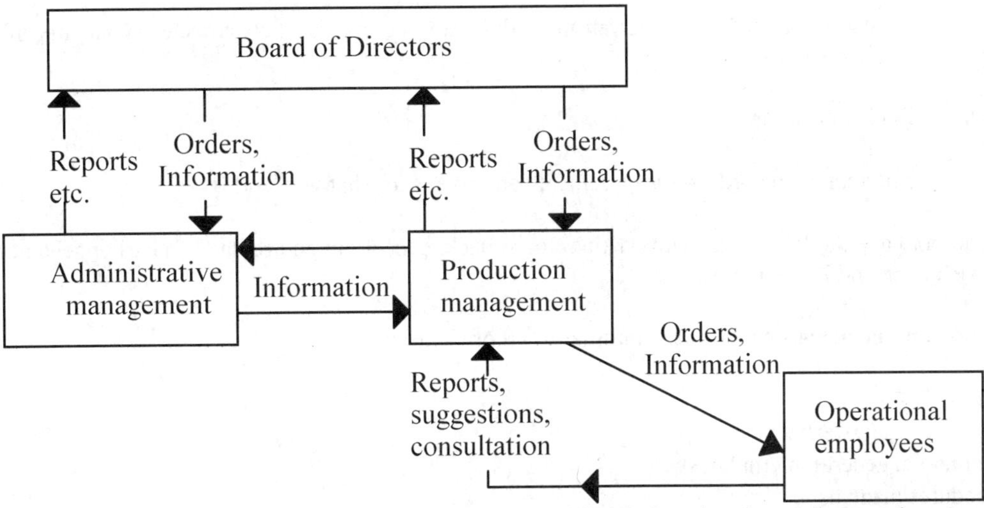

Downwards - from managers with broader responsibilities for planning and control to managers and other employees whose responsibilities are limited to particular functions or operations within the business. A common purpose of downward communication is the issue of orders, instructions and rules.

Upwards - is of equal importance, and will include the following:

- *Reports* on results achieved or problems encountered eg. Material shortages, equipment difficulties, etc.
- *Suggestions* for changes in products, work methods or organisation obtained from experience at the operational level.
- *Information* (for example, about customer reactions to products, employee morale or developments in other companies) which becomes available through contacts;
- *Requests* for consultation on particular working problems;

Horizontal or lateral - for the good of the company, managers should co-operate with each other, and not feel so uncertain of what they are doing or so jealous of their personal reputations that they are unwilling to share their experience with others.

Conclusion Within the organisation communication can flow in three main directions - downwards, upwards and horizontally:

5.4 Communication methods

Communication may be verbal, written, visual or a combination of all three.

Verbal communication - forms a major channel in business communications. Some examples of verbal methods are purely voice to voice eg, telephone conversations and public address announcements. Most methods are face to face, for example:

- interviews;
- lectures and presentations;
- sales visits;
- formal group meetings;
- informal contact and discussions;
- briefing sessions.

Verbal methods have several important advantages:

- There is instant feedback with the opportunity to respond quickly in cases of misunderstanding and disagreement.

- Because of the strong personal aspect, it is a good persuasive medium, which can be used to encourage people to take a certain course of action.

- The message can be unique to you as an individual; no one else is likely to select your mix of words or emphasise the same key phrases.

The obvious disadvantages are:

- There is no permanent record, so disagreement can arise as to what was said.

- We do not have the facility, as with writing, to go back, cancel out and replace an earlier sentence because we wish to amend its meaning.

Written communication - methods are familiar to all of us. Examples are:

- reports;
- letters, general external post;
- memoranda, general internal post;
- procedures manuals;
- notice board, house magazine, wage package inserts;
- forms;
- books.

The major advantages are that:

- it provides a permanent record;

- it enables a difficult piece of communication to be re-worded and rewritten over a period of time, so that the exact shade of meaning can be conveyed;

- the same message is conveyed to everyone;

- it is the cheapest form of contacting a range of individuals.

The main disadvantage is that there is no means of knowing whether the message has been received and understood by the person notified.

Visual communication - includes:

- posters, charts, graphs;
- video, TV, slide projection;
- product demonstration.

The main advantages are that:

- you will notice and remember the picture long after you have forgotten the words and figures;
- a visual communication has the highest retention rate (ie. recall after the event);
- the availability of colour and moving images enables the communicator to add drama and grab attention.

The disadvantages are mainly that:

- it is a limited method in that the amount of content that can be included on one slide, poster, etc. is restricted.
- just as in advertising, where you may remember the advert clearly but forget the product, so with visual communication, the receiver may be interested by the illustration to the extent that the facts become secondary.

5.5 Activity

Because of the advantages and disadvantages associated with each type of communication, organisations use more than one method in conjunction. What methods would you suggest for the sales launch of a new product?

5.6 Activity solution

Initially, visual methods could be used, eg, a film or a mock-up of the TV advertisement, to grab attention and provide impact to the main message. Then verbal methods of briefing, lectures, question and answer sessions may be used to persuade and motivate the sales team, to answer any questions and to show top management's personal backing. Finally, each salesperson could be given a fact pack, containing a written record of all the details, test results, etc. for later reference.

5.7 Effective communication

There are certain basic rules that can be applied to improve the effectiveness of communication. These are:

- **Communication should be to the right person** - specific requests or complaints coming upwards in the chain of management stand a better chance of a helpful response if the approach is made to the person with the relevant functional responsibility.
- **Communication should be accurate and complete** - otherwise wrong conclusions may be drawn or wrong decisions taken.
- **Communication should be timely** - a report that a machine is out of action is of little value if it is delayed while several hours or days of production are lost.
- **Communication should be understandable** - and needs care in its presentation.
- **Communication should be brief** - the length or brevity of communication must be related to the recipient's interest in the subject, the ability to make a logical analysis, knowledge of the subject matter, and the personal preference for a single summary or a fully argued or documented case.

- **Communication should not involve excessive cost** - the benefits expected to result from the communication should be greater than the cost of obtaining the relevant information and putting it into an acceptable form.

Conclusion Good communication helps to advance the aims of the organisation. Failure to impart the right information to the right person at the right time in the right manner is one of the major causes of inefficiency.

6 PROBLEM SOLVING AND DECISION TAKING

6.1 Problem solving techniques

Problem solving and decision taking are virtually part of the same process. Most decisions are made to solve (or forestall impending) problems and most problems have a number of possible solutions. A decision has to be taken on which solution to adopt. A typical problem solving sequence has been defined as containing seven principal steps:

(1) perceiving some need or problem;
(2) gathering relevant facts and identifying the real problem;
(3) looking for new information and analysing the wider picture;
(4) proposing alternative ideas for a solution;
(5) calculating and choosing a final solution which seems the most viable;
(6) implementing the solution;
(7) verifying and checking that the solution is satisfactory over a period of time.

One of the most powerful and yet simplest methods for getting at a problem is to gather all the facts and then ask the questions, for example, 'what is currently achieved/proposed/needed?'

6.2 Decision taking

There are two types of decision - routine and non-routine.

- Routine decisions are ones that are made frequently eg, re-ordering goods out of stock, granting discounts to certain customers. For most of these types of decision there are laid-down written rules and procedures to follow.

- Non-routine decisions require you to go through the process of problem-solving.

6.3 Activity

Draw the problem-solving technique as a system, with input, process and output.

6.4 Activity solution

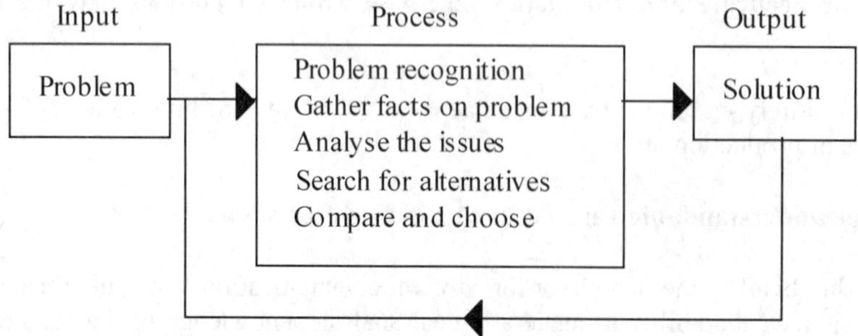

7 MOTIVATING AND MAINTAINING DISCIPLINE

7.1 The link

It is unusual to link motivation to discipline but one has only to think of how the application of discipline tends to discourage interest, reduce effort and lower morale to appreciate that the question of discipline has a bearing on the issue of motivation.

Definition Discipline is about controlling behaviour and motivation is about influencing behaviour.

7.2 Discipline

Any successful organised activity requires that everyone concerned understands what behaviour is expected of them and is able and willing to behave in the required way. From the point of view of management, therefore, discipline is obedience, application, effort and respect. The employee by contrast may view discipline as the necessity to conform to prohibitive regulations and oppressive authority with punishment following any failure to conform.

It is management's job to show that rules are necessary and to convince its employees that the observation of rules is not only a condition of employment but a process that benefits everyone. If the employee understands the requirements of his or her own job, has the requisite skill and knowledge to perform, is convinced of its usefulness to related jobs and to the overall purposes of the organisation, he or she should be suitably disposed to organisational discipline. Provided penalties for poor performance are coupled with competent and fair supervision then employees' tolerance for discipline is unlikely to diminish.

7.3 Motivation

Motivation is all those inner tensions or the needs that we describe as hopes, wishes, desires, fears, intentions - any inner state that activates and moves people. It is the urge or compulsion to do something – eat, drink, seek shelter, make love, throw a punch, win a darts match, become a famous scientist, or produce more and better goods at lower cost. Motivation is seen as a continuous inner process which begins with an awareness of a need or a sense of tension and proceeds through the satisfaction of that need or the dispersal of that tension to the awareness of another need or the sense of further tension and so on.

Definition Motivation is a process that arouses, sustains and regulates behaviour toward a specific goal or end.

Obviously this process is of interest to everyone. To the supervisor, whose job it is to get others to perform tasks, it is vitally important. The supervisor has to become involved with the motivation of the employees so that the performance requirements of the organisation can be met and the employees' needs and expectations satisfied.

7.4 Needs and goals

People can be thought of as having a variety of different needs that influence their motivation. A number of theories - notably Maslow's, have identified needs as the key feature of all human motivation. Needs are seen as varying from basic needs such as food and shelter to more complex needs such as the needs for friendship, self esteem and self realisation. The theories argue that a person with a particular need will be motivated to behave in a way that will satisfy that need. The implication for management is to set up situations in which people are able to satisfy their most important needs by engaging in behaviour most desired by the organisation for effective performance.

Goals also influence motivation. Firstly, a goal provides a target to aim at, something to aspire to, This means the existence of a goal generates motivation in a person to work towards the achievement of the goal. Secondly, goals provide a standard of performance. For goals to be significant motivators, they must be specific, sufficiently difficult to be challenging and they must be accepted by the person as their own particular goals and not as something imposed from outside.

7.5 Maslow

Maslow's needs hierarchy theory is the most important, substantial contribution to the theory of motivation. Maslow argued that people have a complex set of needs that may be arranged in order of priority. This hierarchy of needs is usually depicted in the form of a pyramid, shown in the diagram below.

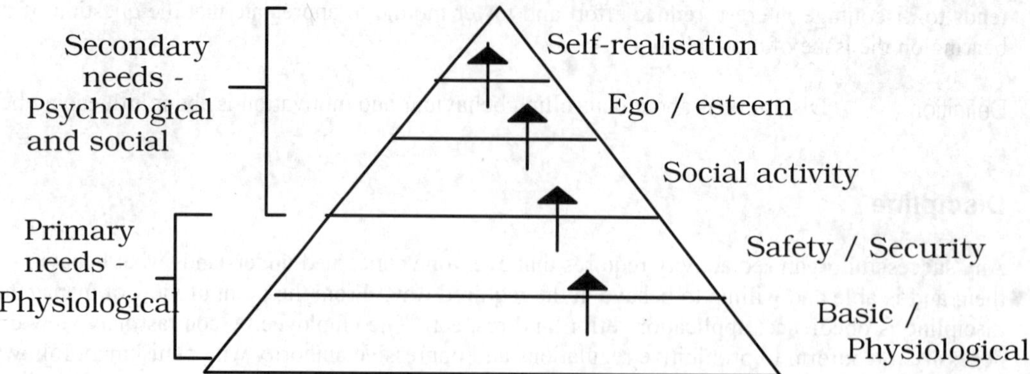

The hierarchy is based on four assumptions:

- A satisfied need does not motivate. When a need has been satisfied, another need emerges to take its place, so people are always striving to satisfy some need.
- The need interactions of most people are complex, with a number of needs affecting the behaviour of each person at any one time.
- In general, primary needs must be satisfied before secondary needs are activated sufficiently to provoke motivated behaviour.
- There are more varied ways of satisfying secondary needs than there are of satisfying primary needs.

Maslow's theory may be summarised and simplified by saying that everyone wants certain things throughout life, and these can be ranked in order of ascending importance:

- Basic or physiological needs - the things needed to stay alive (food, shelter and clothing). Such needs require satisfaction before all other needs and can be satisfied by money.
- Safety or security needs - protection against unemployment and the consequences of sickness and retirement as well as safeguards against unfair treatment. These needs can be satisfied by the contract of employment (pension scheme, sick fund, employment legislation).
- Social needs - people need to belong and it is only through group activity that this need can be satisfied. How work is organised, enabling people to feel part of a group, is fundamental to satisfaction of this need.
- Ego needs - people want the esteem of other people as well as feeling good about themselves. While status and promotion can offer short-term satisfaction, to build up the job itself and to give people a greater say in organising their work (participation) is to give satisfaction of a more permanent nature.
- Self-fulfilment needs - is quite simply the need to achieve something worthwhile in life. It is a need that is satisfied only by continuing success.

The significance of Maslow's hierarchy of needs is that it underlines the relative importance of money. Status has no satisfaction for the man desperate for food and shelter. Equally it demonstrates that money alone is not enough because, when basic and safety needs become satisfied, people are likely to concentrate their attentions on social and ego needs. Motivation of staff depends not only on money but also on the whole employment package embracing:

- pension, sick fund, canteen arrangements;
- nature of the work done;
- interest and challenge in the work;
- scope in the job for self-expression and self-determination;
- style of management used.

7.6 Herzberg

Herzberg developed his 'two-factor' theory of motivation from research into the job attitudes of two hundred accountants and engineers, who were asked to recall when they had experienced satisfactory and unsatisfactory feelings about their jobs. The replies led him to conclude that there are two important factors in work situations, satisfiers (or motivators) and dissatisfiers (or hygiene factors). The term 'hygiene' was derived from the concept of drains. Drains may prevent ill health, but do not in themselves produce good health.

Motivators or satisfiers include:

- achievement;
- recognition;
- responsibility;
- challenging work; and
- advancement.

Herzberg pointed out that these factors were related to the content of work and encouraged managers to study the job itself (ie. the tasks done, the nature of the work and responsibility), and provide opportunities to satisfy the motivating factors.

The hygiene factors, or dissatisfiers, relate to the context or environment of work rather than to job content. The most important hygiene factors were:

- company policy and administration;
- supervision – the technical aspects;
- salary;
- relationships with others;
- working conditions.

7.7 Improving staff satisfaction and motivation

Herzberg defines three avenues that management can follow in attempting to improve staff satisfaction and motivation.

(a) Job enrichment – a deliberate, planned process to improve the responsibility and challenge of a job. Typical examples include delegation or problem solving. For instance, where an accountant's responsibilities for producing quarterly management reports end at the stage of producing the figures, they could be extended so that they included the preparation of them and the accountant could submit them to senior management.

(b) Job enlargement – widening the range of jobs, and so developing a job away from narrow specialisation. There is no element of enrichment.

(c) Job rotation – the planned rotating of staff between jobs to alleviate monotony and provide a fresh job challenge. Trainees might be expected to learn a bit about a number of different jobs, by spending six months or one year in each job before being moved on.

7.8 Process theory

Process theory seeks to explain how motivation occurs given an individual's personal needs and goals. The best known contribution to the process theory of motivation is by Victor Vroom. This theory suggests that motivation is a product of how much one wants something, reflecting preference and priority in personal goals (motivation theorists call this the reward value or valence), and one's estimate of the probability that a certain action will secure it. Therefore valence × expectancy = motivation or the strength of an action devoted to achieving what is desired. This process may be illustrated in the following way:

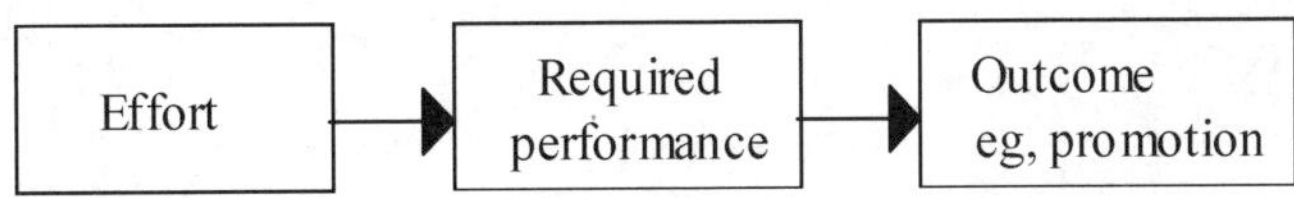

The recommendations to management that go with this model are outlined as follows.

(a) Discover what outcome each employee values most.

(b) Define for employees the kinds of performance that are desired or required, ie, explain what constitutes a 'goal' and an 'adequate performance'.

(c) Ensure that the desired levels of performance are achievable.

(d) Link the outcomes desired by employees to the specific performance desired by management.

(e) Ensure that the overall motivation strategy avoids conflict between the positive expectations it seeks to create and other factors in the work situation.

(f) Make sure that outcome or rewards are sufficiently attractive to motivate the desired level of performance.

Conclusion The functions of a supervisor include: planning; organising; controlling; communicating; problem solving and decision taking; and motivating and maintaining discipline.

8 SELF TEST QUESTIONS

8.1 List the functions of the supervisor (1.3)

8.2 In the hierarchy of objectives are strategic plans higher than operational plans? (2.2)

8.3 What are the 4 M's? (2.3)

8.4 What are the reasons for delegation? (3.4)

8.5 List the tasks involved with the supervision of work in an accounts department (3.5)

8.6 Draw a control cycle (4.2)

8.7 Explain what is meant by 'grapevine' (5.3)

8.8 Outline the advantages of verbal communication (5.4)

8.9 What rules can be applied to improve the effectiveness of communication? (5.7)

8.10 Apart from money, what motivates staff? (7.5)

Chapter 5

OPERATIONAL MANAGEMENT

PATHFINDER INTRODUCTION

This chapter covers the following performance criteria and knowledge and understanding

- Scheduling and planning methods (Element 10.1)
- Time management (Element 10.1)
- Work activities are planned in order to optimise the use of resources and ensure completion of work within agreed time-scales (Element 10.1)
- Contingency plans to meet possible emergencies are prepared with management and, if necessary, implemented within agreed time-scales (Element 10.1)
- Work methods and schedules are clearly communicated to all individuals in a way that assists their understanding of what is expected of them (Element 10.1)
- Understanding that the accounting systems of an organisation are affected by its organisational structure, its MIS, its administrative systems and procedures (Elements 10.1, 10.2 & 10.3)

Putting the chapter in context – learning objectives.

In the last chapter we discussed organising - one of the functions of a supervisor or manager. A part of organising is drawing up a series of plans for all the departments in the organisation and for all the individuals in each department. Co-ordination is needed to ensure that all their efforts move together in the same direction. In this chapter we will be discussing the planning aspects of organising and we will continue with the co-ordination of the plans in the next chapter.

It is essential that work is sensibly and methodically planned at all levels – departmental, sectional and individual. Everybody must be aware of the role they have in attaining the organisation's objectives. The achievement of the objectives involves co-ordination and communication at all levels, coupled with a methodical approach – this is best achieved by sensible planning.

The process of planning is designed to ensure that priorities are established, deadlines adhered to and emergencies limited to the absolute minimum. The use of check-lists, bar charts, activity and time scheduling, action sheets and other systems all facilitates planning.

At the end of this chapter you should have learned the following topics.

- appreciate the need for a methodical and well planned approach to work;
- recognise the principles of effective work planning;
- detail common methods of planning work with the characteristics and applications of each method;
- appreciate the need for identifying priorities and detail the approaches to determining and dealing with such priorities;

1 PLANNING

1.1 Planning and control

The tasks of management are traditionally seen as planning and control. Planning requires management to think ahead. It should generate a climate of awareness throughout the organisation as those involved undergo the discipline of detailed analysis of the following.

(a) What has to be done to attain the objectives of the business?

(b) Who is to be responsible for the various stages of the plans?

(c) When will these stages have to be completed?

(d) How will they be accomplished?

The stages in the planning and control cycle can be shown diagrammatically, as follows:

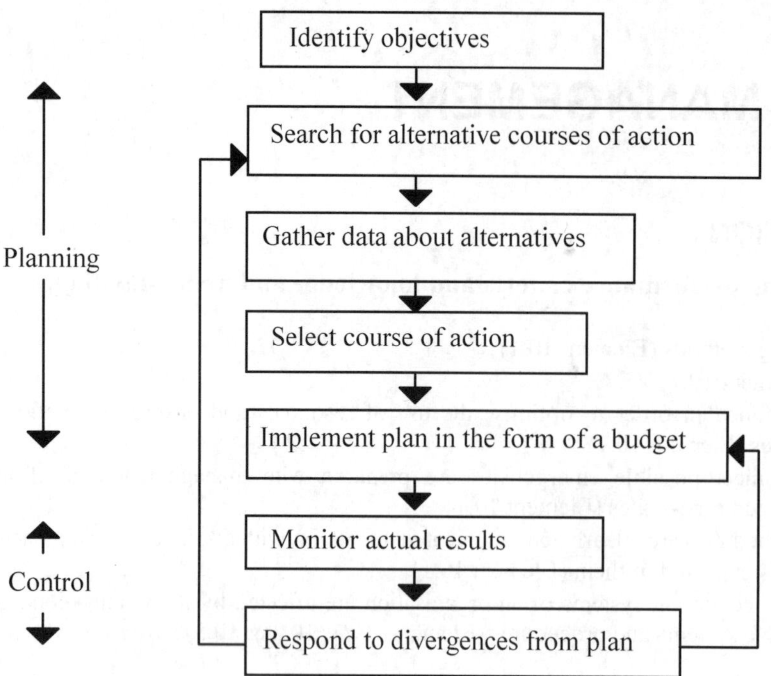

1.2 Management activity

There are three types of management activity: - strategic planning; management control (tactical planning) and operational planning.

Strategic planning - is generally at top management level and involves making decisions about:

- the objectives of the organisation;
- changes in these objectives;
- the resources used to attain the objectives;
- policies governing their acquisition, use and disposal.

Strategic planning is usually, but not always, concerned with the long term. For example, a company specialising in production and sale of tobacco products may forecast a declining market for these products and may therefore decide to change its objectives to allow a progressive move into the leisure industry, which it considers to be expanding.

Management control (or tactical planning) - there are many decisions taken by middle management at this level. They include pricing decisions, distribution decisions relating to purchases and suppliers, stock levels and other aspects of working capital management and fixed asset replacement decisions. Decisions at this level are usually based on financial analysis, money being the common unit of measurement of resources. The control systems are performance reports relating to profit, cost or revenue centres.

Definition Management control is the process by which managers ensure that resources are obtained and used effectively and efficiently in the accomplishment of the organisation's objectives.

Effectively means that resources are used to achieve the desired ends. **Efficiently** means that the optimum (best possible) output is produced from the resources input to the system. Sometimes the word **effectual** is used. **Effectual** means both effective and efficient.

Operational planning- this represents the lowest level of planning and involves line manager, supervisory and foreman levels in the setting of specific tasks. Operational planning takes place within the context of the strategic and tactical plans. To be operational, objectives such as 'to make a profit' or to 'be more efficient' should be translated into more specific terms. When goals can be quantified they can be translated into clear plans by which performance can be measured. The focus of operational plans is on individual tasks eg, scheduling individual works orders through a production planning system.

Definition Operational planning is the process of ensuring that specific tasks are carried out effectively and efficiently.

1.3 Planning and direction

Planning of any kind requires commitment. Commitment implies direction, and direction can best be achieved by:

- Effective inspiration of subordinates towards organisational goals.
- Harmony of objectives, or goal congruence. The more effective the direction, and the better the communication, the more will individuals see that their personal goals are in harmony with enterprise objectives.
- Direct supervision. The more personal the contact, the better the direction. The more levels there are between supervisors and those who are supervised, the greater the risk of confusion of instructions. Face-to-face contact makes people feel that the supervisor is interested in them. Instructions and communications are improved, as are feedback, problem-solving, and sources of new ideas.
- Understanding what motivates people. Having identified what motivates subordinates, this can be reflected in management decisions.
- Recognition of appropriate direction techniques. This requires identification and selection of the most efficient means of stimulating outstanding performance.

Conclusion All levels of management are involved in planning. Top management concentrate on overall strategies and long term plans. Middle management draw up tactical plans that outline how the strategies are to be achieved and supervisors plan work activities and decide what each of their subordinates will be doing at any given time.

2 WORK PLANNING

2.1 Planning for the achievement of objectives

Definition The work plan determines how work should be done and establishes policies and procedures, work methods and practices to ensure that predetermined objectives are efficiently met at all levels.

The basic steps and objectives in work planning include the following:

- the establishment and effective treatment of priorities (considering tasks in order of importance for the objective concerned);
- scheduling or timetabling tasks, and allocating them to different individuals within appropriate time scales (eg, continuous routine work and arrangements for priority work with short-term deadlines), to achieve work deadlines and attain goals;
- co-ordinating individual tasks within the duties of single employees or within the activities of groups of individuals;
- establishing checks and controls to ensure that priority deadlines are being met and work is not 'falling behind', and routine tasks are achieving their objectives;
- agreeing the mechanism and means to re-schedule ordinary work to facilitate and accommodate new, additional or emergency work by drawing up 'contingency plans' for unscheduled events. Because nothing goes exactly according to plan, one feature of good planning is to make arrangements for what should be done if there was a major upset, eg. if the company's computer were to break down, or if the major supplier of key raw materials were to go bust. The major problems for which contingency plans might be made are events that, although unlikely, stand a slim chance of actually happening.

The overall aim encompassing the steps and objectives outlined above is to instil method into work – by working methodically, existing systems can be improved and new systems will be effective from the date of implementation.

2.2 The role of policies and procedures

Planning is an activity that involves decisions about:

- organisational aims and objectives;
- means or policies; and
- results.

Definition A policy is a general plan of action that guides the members of an organisation in the conduct of its operations.

Once an organisation has established its strategic objectives, it can begin to say in what manner it intends these to be achieved. Policies cause managers to take actions in certain ways, but they are not actions in themselves.

Procedures may be defined as:

Definition The formal arrangements by which the principles stated in policies are put into effect.

Procedures provide a sequence of activities that executives are required to follow when implementing policy.

2.3 Working methodically

The majority of organisations approach work planning methodically. Employees, however, often do not realise that if they do not plan their own individual and personal approach to work then the results desired by the organisation will not be achieved despite the efforts of the organisation.

A well-organised employee should endeavour to ensure that as a general guideline the following factors are considered:

- Neatness and tidiness - if the desk, shelves, cabinets, etc. are tidied in order it aids retrieval and efficiency as well as having the advantage of a pleasing appearance.

- Order - there are advantages to be gained from ensuring that tasks are tackled in some semblance of order, be it chronological or priority. Efficiency is improved if work is grouped into batches of the same type and carried out at the same time.

- Routine - it is important that routine in all aspects of the employee's work should be established. For those tasks that need to be done each day, a routine should be established so that they are done at the same time each day. Important and difficult tasks should always be attempted when the employee is fresh, normally during the morning. Tasks, requests and instructions should be written down; memory often proves defective. The adage 'never put off until tomorrow what can be done today' should be put into action. The regular routine, once established, should be written down. This will enable the employee to use it as both a reminder and a checklist. Additionally, if the employee is absent or leaves the organisation the written routine will enable a substitute or replacement to function more effectively.

Although emphasis has been placed above on the employee working methodically it must be remembered that the method employed by the organisation in devising, implementing and operating administrative systems and procedures is of equal importance.

2.4 Principles of planning work

The planning of work involves the allocation of time to the requirements of work to be done. This must be applied to the organisation as a whole, to individual departments and sections and to single employees. An important feature of the principles is the role of time. Planning must be geared to terms of time and the degree of flexibility built into planning will vary according to the length of time being planned for. The principles of planning will revolve around:

(a) the determination of the length of time the plans will be concerned with;
(b) planning by departments and groups of individuals;
(c) planning by individuals;
(d) the implementation of planning principles;
(e) the updating of and alterations to plans.

2.5 Time ranges

There are three time ranges involved in the planning of work: long-term, medium-term and short-term. These three terms are really only expressions of convenience. Different organisations will include different lengths of time under the same heading. For example, a length of five years might be considered long-term for a factory producing footwear but short-term in, say, the aviation industry. It must be remembered that all time ranges are relative.

The allocation of work to time should be undertaken periodically with the ultimate aim of attaining the objectives of the organisation. Planning in the long term involves forecasting and as such may be somewhat inaccurate and is, therefore, normally expressed only in general terms. Medium-term plans are likely to be less inaccurate and less forecasting is required. It is likely that plans have already been put into practice, and the likelihood of medium-term objectives being attained may be measured against the results of these plans. In the short term, forecasting will be fairly accurate and the plans made will probably be adhered to without alteration.

2.6 Planning by departments and groups of individuals

Within organisations departmental plans are devised to meet specific objectives, the origins of those objectives stemming directly from the goals, aims and objectives of the organisation as a whole. There are two aspects that should be considered here:

- the internal departmental/group planning via the determination of schedules etc;
- co-ordination of the work of all the departments/groups within the organisation to ensure that the overall objectives of the organisation are attained.

It is essential to that the objectives of the organisation will only be met in any time span if individual organisation members (employees) plan and implement appropriate actions effectively. The individual should plan for the long term by ascertaining the requirements over, say, the coming year. The equivalent of medium-term planning would be perhaps on a quarterly basis and this would be broken down into monthly, weekly and daily plans – the equivalent of short-term planning. Priorities must be identified.

Conclusion Departmental plans are devised to meet specific objectives, the origins of those objectives stemming directly from the goals, aims and objectives of the organisation as a whole.

2.7 Periodic reviews of plans

The process of planning involves forecasting. Even at the best of times forecasting, particularly long-term, will never be totally accurate. In order to overcome this inaccuracy factor, periodic reviews should be undertaken. In this way plans may be changed to take account of changing, different or previously unforeseen circumstances, and new priorities can be established. This process is based on an approach commonly termed cyclical planning and involves the following steps:

- determining the long-term plan eg. 5 years;
- periodic review and, if necessary, updating of plans. This would normally be at intervals of between 6–12 months;
- inclusion of increasing detail as deadlines approach. Years 3 and 4 in a 5 year plan would be planned in outline whilst years 1 and 2, being nearer, would be planned in some detail.

It must be remembered, of course, that any changes made must be communicated to heads of departments/groups who in turn must inform individuals.

3 PRIORITIES

3.1 Identifying priorities

Much office work is of a routine nature although there are exceptions. Priorities must be established with regard to the cyclical nature of routine work and unexpected demands.

The cyclical nature of routine work often means that certain tasks have to be completed by a certain time. In such cases other work may have to be left in order to ensure that the task with the approaching deadline date is given priority. Such tasks might include:

- the preparation of payroll sheets for a weekly computer run;
- the despatch of monthly statements to account customers;
- the checking of stock levels at predetermined intervals and appropriate action such as re-ordering.

Unexpected demands are often made at departmental, sectional or individual level. If management requires urgent or additional work to be carried out then, obviously, some other tasks will have to be postponed.

Given that routine tasks may be anticipated and that unexpected demands cannot, this area of priority identification can be divided into routine tasks which can be accommodated within normal sensible planning and 'emergency-type' tasks which must be performed at short notice. Routine work usually includes a number of tasks which, as a matter of course, fall into a natural order in which they should be performed. This 'natural order of events' approach can usually be incorporated into the normal routine of the office and/or the individual to such an extent that often it is not apparent that there has ever been a problem with the identification of priority tasks. Where tasks/events of an 'emergency-type' nature arise the main problem facing an individual will be that of deciding which of the routine tasks should be postponed. Additionally, it must be remembered that the postponement of one routine task will automatically delay successive tasks.

3.2 Guidelines for determining priorities

In determining priorities, the following should be noted.

- Wherever it is possible for a priority to be anticipated, such as in the case of the 'natural order of events' described above, then associated difficulties will usually be overcome by sensible, logical planning.

- If an 'emergency-type' task occurs, then normal routine work will automatically take second place. It is here that decisions must be taken to decide which routine tasks should be postponed. Also, plans should be formulated and implemented to ensure that the routine work postponed is carried out as soon as possible, resulting in minimum disruption to the normal routine.

- Often there may arise situations where one priority comes into conflict with another. Here the task deemed more important by a responsible individual should take preference.

- It should be remembered that individuals within one department or section often become blind to the needs of other departments or sections. A task that is classed as low priority within one department or section may be of the utmost priority to another. Thus in arriving at any decision the individual making that decision must ensure that the effect on each department is included in the decision-making process.

- Priorities should be determined by a responsible individual. Often, especially in the matter of routine cycles, the individual responsible for that work will be qualified to determine any priority. However, the greater the effect and the wider the span of influence of priority determination, the more responsible the individual should be.

3.3 Setting priorities

Activities need to be sequenced and scheduled. There may be conflict between the two planning tasks since the best sequence of activities to put the plan into place might not be consistent with the schedule of when particular activities need to be completed. The sequence of activities may be determined by the following:

- An activity must precede another when it is a pre-requisite for later activities. Assembly of a car cannot precede the manufacture or purchase of its components.

- The sequence of activities may be dictated by the ease with which they can be done. New products or services are often introduced into the most receptive parts of the market first.
- An activity may be considered more important than others, eg, in the building industry priority will be given to outdoor work when the weather is favourable to minimise the risk of delays later.

The organisation's operations require proper scheduling of resources to run efficiently and avoid periods of over and under utilisation. Some activities must occur at precisely the right time, eg specific day and time slot for advertising a new product. The scheduling of tasks can also affect customer service in terms of delivery.

4 CONTINGENCY PLANNING

4.1 Introduction

In an uncertain world, events not planned for may occur. Totally unforeseen events are, by their nature, impossible to plan for. The aim is to manage the risk and prepare contingency plans.

Definition Contingency planning means making preparations to take specific actions when an event or condition not planned for in the formal planning process actually takes place.

We all have fire drills and know what to do if we see water coming through the ceiling, but what happens when a tube strike means that 80% of the staff that work in accounts are unable to get to work as normal?

The contingency plan will outline the standby procedure to cope with the disruption and will also set out the procedure to return to normality and catch up with the routine work. The plan will be communicated to all employees along with the name or post holder designated to put the plan into action. As with fire drills, the plan should be tested to make sure that all staff are aware of the procedure.

4.2 Managing the risks

As with all risk management, the key objective is to introduce measures that cost less than the potential damage which might arise if the risks identified occurred.

Specifically, risk management involves three steps: risk assessment, risk management and risk transference.

Risk assessment - all potential problems that can be thought of should be listed and broken down under headings eg, physical, human and systems or employees, computers, operating conditions and criminal activities.

Physical	Human	Systems
Fire, flood or terrorist action	Staff on strike	A computer virus which destroys all the files on the hard disk
Currency devaluation in your main trading country	Payroll theft	Accounting error due to posting a wrong amount
Power cut	Employee has heart attack	Snow breaks telephone lines

These risks should then be assessed as to the impact and damage they would cause to the business if they occurred. The risk should be quantified as far as possible, eg the failure of a particular computer on the network might result in the loss of half a day's sales and the time involved in re-keying information. The qualitative nature of the risk needs to be noted as well. During the 1980s, someone was able to 'hack' into Prince Philip's private mailbox on the Telecom Gold Network. While no actual 'financial' loss occurred, the damage to the mailbox service was apparent and may have resulted in the future loss of revenue.

Risk management - once the potential damage has been assessed, steps are taken to minimise the damage. It is a vital element of risk management that the cost of the steps must be commensurate with the damage avoided. Management can attempt to reduce the risk through good work practices, quality specifications and standards, backup systems and contingency plans. The remaining risk may be an insurable risk.

Risk transference - ultimately, there are some areas where the risk is small in terms of its probability but high in the damage that would be incurred. An example might be earthquake damage in most of the UK, or losses arising due to fire, etc. Whilst steps can be taken to ensure the integrity of data, the most sensible way of dealing with the rest of the risk to the systems is to transfer, or share the cost via insurance or some other form of contingency plan covering the area of 'disaster recovery'.

4.3 Disaster affecting the computer system

In computing terms, a disaster might mean the loss or unavailability of some of the computer systems. In a modern business there are few areas unaffected by computing, and consequently few that will not suffer if its performance is impaired. Also, risks are increasing, an organisation now has to cope with the risks of hacking, virus infection and industrial action aimed at the computing staff.

Losses that can be expected due to the non-availability of computer systems increase with time; it is therefore important to make plans to keep downtime to a minimum.

Management commitment is an essential component of any contingency plan because it will almost certainly involve considerable expense.

Various stand-by plans must be considered; the choice will depend on the amount of time that the installation can reasonably expect to survive without computing. The types to be considered include:

- distributed support, where computing is spread over several sites so that, if one site is lost, the others can cope with the transferred work; this approach implies compatibility and spare capacity to cope with the loss of the largest installation.

- use of another's equipment, which is popular but often not effective, as it relies on continuing compatibility and spare capacity, both out of the control of the installation needing stand-by.

- the spare computer room, either empty, or with an operational computer already installed; the former depends on suppliers acting rapidly to install a machine when required; the latter are obviously more expensive, although subscription to a shared room will reduce costs; a facilities management operation may be of relevance here.

- portable computer rooms, which can be installed at the user's site, but only provide space and facilities for the smaller computers, and are not ready for immediate use.

The key feature of any disaster recovery plan is the regular back-up of data and software. If, at the time of disaster, there are no back-up copies, then no amount of stand-by provision will replace them.

The contingency plan must specify what actions are to be taken during a disaster and during the time that computer systems are unavailable up till the time that full operations are restored. The plan must be as detailed as possible; should state who is responsible at each stage, when it should be invoked, and where copies may be found.

The more care that is taken with a contingency plan, the better the organisation will be able to survive a computing disaster; it also concentrates the mind on computer security and the risks faced, with an increased likelihood that counter measures will be installed which will reduce the risks.

4.4 Contingency, strategic or no planning

Contingency planning cannot deal with events that are not currently foreseeable nor can it deal with every event that could conceivably occur. Consequently there is a need to sieve out the unimportant events. The stages in such a sorting mechanism may be to:

- deal specifically with items of lower probability - the big probability events should already be covered by the strategic plan;

- identify those variables that could seriously damage the organisation, or present an important opportunity, if they occur - these variables are described as 'critical' and should be explicitly covered by the contingency plan;

- exclude events that cannot be coped with - for example, total collapse of the market.

4.5 Advantages and disadvantages of contingency planning

The main argument in favour of contingency planning is that it places the management team in a better position to cope with the change by eliminating or at least reducing the time delay (and hence lost profits) in making a response to an emergency. The emergency may be a lost opportunity or a definite threat. Specific reserve plans help managers to respond more rationally to the event. A crisis can lead to decisions being made within a very short time span and without full information. Early evaluation of the demands of low probability events and the alternative remedies allows more detailed consideration and consequently should reduce the likelihood of panic measures.

Although contingency planning does force managers to consider unlikely events that can result in beneficial spin-offs, it can also result in negative attitudes. Events with low probabilities may be threats and focusing attention on these threats could be demoralising and demotivating.

5 ALLOCATING WORK

Because departmental managers and supervisors have a complete understanding of both the nature and volume of work to be done and the resources at their command, it will be their job to divide the duties and allocate them to available staff and machinery.

Planning is essential in this division of labour because, although there are some obvious work allocations, those of specialist tasks to specialist workers eg computer programmers, and accountants, others may be more complicated. Some areas that need consideration are outlined below.

Peak periods in some tasks may necessitate redistribution of staff to cope with the workload and there should be flexibility in who does, and is able to do, various non-specialist tasks. It is quite usual for staff to be pulled off one job and asked to help out somebody else who has a backlog of work.

Staff attitudes and status must be considered. A hierarchical organisation structure with job grades and different levels of authority and seniority can work towards efficiency, providing close control, motivation etc., but it can also cause planning problems. Flexibility in reassigning people from one job to another or varying the work they do may be hampered by an employee's perception of his or her own status. 'Helping out' or 'covering' for others may be out of the question. Planning must take into account seniority and experience when allocating tasks, but it must also recognise that junior employees may need and expect challenges and greater responsibility to avoid boredom and frustration.

Individual abilities and character differ, and work should be allocated to the best person for the job. Planning should allow for flexibility in the event of an employee proving unfit or more able for a task.

Efforts will have to be co-ordinated so that all those involved in a process (eg. sales orders) work together as a team. Where the team is large, sub-groups may be formed according to activity or skill for closer supervision and sense of unity. Work-sharing will also be more flexible for a unit with common skills and experience, so similar skills should be grouped together.

The hierarchy must function efficiently. There should be suitable team leaders, supervisors and management staff to ensure control throughout the organisation, without an unmanageable span of control or waste of managerial time.

Conclusion — Knowing the human resources under their control means that, in peak periods, supervisors can redistribute staff to cope with the workload and ensure control without waste.

6 WORK GROUPS

6.1 The purpose of a team

An important aspect of work is that it is usually done in groups or teams. It does not matter whether the work is developing a corporate strategy for an organisation, checking insurance claims in an office or building cars in a factory. A team is quite simply:

Definition a number of individuals working together to achieve a common task.

- a number of individuals - a team needs to be small enough to enable the leader to keep in touch with the whole team but large enough to enable each individual to play an effective role without being swamped.
- working together - the members of a team at work should consist of individuals who, while working together, can be more effective than they are working alone.
- to achieve a common task - the task and its objectives must be commonly agreed, clearly communicated and understood by the team.

There are a number of factors that contribute to the performance of teams; for instance, the organisational structure within which the team works, the type of task to be accomplished, resources available and the characteristics of the team and the team members.

6.2 Activity

Is an orchestra a team?

6.3 Activity solution

An orchestra is a team made up of brilliant individualists. The conductor attempts to blend them together to make a superlative team performance.

6.4 Personality types

According to R W Belbin the success of a team, in terms of group morale, behaviour and performance, can depend significantly upon the balance of individual skills and personality types within the group. He has designed a series of questionnaires whereby people can be identified as belonging to a particular group type. He suggests that there are eight main character types that a well-balanced group would contain. These eight types are:

- **the leader** - co-ordinating (not imposing) and operating through others;
- **the shaper** - committed to the task, may be aggressive and challenging, will also always promote activity;
- **the plant**- thoughtful and thought-provoking;
- **the monitor-evaluator**- analytically criticises others' ideas, brings group down to earth;
- **the resource-investigator**- not a new ideas person but tends to pick up others' ideas and adds to them; is usually a social type of person who often acts as a bridge to the outside world;
- **the company worker**- turns general ideas into specifics; practical and efficient, tends to be an administrator handling the scheduling aspects;
- **the team worker** - concerned with the relationships within the group, is supportive and tends to defuse potential conflict situations;
- **the finisher**- unpopular, but a necessary individual; he is the progress chaser ensuring that timetables are met.

Different team roles indicate different types of behaviour which are not necessarily linked to job and task skills. For instance, a person might be naturally imaginative - a 'good ideas' person. Another might be good at checking details to make sure everything has been covered. Yet another might be the person to make sure decisions are implemented and the task carried through to completion. Even though these team roles are not associated with particular job and task skills, they are considered crucial to task and goal achievement in that their presence or absence is said to influence significantly the work and achievements of teams. Consequently, most team role exponents maintain that, for a team to be high performing, it should be 'balanced'; that is, there should exist amongst the typical behaviours of members, the full range of team roles.

The description of Belbin's eight roles does not mean that a team cannot be effective with fewer than eight members. Members can adopt two or more roles if necessary. However, the absence of one of these functions can mean a reduction in effectiveness of the team. With no shaper, the team can get bogged down, with no finisher, important details can be missed, with no monitor-evaluator the team can be swayed by the very bright, articulate and possibly impractical shaper and so on.

Conclusion A successful team consists of carefully selected members who have skills and attributes that can assist the reaching of a desired goal. It will have a leader, subordinates and a task to accomplish.

6.5 Activity

Which of Belbin's personality types do you think you are?

7 TIME MANAGEMENT

7.1 Introduction

Definition Time management implies planning the best use of time, including cutting down on time wasting, devoting more time to the really important issues and completing more in the time available.

Organising tasks and duties are the major functions of the supervisor. However, it is equally as important for managers to manage their own time as to ensure that other people's time is being used efficiently and appropriately. Time management is fundamental to job performance and effective delegation.

7.2 Main influences

The main influences on a person's use of time are outlined in the diagram below:

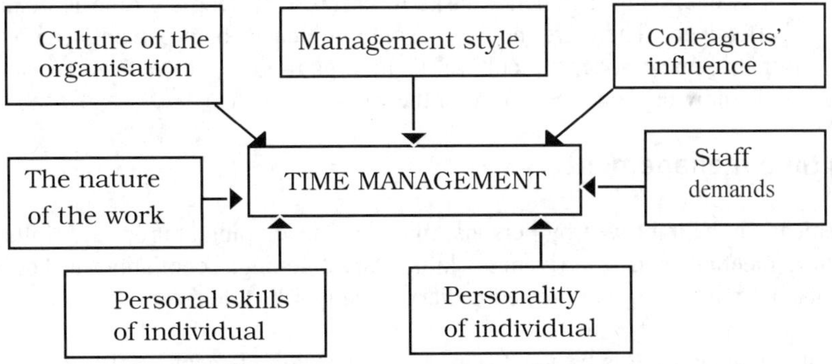

The nature of the work is critical to the amount of control over time management. In established jobs, where the work has become routine and predictable, time management is going to be different from new or developing work. Where a job involves contact with others there is more likelihood of interruptions than a job working with no near contacts.

The physical environment can either help or hinder a person's efforts at time management. Those with offices of their own are able to operate an 'open door' policy for staff communications but a 'closed door' policy when a physical barrier is needed in the interests of personal work efficiency.

Travelling is another major influence on a person's time management. The location of colleagues, customers and suppliers can contribute to time wasted in travelling between appointments.

Culture of the organisation: - some organisation's cultures favour strict adherence to protocol and procedures, discouraging informal contacts. Others encourage an open access communications policy that can be stimulating but time wasting.

The organisations that stress accuracy and quality encourage their employees to take time over their work, as opposed to those organisations that work to tight deadlines and have to risk inaccuracy or occasional errors.

An individual's personal work standards are going to be influenced by the type of decision-making in the firm. Decision-making in some organisations is slow and deliberate whilst in others it is much quicker.

Attributes of job-holder depends on personality and preferences. The differences in attributes and style are due to the fact that some people:

- are more assertive and find it easier to deal with colleagues who waste their time;
- have more skills and experience than others;
- work best in the morning, whilst others work best later in the day;
- are untidy and disorganised whilst others are neat and methodical;
- like to concentrate their efforts into short, intensive periods, whilst others pace their work;
- can deal with several tasks simultaneously, whereas others can only cope with one issue at a time;
- are task-oriented as opposed to people-oriented;
- like to delegate while others prefer to keep the work to themselves;

7.3 The importance of time management

Because time is a valuable human resource - a sort of capital - it should be spent and used in the most effective way. Time management helps to cut down on time wasting, leaving more time to spend on the really important jobs.

Failure to plan properly means that something might be overlooked, causing yet another crisis that, in turn, takes time to put right. An essential objective of looking at time management is to enable the person to save at least some of the time presently wasted to use to tackle jobs that require undivided attention and effort.

Conclusion It is one of management's tasks to ensure that people's time is being used efficiently and effectively. There are, however, some influences on a person's use of time. These include - management style, the culture of the organisation, colleagues, the skills and personality of the individual and the nature of the work.

7.4 Improving time management

Time management can be improved by personal planning, developing appropriate skills (faster reading, report writing, handling meetings and assertiveness skills), target setting, negotiating and delegating. Planning aids also assist in planning the day's activities eg, a diary or daily schedule form.

Another way of managing time is by identifying significant job elements (SJE's). This is done by examining the job description and selecting from it three or four key activities or SJE's, and listing the tasks and duties for each one. For a supervisor these could be:

- organising staff;
- maintaining a constant flow of materials to a given point;
- recording and storing information;
- developing and maintaining a safe and healthy environment.

The time spent each month to complete the tasks and duties under each SJE is then calculated and a labour cost attached. Once these figures are reviewed a decision can be taken on whether to increase or decrease the time spent based upon the costs incurred.

7.5 Activity

Could you identify three significant job elements in your work and work out how much time you spend a month on them?

8 METHODS OF PLANNING WORK

8.1 Methods and systems

It is important to recognise and understand that different types of organisation and different individuals have individual characteristics, tastes, styles, preferences and objectives. These particular objectives may well be attained via different methods and systems. It is thus difficult to state categorically that all methods apply to all organisations. All that can be given are guidelines to the methods available.

The following methods and systems are probably the most common:

- checklists;
- bar charts;
- activity scheduling and time scheduling;
- action sheets;
- other systems including planning charts and boards, requisition forms and diaries.

Each of these methods and systems will be discussed individually below. It should be remembered, however, that any combination may be in use at any one time within an organisation or, indeed, by an individual employee. It is vital therefore that these efforts are co-ordinated - not only with each other but with all actions taken.

8.2 Checklists

Definition Checklists are a list of items or activities.

The preparation of a typical checklist would involve:

- making a list of activities and tasks to be performed within a given period;
- identifying urgent or priority tasks;
- maintaining a continuous checklist adding extra activities/tasks when required.

Typical uses of checklists would include:

- purchasing requirements (shopping list);
- points to cover at an interview;
- points to cover at a meeting eg, an agenda;
- organising a conference or meeting.

8.3 Bar charts

A bar chart has two main purposes:

- to show the time needed for an activity; and
- to display the time relationship between one activity and another.

Bar charts are particularly useful for checking the time schedules for a number of activities that are interdependent. The example shown below depicts a bar chart for the building of a house extension over a period of six months:

	March	April	May	June	July	August
Dig foundations	———					
Walls/floors		———				
Windows			———			
Door frames				———		
Roof				———		
Electric wiring				———		
Plumbing			———			
Glazing					———	
Plastering					———	

This illustrates the importance of bar charts in showing the overall progress to date, thus assisting in monitoring the progress attained at an individual stage of a multi-stage process.

8.4 Scheduling

There are two aspects to scheduling - activity and time.

Activity scheduling may be used for any task that involves a number of actions, which must necessarily be undertaken in some sequence. It involves identifying key factors and assembling them on a checklist.

Definition Activity scheduling is concerned with the determination of priority and the establishment of the order in which tasks are to be tackled.

Establishing the order in which tasks are to be tackled is not as easy in practice as it appears in principle because some tasks:

- must be completed before others may be commenced
- may need to be carried out at the same time as others
- may need to be completed at the same time as others but factors such as finance or manpower may prevent this.

A problem that is suited to activity scheduling is the arrangement of an interview where, say, three panel members are required and six candidates have been short-listed for interview. Obviously mutually convenient dates must be found when all six parties are available and to add to the burden, the room which is to be used for the interview must be available on the days when the six parties are available.

Time scheduling follows the preparation of an activity schedule and involves the determination of time required for each activity. Effectively, a time schedule determines the order in which activities are scheduled on a checklist with the time required for each activity also being shown alongside each item.

The process of time scheduling commences with the determination of the time required to perform each activity. The total of the individual activity times, with allowances for simultaneous activities, will produce the time allowed for one complete group of activities. It is particularly useful in the process of planning especially as it enables deadlines to be set.

8.5 Activity

Draw a schedule for a car journey that you might take.

8.6 Activity solution

Using a route planner to get from Liverpool to Manchester shows the time required is 34 minutes, not allowing for any delays. The stages in the journey are as follows:

Time		Road	For	Direction
00.00	Depart Liverpool	A57	4 miles	East
00.04	Turn off onto	A5080	1 mile	SE
00.05	At M62 junction	M62	24 miles	E
00.31	Turn off onto	M602	5 miles	E
00.32	Turn off onto	A5063	0.25 miles	S

8.7 Action sheets

This system is a natural progression from activity and time scheduling. Action sheets really represent a summary of the time each stage of a particular task should take and the relationship of that time both to the total time necessary to complete the task and to the time of individual stages.

The example below depicts an action sheet for a celebration such as a wedding:

Activity number	**Detail**	**No. of weeks in advance**
1	Book church	26
2	Book reception hall	26
3	Send out invitations	12
4	Receive replies	4
5	Order food/refreshments	3
6	Check arrangements	2
7	The big day	-

8.8 Other systems

Planning charts and boards - usually show information in summary form. Their main feature is that any required item of information may be seen at a glance. They are often used to show details of future events that affect departments, for example, to plan staff holidays.

Work requisition forms - a requisition form is essentially a document that itemises work that needs to be done. It usually requests the recipient of the form to carry out certain tasks as clearly indicated on the form. It is essential that careful thought goes into the design of such forms to ensure that all the necessary information required to complete any particular task is included.

Diaries - the diary is an obvious and consequently often overlooked aid to planning. Diaries range from the small pocket-sized type to large diaries with a page for each day.

Arranging appointments - the failure to note down full and appropriate information regarding a particular appointment could have serious repercussions for the organisation, particularly if an appointment is missed altogether. It is sensible to have a routine for making appointments and that the following information is obtained:

- the full name and title of the person you intend or are required to see;
- the full and precise name and address of the relevant organisation;
- the telephone number and the extension of the person you must see;
- the time, date and anticipated length of the meeting;
- the location of the meeting eg, which room on which floor in which block;
- outline details of the matter to be discussed;
- travel directions and details of entrance points and security procedures.

It is, of course, equally important for those details to be sent to people who may be intending to visit you.

Conclusion Objectives may be achieved via different methods and systems. Some of the methods available include checklists, bar charts, activity and time scheduling, action sheets, planning charts, requisition forms and diaries.

9 SELF TEST QUESTIONS

9.1 What are the three types of management activity? (1.2).

9.2 Outline the basic steps in planning work (2.1).

9.3 Give a definition of a policy (2.2).

9.4 What happens to normal routine work when an emergency arises? (3.2)

9.5 How would the sequencing of activities be determined? (3.3).

9.6 What is contingency planning? (4.1).

9.7 List the personality types identified by Belbin (6.4).

9.8 Explain two of the influences on a person's use of time (7.2).

9.9 Give an example of a use for a planning chart or board (8.8).

Chapter 6
CO-ORDINATION

PATHFINDER INTRODUCTION

This chapter covers the following performance criteria and knowledge and understanding

- Scheduling and planning methods. (Element 10.1)
- Purpose of the work activity and its relationship with other related work activities. (Element 10.1)
- Work activities are effectively co-ordinated in accordance with work plans and any contingencies that may occur. (Element 10.1)
- Work activities are planned in order to optimise the use of resources and ensure completion of work within agreed timescales. (Element 10.1)

Putting the chapter in context – learning objectives.

In a previous chapter we discussed organising - one of the functions of a supervisor or manager. Co-ordination is an essential part of organising rather than a separate function. A part of organising is drawing up a series of plans for all the departments in an organisation and for all the individuals in each department. Co-ordination is needed to ensure that all their efforts move together in the same direction.

At the end of this chapter you should have learned the following topics.

- understand the necessity for co-ordination and control within the planning process

1 CO-ORDINATION

1.1 Introduction

The essence of organisation is to combine and co-ordinate the varied parts to make an effective working unit.

Definition — Co-ordination is the process of integrating the work of different individuals, sections and departments in an organisation towards the effective achievement of the organisation's goals

All parts of an organisation are very much dependent on each other for doing their job properly. They are all intertwined and have links with one another. The marketing manager must prepare the sales budget, which must be discussed with both the manufacturing and finance departments, and he or she will also be aware of the costs of sales promotion and of the sales staff. All these various and different parts of the organisation must decide on the best course of action to take. This means that the chief accountant must discuss with other managers the various ways in which the organisation should carry out its tasks in order to maximise its use of financial resources.

1.2 Integration of activities

Co-ordination is the integration of the activities of groups/individuals to provide harmonious working with least effort and maximum efficiency.

Co-ordination requires the various functions to work together as a team, to co-operate and communicate. It requires both a definite, planned system of cross-functioning between the departments and an acknowledgement of informal methods perhaps facilitated by management (such as open-plan offices).

Examples of co-ordination often cited are:

(a) sales and market research linked to production;
(b) research and development linked with market research.

Inevitably the situation will develop where there is contact up and down and across the organisational hierarchy lines, since problems frequently affect more than one function. For example, a major export contract will affect sales, but:

- can production meet the deadlines and match the specification?
- will modifications need to be made to suit local requirements (development and technical)?
- what about payment and the implications on working capital (finance)?

1.3 Co-ordination in practice

Ways in which co-ordination can be achieved in organisations include the following:

- an organisation structure that ensures that all sections of the business are pursuing common objectives.
- clearly defined job descriptions, to improve appreciation of the interrelationship of tasks; it should prevent overlapping, or areas of responsibility being missed.
- standard instructions and procedure manuals that reduce the risk of conflicting practices within the company. (But care must be taken to avoid the risk of stifling initiative.)
- regular meetings between departments may prevent them acting in a parochial manner to the detriment of the organisation as a whole.
- training in group practices may accustom executives to a uniform approach to organisational problems, gaining an appreciation of the benefits of co-ordination as well as of the culture of the organisation.
- financial co-ordination can be achieved by a sympathetic use of budgetary control procedures, in which participation in budget preparation is encouraged.
- good communication will minimise misunderstanding about the motives of the organisation and its managers on the part of supervisors and workers.

1.4 Internal co-ordination

Up to now in this textbook, the term 'organisation' has been broadly used. Another interpretation of this term may be made if organisation is regarded as being the co-ordination of all the procedures, systems and functions within that organisation. If all these are indeed co-ordinated then the organisation will function effectively, efficiently and economically. This seems eminently logical and sensible and indeed formal recognition appears frequently in the writings of noted management specialists. For example:

O'Shaunessy defines organisation as:

Definition 'a matter of dividing work among people whose efforts will have to be co-ordinated'.

And Henri Fayol, often termed 'the father of modern management', defines organisation as:

Definition 'the bringing together of the necessary factors of production – the requisite capital, materials, equipment and manpower – and maintaining them to enable the business to continue'.

These versions show that to organise really means to co-ordinate all aspects of an organisation.

1.5 Formal types of co-ordination

Many organisations endeavour to set up formal systems of co-ordination to ensure that individuals, groups and functions work effectively with each other and that the parts, although existing individually, operate in harmony. This is usually attained by the setting of an overall organisational goal that is broken down into supporting objectives for individuals, groups and functional areas.

Co-ordination covers aspects such as:

- the planning and direction of activities (allocation of human, money and material resources) for maximum efficiency and effectiveness;
- synchronising the timing of activities for maximum usage of labour, machine hours and effort;
- ensuring that service or staff functions provide the basis and backup for the line departments of production, marketing and finance, so that they can meet objectives;
- implementing control procedures for comparing actual with desired results.

These aspects are important – it is of little value to have a stock control system which appears to work for both raw materials and finished goods and an apparently efficient production department system if the two functional areas are not co-ordinated. If the right type of raw materials cannot be issued to the production department at the right time then, however efficient the production department may be internally, it will not be able to contribute effectively to the organisation as a whole. In turn such failure will mean that the production department will be unable to furnish the stores section with the required quantity of finished units to meet customers' orders.

Legal proceedings, the processing of data for decision-making, recruitment of key personnel, typing of documents, retrieval of files – are all service activities that may affect speed, cost and quality of the production or marketing operations that are the main activities of the organisation.

Formal systems of co-ordination are required to ensure that the goals of the organisation are achieved and not hampered.

1.6 Informal types of co-ordination

It is to the credit of many individuals within organisations that they recognise instinctively the relationship between different procedures, systems and functional areas and implement them. This is usually achieved without formal modes, within small groups and sections where, having identified the goals of the particular group/section, the group/section leader and individuals devise suitable and logical ways of attaining the required goals. This is normally achieved informally whilst the co-ordination of a number of groups or sections requires attention of a more formal nature.

1.7 Co-ordination and communication

Communication is the prerequisite that must exist before co-ordination can be attempted. Individuals must know how relevant their work is to the goals of the organisation as a whole and also to the aims at departmental level. Departments and sections must also be shown how the results of their work fit together and are effective in attaining required goals. Communication may be, perhaps, rather obvious but it is often ignored and yet it is vital for effective co-ordination.

1.8 Co-ordination through planning

As indicated previously there are formal and informal types of co-ordination, but even before co-ordination is considered there needs to exist information upon which co-ordination can be based. This will involve planning and perhaps the three most important plans, or forecasts are:

(a) the business plan;
(b) the manpower plan;
(c) the organisation plan.

These are listed in what would appear to be a logical order given that the business must know first where it is going and what it is trying to attain and secondly the type of staff required to help attain those goals effectively. Once these two aspects have been adequately planned for, the organisation or co-ordination of work may be attended to.

2 THE BUSINESS PLAN

2.1 Introduction

A business plan is a control mechanism in a work organisation. The business plan indicates all the various aspects of work to be carried out or equipment to be purchased by the organisation and outlines the number and estimated cost of the staff required. It can be defined as:

Definition The forecast made by an organisation at certain stipulated intervals of its financial assessment of future activities, both in the short term and the long term.

2.2 Overall business plan

The management of any concern should have some corporate objectives in which they will put forward what is called the overall business plan. This will mean looking at every aspect of the work carried out by the organisation, and planning a forecast of what it will do in the future, probably giving a one-year (short-term) forecast and perhaps a five-year (long-term) forecast. This planning will have to be carried out at least once a year, although most organisations monitor or update the plan at shorter intervals, usually every three months.

Such a plan often depends on what is known as a key or limiting factor, a factor which will, in essence, prevent it from producing and/or selling as much of a product as it would like. For example, a concern may have the capacity to produce one million units a year, but if the potential sales market is only half a million units then sales becomes the limiting factor and will determine the shape of the business plan. Again if a particular type of skilled labour is in short supply, production and hence sales will be limited – the shortage of skilled labour will become the limiting factor and will determine the shape of the business plan. Such limiting factors could influence adjustments to and realignments of existing business plans by forcing concerns to look to other markets with, perhaps, other products. Whatever the result, the organisation must know where it is going and how it is going to get there.

2.3 The importance of the business plan

A business plan is important to an organisation because its contents can be monitored from month to month to see whether the forecast is within reasonable bounds. It would be of no use having a business plan without it being subject to controls, which are usually exercised by the finance department. For instance, if costs exceeded the forecast and income was less than forecast, then this information would need to be acted upon quickly by the finance department, because if the trend continued then the organisation would find itself in such a position that it could no longer trade. Changes within and outside an organisation can take place very quickly and consequently business plans have to be monitored and amended from time to time. The important point is that planning must not only be carried out, but it must be continually monitored if an organisation is to succeed.

3 THE MANPOWER PLAN

3.1 People resources

People resources are required to fulfil the needs of a company in relation to its current operations and its future plans. People resources are costly and like all other resources of the company have to be carefully planned. We can define a manpower plan as:

Definition The internal manpower requirements of an organisation that takes into consideration the number and type of staff required to carry out the tasks required during a future period of time.

Not only is there a need to plan what the business is going to do with its resources, there is also a need to plan on the number of staff required. Whilst this may seem to be a simple matter there are many aspects which need to be considered. It is not just a matter of counting the number of bodies required, but sorting out the number of retirements expected, the number of vacancies proposed, whether recruits can be obtained and if so, what rate is required.

There may also be discussion with departmental managers to find out and to settle the number of staff they require. They may decide that certain work streams are necessary at certain times and all this information will affect the manpower plan. Since there will be a need to retain existing staff, a staff bonus scheme may also be considered. There is also the question of training and what to do with surplus staff. Not only is there a need for a manpower plan which is very often combined with the business plan, but there is a need to monitor and control the staff requirements. This is usually left to the staff group or personnel group to do in conjunction with the finance group.

3.2 Objectives of the company manpower plan

Manpower planning is a fundamental part of the overall corporate plan, and its objectives will be related to overall objectives. Manpower plans and corporate plans cannot exist in isolation, since each will automatically influence the other.

Heads of all organisation functions are therefore involved in the process of considering the changing staffing needs over the period of the corporate plan, starting from the present position. Personnel management's responsibility is that of drawing the functional requirements together within the framework of company manpower policy including funding. The basic aim is to assess the quantity and quality of people required at each level within each department of the business and to ensure that these positions are filled on a continuous basis.

Effective manpower planning will, therefore, help to remove the need for redundancies and avoid shortages of labour; and age planning as part of manpower planning can deal with some of the people problems arising from time to time.

3.3 Steps in manpower planning

The steps in devising the plan are:

- manpower objectives are agreed within the corporate plan;
- manpower resources are assessed or evaluated;
- manpower forecasts are prepared for each significant manpower group, which will identify surplus staff as well as shortages;
- policies and plans are drawn up, in detail, to overcome shortages in labour numbers and skills;
- recruitment sources are identified and agreed;
- staff development, succession, career and promotion plans are prepared;
- education and training plans are agreed;
- strategies for reducing surplus staff are agreed.

When assessing or evaluating present manpower resources, staff should be classified as to:

- age - to assist with retirement plans, labour turnover forecast, or as one of the promotion factors;
- ability - it is essential to know the degree of ability of each employee;
- skills - it is important to detail all the skills of an employee, even if in his present role he or she is not utilising all of them. For example, the increasing opportunities for companies arising from the UK's trade with Europe has heightened the need for employees to speak/correspond in European languages;
- any other key factors relevant to the company.

From the available information it would be usual in assessing present resources to detail them within significant manpower groupings, eg, managers, supervisors, skilled, semi-skilled, clerical, professional etc. Other information brought to the assessment would include the output from development and training schemes and labour turnover statistics and costs. The increase in computer technology has meant that this information can be gathered and maintained relatively easily.

3.4 Secondary aspects of manpower planning

Secondary factors to the three key ones are the employment considerations and effective recruitment.

It is expensive to employ staff. Not all the costs relative to an individual are apparent at first consideration; obviously the annual salary plus any pension or related government costs form part of the expenses of employment. However, in addition, training, sickness, holiday and initial recruitment costs and even the cost of the poor work an unsuitable recruit might do must be taken into account. Contemplation of such costs leads to the realisation of the need for effective recruitment. If the wrong person is recruited for a job, he or she may either leave after some of the costs of employment have been incurred, or may become a disciplinary case where dismissal for incompetence, with all its inherent problems may arise.

Either way, it is important that the manpower planning function offers a high standard recruitment service. It is essential that the recruitment officer is sure of the suitability of the prospective employee before making any offer.

3.5 Activity

Outline an advantage of planning the manpower requirements in advance of their being required.

3.6 Activity solution

The advantage of planning manpower ahead of requirements is the time that becomes available for effective action. For example, in a situation of surplus staff, the strategies agreed will come into play. The possible strategies include:

- stopping recruitment;
- the identification of normal wastage, ie, staff coming up for retirement or the normal known percentage of female workers leaving within a particular period;
- the encouragement of early retirement with enhanced benefits; and finally
- the declaration of redundancies.

4 THE ORGANISATION PLAN

Having identified where the organisation is going and how it is going to get there via the business and manpower plans, the necessary work must be identified, divided and co-ordinated. To ensure that the organisation is functioning effectively as a whole and within separate units a control mechanism must be implemented.

Definition In conjunction with the manpower plan and the business plan, the organisation plan effectively considers the requirements of the individual departments.

For example, if the organisation proposes to purchase a large number of personal computers in order to sell them, it will have to plan the type of organisation it requires. It will need to consider the number of staff required for:

(a) dealing with the number of items of equipment received each week from the factory;

(b) the storage of equipment;

(c) the shipping of equipment to agents or retail outlets;

(d) the accounting work necessary.

Whilst these are the major areas which spring to mind, you may also consider others which could be added. All the various departments have to plan what they wish to do and it is usual for an organisation's plan to change from time to time to take account of the increased opportunities in some areas and of the reduction in others.

5 ASPECTS OF CO-ORDINATION

5.1 Linking work flows

Command, direction and supervision are the key functions that underlie the linking of work flows. Managers seek to optimise the output by linking several operations into a scheduled workflow. This means that the output from one workstation becomes the input for the next. In attempting to schedule this, the manager may be faced with either great rigidity or reasonable flexibility. This will depend upon

- the type of work;
- the evenness of work spread;
- timetables;
- output rates;
- manning quality and versatility;
- manpower attendance.

It is often difficult to integrate work flows between specialists who are unable or unwilling to widen their scope of skills. This problem would be compounded if some people were overloaded whilst others were generally under-utilised. Such a situation would breed rigidity. However, where people have wider skills and are involved in the total job, rather than one small aspect, they are more likely to be flexible in their approach to work.

To link workflows effectively, a manager needs to know:

- capabilities of staff members;
- probable output rates;
- timetable constraints;
- target performance (possibly, time/quality/output).

5.2 Co-ordination and control

Control is necessary to ensure that what management requires to be done is being done. For example, there must be a means of checking that employees are doing what they are supposed to be doing, and that it is done effectively and efficiently. The flow of information represents another example – is the right information reaching the right people at the right time? There must be an established means of ensuring that this is so.

In principle, control requires four basic elements. They are:

(a) standards of performance that are verifiable, achievable and clearly stated;

(b) relevant, adequate and timely information to monitor the system at work;

(c) detailed analysis of deviations from standard, applicable to favourable as well as adverse variances;

(d) 'attention-directing' information – control includes putting right what may have gone wrong. Information systems should highlight areas needing attention and, later, confirm that any errors have been corrected.

As we have previously noted, there are two approaches to control:

- an emphasis on financial values – budgetary control.
- an emphasis on physical values – quality and output control.

Most organisations adopt both approaches.

5.3 Co-ordination and conflict

Inevitably the work required to achieve the right level of co-ordination between functions in the organisation will encounter difficulties:

- there may be poor communications both horizontally and vertically within the organisation;

- different departments and managers may have varying views as to the plans for the organisation. They may be pursuing different objectives and have different priorities leading to a lack of goal congruence;

- time pressures can vary between different parts of the organisation;

- differences in leadership style can mean that two departments may have very different ways of doing things and very different time pressures to work under;

- organisation structure may hinder co-ordination – particularly where there is a complex or matrix management structure, and where there is no unity of direction;

- personal or interdepartmental jealousies/dislike can prevent co-ordination and cause conflict;

- there are often difficulties in creating an effective management team with people from varying disciplines – eg. a production management team must bring together people with technical skills (engineering, quality control), financial skills (budgetary control, cost reduction), personnel skills (recruitment and training) and planning skills (production planning).

5.4 Synergy

Co-ordination is the main purpose of organisation. Its main aims are shown below:

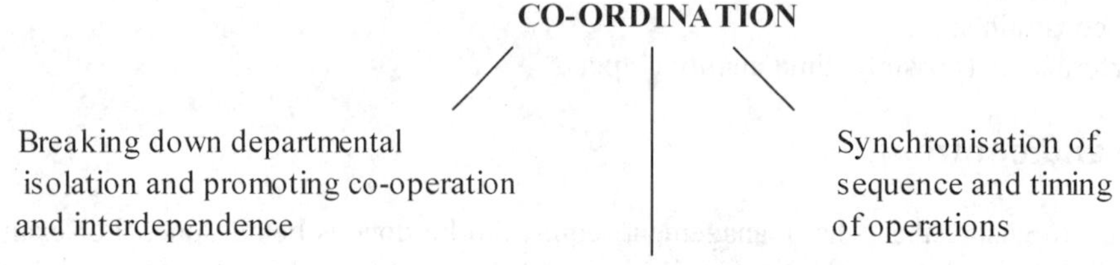

Through co-ordination we obtain a synergy - a whole that is greater than the sum of all of its parts.

6 CO-ORDINATION OF FUNCTIONS

6.1 Work organisation: co-ordination and control

Within any organisation (when seen as an entity), departments, sections and individuals must all be organised in such a fashion as to ensure that:

(a) the overall objectives of the organisation are attained;
(b) each department, section and individual makes a valid contribution.

It is therefore essential that the efforts of each contributor are co-ordinated to ensure that objectives are met.

The function of an organisation, ie. attaining a set objective, is operated via the attainment of contributory objectives by departments, sections and individuals. This is why efforts at all levels must be co-ordinated.

In addition to the initial communication of expected objectives to contributors, it is essential that the organisational structure permits the flow of required information in all directions to ensure that attainment and achievement may be measured or forecast at any one moment.

The co-ordination and communication highlighted above may be implemented by reporting procedures. Top management, having decided on the required objectives and structure, will expect executives and managers to report the requirements throughout the organisation. This will ensure that everybody within the organisation is aware on an individual basis of what is required, how it is to be achieved and when and where. Reporting procedures should be initiated to ensure that progress is constantly monitored and that the work plan is kept to schedule.

Conclusion Functional plans cannot proceed without regard for those of other functions. There must be co-ordination between them and an integration of all towards successful performance.

6.2 Divisions and links within an organisation

As we have seen earlier in this textbook, it is difficult to visualise an organisation structure in its entirety, so it is usual to represent these divisions and links by means of an organisation chart. A typical presentation for a manufacturing company might be:

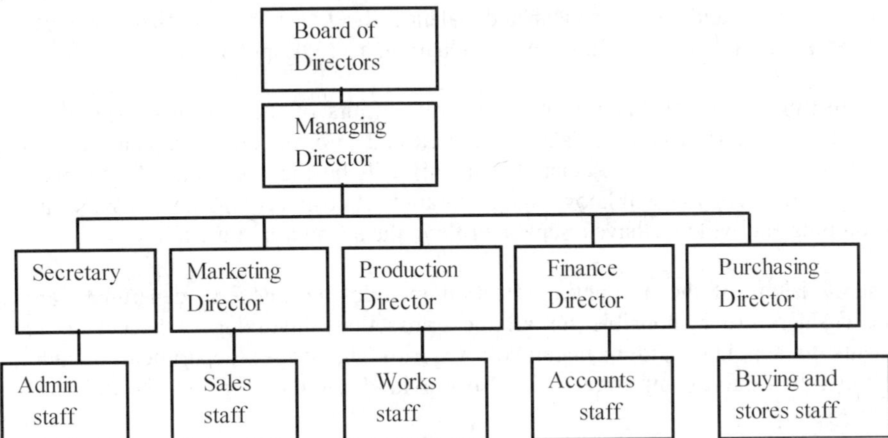

Of course, there will be different titles used and many variations upon the relationships depicted above. For example internal audit might appear as a separate function for some businesses, buying and stores staff may report to the production director in others, and so on. What is usual, however, is the relationships suggested for the various functions. Within each function there will be the line relationships such as that between the chief buyer and assistant buyers, as well as the functional relationships between specialists such as that between the production director and the finance director.

If we briefly consider the role of the accounting function we can see that it has a relationship with other major areas. The accounting department can be viewed as having responsibility for handling and processing information within the organisation. This information and any control procedures is provided as a service to the other departments.

6.3 Relationships within the accounts function

Again it must be recognised that there will be many different approaches to how work is divided and responsibilities allocated within a particular function and the accounts department is no exception. However, dependent upon the objectives laid down for the function and the particular characteristics of the organisation, it is possible to suggest a basic structure:

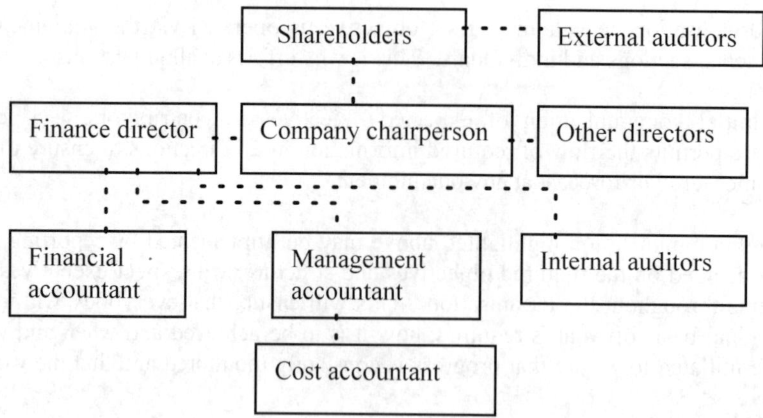

Initially we can distinguish between two divisions of accounting. Financial accounting is concerned with the recording and processing of transactions which have taken place, while management accounting involves the preparation and presentation of accounting information in such a way as to assist management in formulating policies and planning and controlling activities.

Financial accounting - is concerned with maintaining records of events of a financial nature as they occur. Accounts are kept of all debtors and creditors transactions and of all moneys paid by them to the business. Coupled with this will be the preparation of the annual accounts in the forms required for both shareholders and the Inland Revenue and also periodic financial statements, eg. cash flow statements, debtors and creditors balance, draft monthly profit and loss accounts and balance sheets. For these there will be the need to incorporate adjustments such as for depreciation, asset valuation, accruals and provisions.

Management accounting - is involved only in the internal affairs of the business. Based mainly on the information provided by the cost accounts, data is analysed and information is presented to management to provide a basis for decision making. Associated with this will be the operating of systems of budgeting control and standard costing. As you will know, the preparation of cost accounts involves a separate approach from financial accounting and will thus have a separate role in the accounting function.

Normally other subdivisions of the accounting function include the cashiers' department and the wages department. The cashiers are responsible for all the transactions involving cash such as receipts from customers, payments to suppliers and payments of wages. The wages department, in addition to the calculation of remuneration due to employees, will also provide basic data for both the financial and costing systems.

Because of their association with accounts and the knowledge of the work processed by the accountant, these two departments are usually seen as natural subdivisions of accounting. In many organisations the same arguments apply to the recognition of computing services as a section of the accounting function. Much of the data processed is of an accounting nature and computing skills have been developed by accounting staff in many instances. However it must be recognised that, as the provision of computing services expands, there will be many cases of separate departments being established but still maintaining close links with the accounting function.

6.4 Location of accounts department

For organisations with different sites the overall policy on centralisation versus decentralisation and organisational structure will have important effects on the location of the accounts departments. In some cases the accounting function may be carried out entirely at the head office; in others each location would be responsible for all its own accounting procedures, with only interim and final financial statements being forwarded to head office.

With centralisation there is the opportunity to employ specialist accounting staff and advanced EDP systems more effectively and economically. When staff are in one central office, supervision may be improved and there is greater flexibility of staff and easier handling of peak loads. However day-to-day control over financial control systems may be lost and there may be delays in the flow of information and documents. In addition head office staff are quite often regarded with suspicion and resentment and there may be the danger of head office becoming out of touch with the peculiar characteristics of the methods of working at each location.

Organisational structure may determine the location of departments. A divisionalised structure with different activities within the group may lend itself to separate accounts departments at each division. On the other hand a major chain of retail stores may install strong control systems at each outlet, with basic data being transmitted daily for processing and reporting by a centrally located accounts department.

6.5 Co-ordination between functions within the organisation

We have examined the organisational details of the accounting function. A similar requirement exists for other parts of the organisation, such as manufacturing, information processing, despatch, purchase, marketing and personnel. They all need to analyse what is required for their own particular area, taking into consideration the financial decisions made by the organisation. The manufacture would only go ahead if the factory manager knew that the products could be sold. He or she would have to depend on the advice from the marketing manager as to the level of production that is expected to be sold and on the sales staff for bringing in more orders. The purchase manager would also have to plan for the amount of stock required by the factory and the despatch manager for making certain that the finished goods are delivered as cheaply as possible and by the quickest means. They are all dependent on obtaining the right type of staff to carry out the various tasks, and this is where the personnel function comes into its own, to interview the staff and decide how much each individual should be paid.

6.6 Accountants as co-ordinators

Accountants often act as co-ordinator in the information processing system, for example:

(a) **The budget controller function** - the accountant often acts as budget controller/ co-ordinator by carrying out the following tasks:

- assisting managers to develop their budgets for costs/activities under their control;
- translating non-financial budgets (eg. production estimates) into financial terms;
- ensuring that all budgets are properly interrelated;
- co-ordinating all budgets into one master budget.

The accountant is admirably placed in the organisation to act as a 'link man' for this process as the finance function inevitably interfaces with all other functions. The accountant is also in a position to see where there are problems within the system and to suggest improvements or enhancements to bring about savings.

(b) The monthly management information 'package' - most companies of any size rely upon a monthly reporting system which produces, systematically, information in a standard format and content which is designed for:

- performance evaluation;
- motivation;
- historical purposes.

This monthly package of information may consist of both financial and non-financial data, designed to enable management to:

- report deviations from the business plan ('feedback');
- analyse causes;
- suggest corrective measures;
- re-forecast the future trend of results ('feedforward').

(c) Producing ad hoc reports for the management - in order to make informed decisions prompt, accurate and relevant information is required. As practically every decision has some financial consequence the accountant is often regarded as a prime source of relevant data. Examples of *ad hoc* reports are:

- make or buy decisions (is it better to make the item or purchase it outside the business?);
- special contracts for marginal business (how can we maximise our short run revenues?);
- evaluating the financial effect of some course of action, (closure of a department).

6.7 Information technology and the accounting technician

There is no doubt that the accountant technician falls into the category of an 'information worker'. An information worker can be described as:

Definition A person whose primary occupational task is the production, processing or distribution of information.

It is therefore natural to consider the ways in which technological support is given to the information worker. When the tasks of the information worker are analysed they can be seen to consist of the following:

- creating text;
- completing paperwork;
- filing and retrieval of paperwork;
- routine decision-making;
- 'communication' - internal/external; textual/oral.

7 SELF TEST QUESTIONS

7.1 Outline the different ways that co-ordination can be achieved in an organisation (1.3)

7.2 What is a business plan? (2.1)

7.3 Why do organisations need manpower planning? (3.2)

7.4 What sort of conflict might be encountered in trying to co-ordinate activities in an organisation? (5.3)

7.5 Compare and contrast financial and management accounting (6.3)

7.6 Define an information worker (6.7)

Chapter 7
CONTROLS

PATHFINDER INTRODUCTION

This chapter covers the following performance criteria and knowledge and understanding

- The range of external regulations affecting accounting practice. (Elements 10.2 & 10.3)
- Quality management, quality circles. (Element 10.2)
- Overview of the organisation's business and the critical external relationships. (Elements 10.2 & 10.3)
- Work activities are closely monitored in order to ensure quality standards are being met. (Element 10.1)
- Methods of operating are regularly reviewed in respect of their cost effectiveness, reliability and speed (Element 10.2)
- The system is updated as directed in accordance with changes in internal and external regulations, policies and procedures. (Element 10.2)

Putting the chapter in context – learning objectives.

We have already looked at control systems in chapter 3 and, in this chapter, we are going to discuss controls specified by both the organisation and the UK regulatory framework which imposes controls on certain functions within it.

Any system in an organisation should be regularly reviewed and have control procedures to identify problem areas.

At the end of this chapter you should have learned the following topics.

- Understand the necessity for co-ordination and control within the planning process.
- Explain the concept of quality.
- Outline the difference between 'quality control' and 'quality assurance'.
- Analyse the role of total quality management

1 ORGANISATIONAL CONTROL

1.1 Introduction

Control is concerned with:

Definition regulating the activities within an organisation so that the causes of deviations from standards specified in policies, plans and targets are identified and corrected.

The purposes and methods of organisational control are therefore to:

- standardise performance – eg. by quality assurance and control systems, supervision, procedure manuals, production schedules;
- obviate losses through theft, fraud, wastage or misuse, eg. by record keeping and audit procedures;
- correct deviance's, eg. by statistical quality control, supervisory management, disciplinary procedures;
- define and limit authority by job descriptions, policy statements, rules and procedures;
- define and direct performance by management, by objectives, budgets, sales and production targets.

1.2 The control process

The main stages are:

(a) Determining and agreeing objectives;
(b) Translating objectives into plans and performance standards;
(c) Communicating plans and standards to those concerned with their implementation;
(d) Measuring actual performance against agreed standards;
(e) Ascertaining the reasons for deviations;
(f) Taking appropriate corrective action.

A more detailed cycle of control is illustrated below:

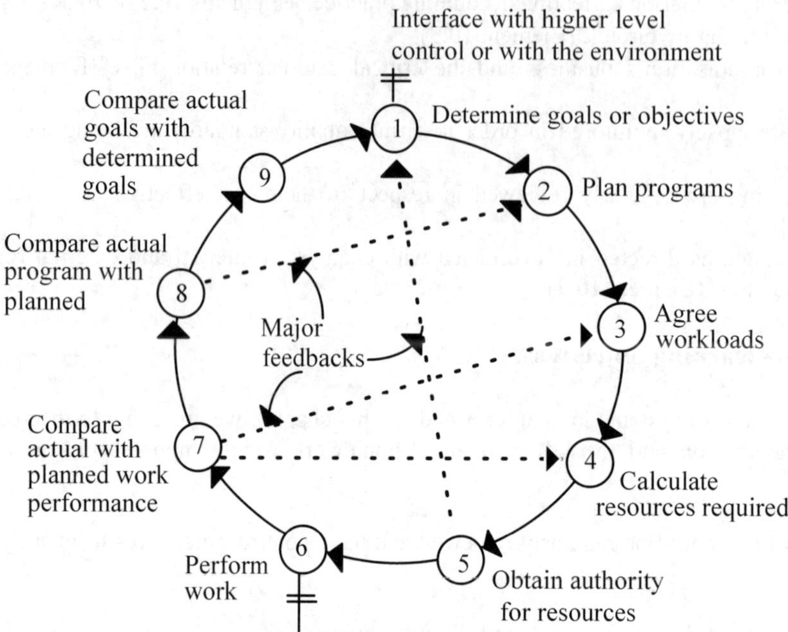

1.3 Planning and control distinguished

Planning is aimed at bridging the gap between the present and the desired position of the organisation. The planning function involves:

- research;
- forecasting;
- consultation;
- flow of information;
- appraisal of the company's present resource capability and its desirable resource capability, including its technical and human strengths and weaknesses;
- the consideration of the means of attaining the desirable resource capability, known as its 'critical mass', needed to attain objectives.

The planning function is preoccupied with these factors which underlie and determine the strategy and tactics of the company. It is primarily concerned with the relationship between objectives, which are needed in every area where performance and results have to be set, and the resources needed to achieve them.

It is contrasted with the control function, which is designed to effect corrective action where targets are not being achieved.

Both planning and control depend on the flow of information to decision takers.

1.4 The characteristics of good control procedures

The characteristics of good control procedures have been identified as follows:

- **Relevance** (tailored to plans and people) - the control system should be adapted to the specific plans, positions and people to which it applies; no one system effectively controls every activity under all situations.
- **Flexibility** - controls should be capable of change to deal with new plans, changed environmental circumstances and shifts in personnel.
- **Focus on critical points** - control systems should be applied at strategic points that are crucial to the final outcome.
- **Timeliness and reporting speed** - the better control systems warn of deviations immediately so that corrective action can be taken before the deviation continues to grow.
- **Simplicity and clarity** - For control systems to work well, those who apply them must understand them, including the standards, measures, corrective actions and nature of operation.
- **Cost effectiveness** - controls should produce savings at least the equal of their costs.
- **Suitability for corrective action** - control systems should be designed not only to identify deviations from standard but to point to appropriate corrective actions.

Conclusion The control function of management is closely linked to the planning function. Plans give rise to actions and these have to be monitored to make sure that they reflect the aims and intentions of the plans. This monitoring of performance is the central core of the control function. Control establishes standards of performance, measures performance against the appropriate standards and identifies corrective action where required.

2 INTERNAL AUDIT

2.1 Internal control

Primarily the responsibility of internal audit is to examine systems of control. Internal control can be defined as:

Definition The whole system of controls and methods both financial and otherwise, which are established by management to:

(a) safeguard its assets;
(b) ensure reliability of records;
(c) promote operational efficiency;
(d) monitor adherence to policies and directives.

Internal controls can be divided into two main categories:

- financial controls, which are primarily concerned with the legitimacy of expenditure and the security of assets and income; and
- other controls, which are created and maintained by management to ensure that an activity is relevant to the needs of an organisation and is carried out in the most effective manner.

These categories are interdependent, and should not be regarded in isolation as both have an impact on the performance of activities and their consequent cost and value to the organisation.

The main areas of internal control can be more closely defined as financial control and management control.

2.2 Financial control

Financial control includes:

- *Budgetary control*: - the organisation should plan and control its expenditure and income to meet its predetermined objectives.

- *Legitimacy of income and expenditure*: all income and expenditure should be in accordance with the policies of the organisation, should be properly authorised and should be within the law.

- *Security of assets*: the assets of the organisation should be kept in proper custody and not wrongly applied, either by error or intent.

- *Accounting controls*: all transactions should be correctly recorded and accurately processed, and control accounts maintained.

2.3 Management control

The nature of management controls will vary widely according to the type of activity that is under review. However, there are several basic control areas that should always be in evidence.

- *Objectives*: - relating to any operational activity, and the methods needed to achieve them should be reviewed regularly. An audit may show inadequate controls on the supply of information to management for decision-making.

- *Procedures*: - staff at all levels need to be informed both of their overall objectives and the organisational procedures which are to be followed to ensure the achievement of the operational activity.

- *Organisation*: - the organisational structure should be clearly defined so that the staff appreciate their role, responsibilities and obligations.

- *Management information*: - needs to be continually informed, with relevant and up-to-date data, of the financial and operational performance of any activity under its control.

- *Supervision*: - systems of supervision and internal check (eg, division of duties, independent checking of work, quality control, etc) should be maintained to ensure that breakdowns, including irregularities and fraud, or weaknesses within the operation are revealed at an early stage.

- *Reviews of operational effectiveness*: - management should regularly review the effectiveness and efficiency of operations under its control, and consider their continued relevance in the light of changing circumstances.

2.4 Organisational and operational control systems

Many writers classify control systems into the following two principal groups - Organisational control and operational control

Definition **Organisational control** emphasises the nature of the organisational or systems design.

Organisational control is where we might examine an existing system and ask 'how effective and efficient was the design or why did it fail?' An important consideration in such an examination is to determine whether the system objectives are being met. Where there are no clear-cut objectives it is very difficult to evaluate any system. Also note that, while a system might be achieving its objectives, it could be using an unreasonable amount of resources in the process.

The accountant's role in organisational control is much more fully documented and more familiar in practice, since it involves the use of budgetary control and of costing systems appropriate to the particular business concerned.

An operational control system is where action to be taken is determined by a set of logical rules. Operational control systems, as with any other systems, need information. Such information is primarily non-financial, for example, data is often expressed in man-hours, numbers of items, weight of scrap etc.

Definition **Operational control** is the process of ensuring that specific tasks are carried out effectively and efficiently.

The accountant's role will be to produce the operational control reports. These will be mainly statistical and must be completely accurate and produced immediately the facts are available.

2.5 The supervisor and cost control

The supervisor's role in cost control derives from the responsibility for resources – people, machines, materials, work in progress or whatever. They are in charge of activities that incur costs and have therefore a cost responsibility. They have the job of controlling costs within specified parameters or against clear cost standards. They may even be charged with reducing or eliminating costs. Where they have a cost responsibility they must know what costs are theirs, how they are determined and the nature and characteristic behaviour of those costs. This information is usually provided by the cost department or by a section of the finance function. It is, however, important for supervisors to know and to interest themselves in the basic costing procedures that apply to their area of activity. The supervisor is, of course, a provider of much of the data used by the cost personnel – time sheets, piecework tickets, stores requisitions and so forth – and as such will appreciate the importance of:

- reliable cost data and information to effective cost control;
- good relations between supervisors and cost department staff.

In summary, the supervisor should:

- ensure that reliable cost information about their area is provided promptly;
- understand the cost procedures that apply to those activities;
- develop a social, co-operative relationship with cost staff.

The costing procedures that the supervisor needs to know and understand derive from some type of cost analysis or classification. The type chosen depends on the business and organisation of the enterprise but in most costing systems, of manufacturing organisations, costs are typically identified in the following way.

(a) The cost of materials embraces all purchases of new materials, components, stores and other commodities except the fixed assets of the firm.

(b) The cost of labour or 'wages' encompasses the remuneration of all employees and managers and includes commissions and bonuses.

(c) Expenses cover the cost of services and benefits to the concern other than those provided by the firm's own employees and the notional costs of the use of its assets in land, buildings, plant and equipment (depreciation).

There is no strictly mechanical way in which a supervisor or anyone else can control costs. Of course, the computer makes possible a continuous flow of data and information about performance and deviations from standards, and may seek to influence directly the response of people to these signals. In the final analysis, however, the most potent influence, the best method of control is human - the manager and supervisor.

Effective control is highly dependent on positive opinion and attitudes among employees and management on every level. Supervisors, by their own application and diligence, can influence the behaviour of their subordinates in ways that will keep 'lost time' and 'non-productive time' at a minimum and thereby help to control labour costs. Similarly, they can, for example, by giving advice, control material cost and overhead cost by keeping scrap levels and the misuse or over-use of consumables down.

Conclusion Supervisors can only control costs if they are given realistic standards to work to and reliable information about performance, especially about any variance or deviation that occurs. The standards should be derived from a thorough analysis of the job, the methods used and the efficiency of performance.

3 BUDGETARY CONTROL

3.1 Budgets

A budget is an action plan for the immediate future, representing the operational and tactical end of the planning chain. It can be defined as follows:

Definition A budget is a statement, usually expressed in financial terms, of the planned performance of an organisation in the pursuit of its objectives in the short-term (generally one year).

Budgetary control takes the targets of planned performance as its standards, then systematically collates information relating to actual performance, and identifies the variance between target and actual performance. Thus, whereas budgets in themselves are primarily tools of planning, the process of budgetary control is both a planning device and a control device.

Throughout the whole of the forecasting and budgeting exercise it is important for people who will be responsible for achieving budgeted sales or controlling budgeted costs to participate in their preparation. If managers gain the impression that the budgets are simply documents produced by the accounts department, they will never feel responsible for achieving the figures shown in them. Managers must be made fully aware that the budgets which are being prepared are their budgets and that any accounting staff involved in the preparation of them are simply providing a service.

3.2 Variance analysis

Variance analysis is the phrase used to describe the comparison of:

- actual financial performance at different levels against that planned;
- actual usage against budgeted;
- actual output against planned.

When the controller considers these variances which may appear as computer tabulation, the bare figures do not give the **reasons** for the variances. The controller has to determine these, consider whether the differences were of a category that arose through circumstances outside the control of management, or whether they occurred through failure within the company. In some circumstances, the variance will be known before it is tabulated and action may already have been taken. In other cases, action remedying the situation will follow. Sometimes, nothing can be done immediately. The variance arose because of an action outside the company and in the short term has to be accepted.

Unexpected changes in taxation, the imposition of a new tax, an extraordinary rise in the price of oil, a sudden plunge in the value of the pound are all examples of circumstances/actions outside the control of management. A marked rise in products rejected by internal **quality control** procedures, a marked fall in productivity on the shop floor indicated by **production control** returns are examples of variances within the control of management.

In all examples the speed of flow of information to decision takers is a key requirement of the control function. It is as important to determine any circumstance which delays, suppresses or distorts the flow of information needed for corrective action as it is to set up a control system which will eventually record the variance. The earlier the information is available to decision takers the better.

3.3 Budgetary control system

The aims of a budgetary control system are to:

- establish short-term business plans;
- determine progress towards the achievement of short-term plans;
- ensure co-ordination between key areas of the organisation;
- delegate measurable responsibilities to managers without loss of control;
- provide a controlled flexibility for meeting change in the short term.

A budgetary control system for a manufacturing company would contain the following:

(a) **Forecasts** – these are statements of probable sales, costs and other relevant financial and quantitative data.

(b) **Sales budget** – is prepared based on an analysis of past sales and a forecast of future sales in the light of a number of assumptions about market trends. The resulting budget is an estimate of sales for a given budget period.

(c) **Production budget** – is prepared on the basis of the sales budget. This involves an assessment of the productive capacity of the organisation in the light of the estimates of sales, and a consequential adjustment of either, or both, to ensure a reasonable balance between demand and potential supply. Production budgets will include output targets, and cost estimates relating to labour and materials.

(d) **Capital expenditure budget** – is drawn up to cover estimated expenditure on capital items (fixed assets) during the budget period.

(e) **Cash budget** – is prepared by the accountant to ensure that the organisation has sufficient cash to meet the ongoing needs of the business. This budget reduces the organisation's transactions to movements of cash and indicates shortfalls or excesses of cash at particular periods of time.

(f) **Departmental budgets** are drawn up individually after the production of the sales and production budgets.

(g) **Master budget** – is effectively a statement of budgeted profit and loss with a projected balance sheet.

Before any figures can be adopted as the budgets of the business, the budgets for each function must be co-ordinated. The most obvious example of this is the need to ensure that the quantities, which the sales department is forecasting that they will sell, are in line with the quantities which production are budgeting to produce. It is necessary to check that the budgeted production volume of a component made in one department and to be used in another agrees with quantities budgeted to be used by that other department. It is also necessary to ensure that the financial implications of the individual budgets are co-ordinated, eg, capital expenditure proposed by operating departments must be reconciled with the cash available for capital expenditure as shown by the cash budget. The main responsibility for ensuring proper co-ordination of the budgets will rest upon the budget controller and the budget committee. Where the proposals in two budgets cannot be reconciled, the budget committee will be responsible for recommending to the managing director what action should be taken.

3.4 The budget manual

It is desirable to have a budget manual setting out the principles and procedures to be followed in preparation of the budgets, collection and comparison of the actual figures and the action to be taken on the variances. It will include:

- the organisation structure, clearly allocating responsibilities and authority;
- timetables for preparation of budgets;
- budget period and control periods;
- instructions on the documentation to be used;
- procedures to be followed;
- classification and coding to be used.

The manual should also give the name or post holder to ask if you have any queries about your work in this area.

3.5 Activity

Does your accounts department have a budget manual? If not, would the effectiveness of the department be improved if one was drawn up?

3.6 Examples of planning and control systems at different management levels

Although planning and control are discussed separately, it is not easy in practice to say where planning ends and control begins. Let us take an example of a budgeting system: the issuing of budget guidelines and initial work of preparing the budgets is clearly part of a planning system, whereas the subsequent measurement of actual expenditure compared with budget is part of a control system. In order to provide an overall idea of planning and control systems, a few typical activities, at different management levels, are set out below:

Strategic planning and control systems	Management planning and control systems	Operational planning and control systems
	Activities	
Selecting company objectives	Preparing annual budgets	Scheduling production runs
Setting financial policies	Cash management planning	Credit control
Setting marketing policies	Planning advertising budgets	Controlling advertisement bookings
Setting research policies	Deciding on research projects	Project cost control procedures
Preparing take-over plans and policies	Reorganising production as required	Rescheduling plant maintenance
Selecting personnel policies	Manpower budgeting	Implementing personnel policies

4 QUALITY

4.1 Quality control

By developing the right approach to quality, organisations can benefit by 'getting it right first time' and avoiding the problems those faulty goods and dissatisfied customers can bring.

Management has a duty to ensure that all tasks are completed consistently to a standard that meets the needs of the business. To achieve this they need to:

- set clear standards
- plan how to meet those standards
- track the quality achieved
- take action to improve quality where necessary.

4.2 Activity

In the control cycle outlined above, which step forms the feedback?

4.3 Activity solution

The feedback is the tracking the quality achieved (or not achieved).

4.4 Setting standards

To manage quality everyone in the organisation needs to have a clear and shared understanding of the standards required. These standards will be set after taking account of:

- the quality expected by the customers;

- the costs and benefits of delivering different degrees of quality;

- the impact of different degrees of quality on the customers and their needs, the contribution to departmental objectives and employee attitude and motivation

Having decided on the standards these must be communicated to everyone concerned to ensure that the right standards are achieved. Documentation of the standards must be clear, specific, measurable and comprehensive.

The British Standards Institution, through its Certification and Assessment Services, provides industry with first class product certification and company quality assessment schemes. When an organisation operates to BS5750 it is a way of demonstrating that the organisation is committed to quality and has been assessed accordingly.

There are three parts to the BS5750:

(a) Specification for design, manufacture and installation
(b) Specification for manufacture and installation
(c) Specification for final inspection and test.

4.5 Meeting the standards

Having decided on appropriate quality standards, management should then:

- agree and document procedures and methods to meet the standards;
- agree and document controls to ensure that the standards will be met;
- agree and document responsibilities via job descriptions and terms of reference; and
- prepare and implement training plans for employees to ensure they are familiar with the standards, procedures, controls and their responsibilities.

Employees within the organisation have a huge influence on the quality of their work and to gain their commitment and support the management should:

- publish the quality being achieved;
- meet regularly with the staff involved to discuss the quality being achieved as well as the vulnerabilities and priorities as they see them. Agree specific issues and action points for them to work on to improve quality;
- encourage ideas from the staff about improvements and consider introducing short-term suggestion schemes.

After the process to achieve quality has been set up, an information system to monitor the quality should be set up. This is called quality control.

Quality standards are set after taking note of the quality expected by the customers and the costs and benefits of delivering different degrees of quality.

4.6 Quality control function

Definition Quality control is concerned with maintaining quality standards.

There are usually procedures to check quality of bought in materials, work in progress and finished goods. Sometimes one or all of these functions is the responsibility of the research and development department on the premise that production should not self regulate its own quality.

Statistical quality control through sampling techniques is commonly used to reduce costs and production interruptions. On some occasions, customers have the contractual right to visit a manufacturer unannounced and carry out quality checks. This is normal practice with Sainsbury and Tesco contracts with manufacturers producing 'own label' goods (eg. Tesco Baked Beans).

In the past, failure to screen quality successfully has resulted in rejections, re-work and scrap, all of which add to manufacturing costs. Modern trends in industry of competition, mass production and increasing standards of quality requirements have resulted in a thorough reappraisal of the problem and two important points have emerged:

- it is necessary to single out and remove the causes for poor quality goods before production instead of waiting for the end result;

- the co-ordination of all activities from the preparation of the specification, through the purchasing and inspection functions and right up to function of delivery of the finished product is essential.

Managers understand that it is not possible to achieve perfection in products because of the variations in raw material quality, operating skills, different types of machines used, wear and tear, etc. However, quality control attempts to ascertain the amount of variation from perfect that can be expected in any operation. If this variation is acceptable according to engineering requirements, then production must be established within controlled limits and if the variation is more than the acceptable one then corrective action must be taken to bring the variation within acceptable limits.

Quality control may be looked at under the following five headings:

(a) *Setting standards* - includes location of possible sources of manufacturing troubles from trial runs, preparing inspection specifications after sampling, and planning the production and inspection functions based on the results of these preliminary activities.

(b) *Incoming material control* - ensures the availability of the necessary material of the required quality standards during production. Close quality contacts must be made with the supplier to establish quality control at the source. The first deliveries received are subjected to 100% inspection to establish the supplier's level of quality. Information is given to the supplier to allow remedial action if necessary. When the required quality level has been reached, other deliveries are subjected to sampling tests only.

(c) *Product control* - involves the control of processed parts at the production sources so that most differences from quality specifications that may have arisen are put right before any defective parts are produced. The three aspects of product control are:

  - quality mindedness of the operatives and to this end extensive training programmes in quality control are arranged;
  - inspectors and testers with good training and experience help foremen to pinpoint potential causes of defects by showing them how to apply control techniques;
  - applying sampling checks to the finished product before delivery.

(d) *Special purpose studies* - the investigation of the causes of defective products and looking for ways of improving elements of production quality.

(e) *Appraisal* - critical appraisal of the overall results obtained from the programme and consideration of ways to deal with changing conditions.

Quality itself must be regarded as relative to other factors such as price, consistency and utility. The market for a product or service will accommodate itself to various degrees of quality.

The quality control function looks at the process as a continuous operation, a series of trends and rejection rates. Reports from the quality control department to management include:

- analysis of defects by cause;
- comparisons between processes and departments;
- comparison of defect levels with previous levels and standard levels;
- longer term trends in quality;
- reports on customer's complaints;
- developments in quality control practice;
- special reports.

4.7 Quality control audit

Apart from receiving reports, management may also commission a quality control audit to find out:

- What is the actual level of rejects?
- Are the standards fairly set?
- Are the standards achieved at the expense of excessive costs?
- How many customer complaints are received?
- Has the quality control system been modified in accordance with changes in processing, policies, materials and products?
- What are the costs of quality control?
- What is done to improve performance by eliminating causes of poor performance?
- Should a personnel audit on their efficiency and knowledge be carried out?

4.8 Advantages of quality control

The advantages lie in the fact that quality control identifies why faulty work is being produced and the quantity of faulty work produced. Action taken as a result can reduce scrap and the amount of necessary re-work. It shows where a design modification could raise efficiency in manufacture. It minimises the chances of poor materials being processed.

The important factor is that quality control must be applied during processing and not after. The most effective areas where control can be usefully applied in most enterprises are:

- goods inwards;
- inspection at the supplier's business to see the type of plant and the methods used;
- inspection of all new tools and plant;
- inspection of the first part completed at each stage;
- the first part produced at each stage should be inspected;
- inspection should take place between processes;
- a final check should be made at the end of the production line and any minor adjustments made.

It is as much a fault to produce goods of too high a quality as goods of poor quality. The requirements of the customers must be borne in mind and the sales department and market research can advise on this. They will be aware of competitor's prices and qualities and a decision must be taken whether or not to increase quality. To increase quality means increasing costs and at what point will the quality be more than the customer can afford?

Definition of quality is 'a degree of excellence'. It is the correct degree of excellence compatible with costs that management must agree on. If they can arrive at this and maintain it they will have overcome one of the most difficult factors of production.

4.9 Supplier quality assurance (SQA)

Obviously, the student will appreciate that it is necessary to control the quality of components delivered into the organisation, be it factory, health authority or service industry. This is usually done through supplier quality assurance officers, who control the specification of the goods supplied.

This may empower the SQA officer to enter the supplier's plant, to verify that production is to the correct specification, working tolerances, material and labour standards. For example, the Ministry of Defence would reserve the right to ensure that defence contractors produce to specification, since defective work would mean the failure of a multi-million pound aircraft, loss of trained pilots and possibly ground crew as well as damage to civilian life and property. Likewise, a weapons system failure could have disastrous consequences. Students connected with the health service will be concerned about drug production being carried out in acceptable conditions, since impurities in drugs could have far- reaching and disastrous consequences.

One great advantage of SQA is that it may render possible reduction of the in-house quality control headcount, since there will be no need to check incoming materials or sub-assemblies or components.

4.10 Total quality management

In many manufacturing industries, quality standards can be necessary at four levels.

- At policy levels - in determining the desired market level of quality. An interesting example is the food supermarket chains. Typically, as an industry becomes more established, so customers respond to higher quality rather than a cheap pricing policy.

- At the design stage - quality standards must be determined and specified to meet the market level of quality. This is an area where Japanese companies concentrate a great deal of quality effort. Japanese companies are rarely trailblazers in introducing new products. They prefer to wait until the design is perfected so that quality can be guaranteed. Japan has not been a major inventor in compact disc equipment, video recorders or camera/photography industries, yet Japanese companies dominate all these areas.

- At the production stage - when application of quality standards over incoming materials and production operations is necessary to implement the policies and design specifications. This is the traditional quality control area where quality circles have made an important contribution.

- At the use stage - in the field where installation can affect final quality and where the guarantee of quality and performance must be made effective. This stage would include training of client's staff, format of instruction manuals, availability of after-sales service, etc.

Total quality management seeks to define the best available practice and quality in every aspect of the company's operations and creates an employee philosophy that expects high quality throughout.

4.11 Quality circles

Quality circles consist of about ten employees possessing relevant levels of skill, ranging from the shop-floor through to management. They meet regularly to discuss the major aspect of quality, but other areas such as safety and productivity will also be dealt with.

The main aim is to be able to offer management:

(a) ideas connected with improvement and recommendation;

(b) possible solutions and suggestions;

(c) organising the implementation of (a) and (b).

The development of quality circles allows the process of decision making to start at shop floor level, with the ordinary worker encouraged to comment and make suggestions, as well as being allowed to put them into practice. Circle members experience the responsibility for ensuring quality, and have the power to exercise verbal complaint. General productivity is considered as well as reduced frustration and grievances and reduced labour turnover. Quality circles may be applied at any level of organisational activity, being used to cover all aspects and could conceivably involve all employees.

The benefits arising from the use of quality circles are substantial:

- improved quality leading to greater customer satisfaction;

- greater motivation of employees;

- improved productivity;
- shop floor understand and share management/customers problems;
- a spirit of seeking improvements is generated;
- employees become more aware of opportunities for improvement because of training, in areas outside quality circles.

5 COMPUTER SYSTEM CONTROLS

5.1 Sources of error

It is important to identify how errors might occur during the operation of a system other than as a result of failing to establish proper administrative controls. Errors will fall into the following classes:

(a) Data capture/classification errors - These occur before data is ready for input to a system and arise because of:

- incorrect classification of data (allocating a production cost as an administrative cost);
- assessment/measuring mistakes (recording the arrival of ten tons of raw material when only nine tons was delivered);
- incorrect spelling (of a customer's name);
- transposition (recording a receipt as £50,906 instead of the actual figure of £90,650).

(b) Transcription errors - these arise during the preparation of data for processing:

- data which has been written down previously or which is passed on orally may be incorrectly recorded on data input forms;
- where data is converted from one format to another, eg. from a DOS format disk to a UNIX system, and then used for the preparation of customer orders.

(c) Data communication faults - if the system operates over a wide area network (WAN) then the original input at the terminal/PC may become corrupted during transmission either during on-line processing or where the information is stored in a batch file and transmitted over the WAN later for processing. Similar issues need to be considered for local area networks (LANs) but far fewer problems arise due to the greater level of resilience inherent in LANs.

(d) Data processing errors - these can arise due to:

- programming error;
- system design;
- data corruption on the system itself.

Because the above errors are likely to occur throughout the life of a system, with varying degrees of seriousness, we must take specific measures to identify when they occur and to ensure that corrections are made to the data, either before or after processing has occurred.

Conclusion Computer system errors can be due to data capture, transcription, communication or processing.

5.2 System activities

The purpose of the controls is to ensure as far as possible that:

- the data being processed is complete;
- it is authorised;
- the results are accurate;
- a complete audit trail of what was done is available.

The areas in which we would expect controls to be assigned to provide protection to the system are input activities, file processing activities and output activities.

Input activities include:

- Data collection and preparation;
- data authorisation;
- data conversion (if appropriate);
- data transmission;
- data correction;
- corrected data re-input.

File processing activities include:

- Data validation and edit;
- data manipulation, sorting/merging;
- master file updating.

Output activities include:

- Output control and reconciliation with pre-determined data;
- information distribution.

Controls in these areas are vital and must deal with errors or problems as they arise instead of delaying their resolution to a later processing stage. This is because processing inaccurate data represents a waste of both computer time and human effort and may lead to further unforeseen errors occurring and misleading final results.

5.3 Controls over data input

The control procedure will be designed with completeness, authorisation, accuracy and compliance with audit needs. The controls will use the following techniques:

(a) Data validation

- Type checks – Every entry must comply with the prescribed format, eg. dates may be defined as consisting of 2 digits, 3 alphabetic characters and 2 further digits such as 04AUG01. Any other form of input will result in an error.

- Non-existence checks – Data fields requiring entry may have a separate validation table behind them such that the data being input must exist on that table, eg. a supplier account number must exist already before the system will accept that number on an invoice.

- Checks for consistency – Where data is originally entered and does not require on-going maintenance, the fact that it is still consistent with the original data input should be checked within an appropriate time-scale, eg. batch totals should not be altered once input, payee codes for suppliers paid by BACS should be confirmed by print-out against source data on a half-yearly basis.

- Duplication/repetition checks – The system may check, eg. that only this invoice has been received from a supplier with the supplier's invoice number currently being input.

- Range checks – A minimum and maximum value could be established against which input can be checked.

(b) Data verification

This determines whether the data has been properly conveyed to the system from the source (unlike validation which is concerned with whether the data is correct or not)

5.4 Controls on output

Controls are put in place over output to ensure that:

- the output expected from the computer is received by the user or user department;
- exception reports which are used as the basis of action are so used;
- error and data rejection reports are reviewed and actions taken to correct the errors;
- the output received reconciles to the input data provided;
- the users receiving data are authorised to do so and acknowledge receipt of it.

The types of control that should be considered during design include:

- printouts should be numbered starting from 1;
- printouts should show the date and time they were produced, by whom and at whose request if the report has not been produced as part of the normal processing cycle;
- exception reports should be considered for every aspect of the output required to see if long, detailed reports can be avoided;
- sub-totals and final report totals should be included;
- any reconciling information should be shown separately;
- the number of pages produced should be indicated beside the End of Report marker.

Conclusion To provide protection to the computer system, the main areas to control are input activities, file processing activities and output activities.

6 EXTERNAL REGULATIONS

6.1 UK regulatory framework

In the UK, statute law provides a framework which is supplemented by regulations issued by a private sector body, the Accounting Standards Board, while companies which have shares dealt in on The Stock Exchange are subject also to the regulations of that body.

The major elements of the UK regulatory framework comprise:

- The Data Protection Act
- The Companies Acts
- Accounting Standards

6.2 The Data Protection Act

The Act is all about protecting data concerning individuals where this data is processed automatically ie, by computer. Because computers can bring together vast amounts of information, process it rapidly and transfer it instantly anywhere in the world, there is an inherent danger that information could be corrupted, used out of context or lost in the system, with the result that individuals would suffer.

The underlying principles behind the legislation are openness, good practice in obtaining and using data, and an opportunity for redress when an individual has cause for complaint. The Act places obligations on those who use personal data. They must be open about that use - through registering with the Data Protection Registrar, and they must follow a code of good practice - the Data Protection Principles.

6.3 Companies Act 1985

The Companies Act 1985 provides a statutory framework for the preparation of the accounts of limited companies. It contains the following:

- formats;
- fundamental accounting principles.
- valuation rules;
- possible exemptions for small and medium-sized companies.

Formats - companies must prepare their annual accounts in accordance with certain formats. There are two formats specified for the balance sheet and four formats specified for the profit and loss account. These formats specify the items that must be disclosed in the financial statements and the order in which they must be shown, although they do provide some flexibility to relegate details to the notes to the accounts.

Fundamental accounting principles - the law embodies five accounting principles:

- going concern;
- consistency;
- prudence;
- accruals; and
- no offset.

These accounting principles are well known to accountants and the first four are listed as fundamental accounting concepts in SSAP 2 'Disclosure of accounting policies' The fifth principle deals with the idea that assets and liabilities, even those relating to the same transaction, should not be offset against one another. Thus, if a company borrows money to purchase a factory, the factory should be shown in fixed assets, and the loan in creditors.

When the directors depart from these accounting principles, a note to the accounts must provide particulars of the departure, the reasons for it and its effect.

In addition there are two further concepts in existence that are not mentioned in either SSAP2 or the Companies Act 1985:

- Materiality: an item is material if it will influence the reader of the accounts. The misstatement or omission of an immaterial item will not prevent the accounts from giving a true and fair view.

- Economic (or commercial) substance over legal form: items are accounted for with reference to the effect of the transaction and not the strict legal wording. For example, assets acquired under hire purchase agreements are treated as bought even though legal title does not pass until the final instalment is paid.

Valuation rules - the Companies Act 1985 embodies two sets of valuation rules: the historical cost accounting rules and the alternative accounting rules.

- Historical cost accounting rules: - under these rules assets are shown on the basis of their purchase price or production cost. Fixed assets with a finite useful economic life must be depreciated on a systematic basis over their useful economic life. Current assets (eg. stocks) must be written down if the net realisable value is lower than the cost.

- Alternative accounting rules: - under these rules, fixed assets other than goodwill, stocks and short-term investments may be shown at their current cost.

6.4 Small and medium sized companies and groups

The term 'small company' and 'medium sized company' is defined in CA 1985. Companies that qualify as small or medium sized are entitled to various exemptions when preparing company and group accounts. The number of exemptions is increasing, particularly for small companies.

- Small companies may prepare simplified accounts for circulation to their members. Both small and medium sized companies may file abbreviated accounts with the Registrar of Companies.
- Consolidated financial statements (group accounts) need not be prepared by the parent of a small or medium sized group.
- Small and medium sized companies are not required to state whether their accounts have been prepared in accordance with applicable accounting standards.

Although the concept of small and medium sized companies originated in the Companies Act, companies that qualify as small or medium sized under CA 1985 are now exempt from the requirements of some accounting standards. For example, under FRS1 small companies do not have to prepare a cash flow statement.

6.5 Companies Act 1989

The Companies Act 1989 has to some extent increased the volume of disclosure that companies are required to make in their financial statements.

One of the most significant requirements is that the accounts of public and large private companies must state whether they have been prepared in accordance with applicable accounting standards (ie SSAPs and FRSs) and give details of, and the reasons for, any material departures.

6.6 Accounting standards

Accounting standards give guidance in specific areas of accounting. There are two types of accounting standard currently in issue:

(a) **Statements of Standard Accounting Practice (SSAPs)**

SSAPs were created by a body known as the Accounting Standards Committee. The ASC was abolished in July 1990. The Accounting Standards Board (ASB) took over the role of setting accounting standards from the ASC in August 1990. One of the ASB's first acts was to adopt all 22 existing SSAPs. The SSAPs therefore continue to be applicable to all sets of accounts, in so far as they have not been replaced by Financial Reporting Standards.

(b) **Financial Reporting Standards (FRSs)**

The new accounting standards created by the ASB are known as Financial Reporting Standards. In preparing company accounts, both SSAPs and FRSs should be complied with. Failure to do so can lead to the company being ordered to redraft its accounts (S12 CA 1989).

The board consists of nine qualified accountants and is monitored and funded by a body known as the Financial Reporting Council whose members are drawn from accounts user groups (eg. Stock Exchange, CBI) as well as the accounting profession.

6.7 True and fair view

Accounts must give a true and fair view of a company's state of affairs and results. On very rare occasions compliance with the requirements of the Companies Act may mean that the accounts do not show a true and fair view. If this is the case then the Companies Act requirements may be overridden, provided that particulars of the departure, the reasons for it and its effect are given in a note to the accounts.

Conclusion Budgetary control is a method of financial control, quality control is an example of a control of physical standards and the UK regulatory framework also imposes controls on the organisation.

7 SELF TEST QUESTIONS

7.1 Outline the purpose of organisational control (1.1).

7.2 Distinguish between planning and control (1.3).

7.3 Describe organisational control and operational control (2.4).

7.4 What is a budget? (3.1)

7.5 What will the budget manual include? (3.4).

7.6 How are quality standards set? (4.4).

7.7 What is statistical quality control? (4.6).

7.8 How can the level of quality be decided? (4.8).

7.9 List the input activities in a computer system (5.2).

7.10 What are the major elements of the UK regulatory framework? (6.1).

Chapter 8

TRAINING

PATHFINDER INTRODUCTION

This chapter covers the following performance criteria and knowledge and understanding

- Principles of supervision (Element 10.1)
- Principles of human relations, team building, staff motivation (Element 10.1)
- The competence of individuals undertaking work activities is reviewed and the necessary training is provided. (Element 10.1)
- Work methods and schedules are clearly communicated to all individuals in a way which assists their understanding of what is expected of them. (Element 10.1)
- Problems or queries concerning work activities are identified and either resolved or referred to the appropriate person. (Element 10.1)
- Weaknesses and potential for improvement to the accounting system are identified and considered for their impact on the operation of the organisation. (Element 10.2)
- Recommendations are made to the appropriate people in a clear, easily understood format. (Element 10.2)
- Recommendations are supported by a clear rationale which includes explanation of any assumptions made. (Element 10.2)

Putting the chapter in context – learning objectives.

The general purpose of any assessment or appraisal is to improve the efficiency of the organisation by ensuring that the individual employees are performing to the best of their ability and developing their potential for improvement.

Past appraisals or a competence-analysis exercise could determine the existing position of the current and proposed job-holder. From this base, of future need and present capability, a systematic, step-by-step training and development scheme can be defined.

At the end of this chapter you should have learned the following topics.

- explain the process of competence assessment
- outline the purposes and benefits of staff appraisal in the process
- describe the barriers to effective staff appraisal
- list the benefits to the organisation and the individual of effective training and development
- explain the methods used to analyse training needs
- suggest ways in which training needs can be met
- describe methods of staff evaluation and follow-up

1 TRAINING

1.1 Introduction

In a large company, training will be the responsibility of a training and education officer, usually a member of the personnel department. This responsibility would cover the provision of tuition for the requirements of any professional training, as well as induction training for junior newcomers, supervisory and management training, and technical training for the introduction of new technology. Because of the specialised nature of much of the work in accounts departments it is likely that a senior member of the accounting staff would liaise very closely with the personnel department. In many cases it is probable that he or she will play the major role in the determination of courses attended and professional studies undertaken because of the intimate knowledge of the requirements of both the job itself and the developments within the accounting profession.

In smaller firms the accountant will be in charge of training and it must be admitted that in many firms the initiative must come from members of the accounts department staff themselves.

1.2 Induction

When new employees join a large organisation they may go through an induction process. This involves a tour of the offices and factory, talks or films on the history and products of the organisation, and explanation of the policy relating to holidays, sickness, trade union membership, flexitime, etc. When joining the accounts department a new member of staff would then require an introduction to the structure of the departmental organisation and his or her role in it. Details of the methods of working would also be given (much of this may be embodied in an office manual) and instruction given by a supervisor on the requirements of the new post.

1.3 Accountancy qualifications

For staff who are seeking membership of one of the accountancy bodies the selection of the most appropriate qualification and methods of study will have to be determined by discussions between the student, the accountant and the training officer (this may have been agreed at the selection interview). In addition a training programme must be initiated so that the correct practical experience is obtained to satisfy the requirements of the accountancy body.

Within the accountancy profession there is much emphasis on post-qualifying education (PQE) and details of courses provided by all the accountancy bodies and other organisations should be readily available. Staff should be encouraged to attend to keep their knowledge up to date and, in some instances, staff may be directed to attend, eg. to acquire knowledge of a new accounting standard, tax changes, computing course, etc

Staff at all levels should be encouraged to develop their knowledge and abilities to as far as they are capable (and wish). In accounts departments there are many opportunities to specialise and this should be encouraged, in so far as it is compatible with the policies and requirements within the organisation and the need to ensure that there are understudies for all areas of knowledge. Some may wish to concentrate on computers, others on management control systems and yet others on taxation. So long as the knowledge gained is appropriate and there is adequate cover while members of staff attend courses, there should be worthwhile benefits to the organisation from any investment made in training.

2 THE PROCESS OF COMPETENCE ASSESSMENT

2.1 Competencies

Definition Competencies are the critical skills, knowledge and attitude that a job holder must have to perform effectively

Competencies are expressed in visible, behavioural terms and reflect the skills, knowledge and attitude (the main components of any job) which must be demonstrated to an agreed standard and must contribute to the overall aims of the organisation. The term is open to various interpretations because there are a number of competence-based systems and concepts of competence. As a general definition, a competent individual can perform a work role in a wide range of settings over an extended period of time.

Some competence-based systems are development-led - they focus on the development of competence and are linked to training and development programmes to develop people to a level of performance expected at work. Other systems are achievement-led - they focus on assessment of competent performance - what people do at work and how well they do it.

This is an important distinction when considering competence-based systems as the system may include many components, each linking to a different aspect of human resource activity within an organisation.

2.2 Process

For any competence based system the process is the same:

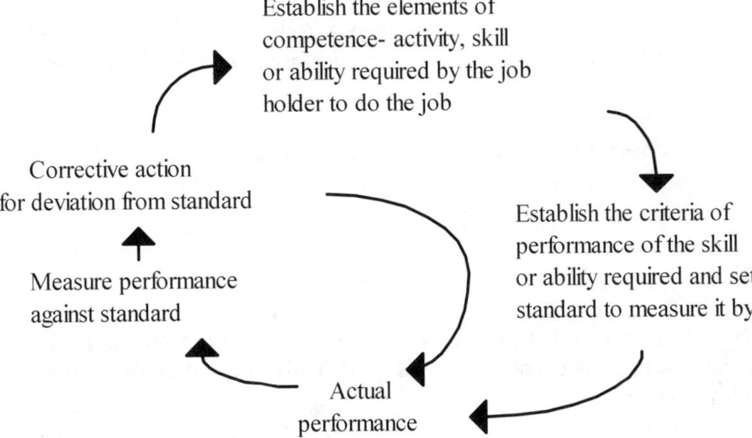

Conclusion Although it is not a work-based activity, think of the process of passing a driving test. It is an observable skill that is measured against set standards. In the case of failure a list which outlines the failed areas is given to the learner driver and is used to form the basis of any corrective action needed before re-applying for the test.

2.3 Standards of competence

For the AAT, highly qualified representatives from different occupational and professional groups formed Lead Industry Bodies to get involved in setting standards.

The Lead Body guidelines, for the units that make up your course, are written as statements incorporating:

- the elements of competence - the specific activities a job holder should be able to perform;
- performance criteria - how well it should be performed;
- a range statement - in what context and conditions; and
- the knowledge and understanding which underpins the competence.

Where there is more than one awarding body who want to offer an NVQ in a particular area then each must base their award on the same standards.

2.4 Assessment

Wherever you work, your performance is assessed. Often this is a casual, subjective and infrequent activity but, increasingly, many organisations (particularly larger ones) have decided to formalise the assessment process and use it to improve performance, assess training needs and predict the potential of employees.

Conclusion A competence is an observable ability to complete a specific task successfully.

2.5 Activity

After studying this section you should be able to explain the process of competence assessment

2.6 Activity solution

Your explanation should include the fact that it is a way of measuring what people do at work and how well they do it.

After analysing a job, there should be a statement drawn up by the supervisor or manager establishing both the specific activities a job holder should be able to perform and the performance criteria detailing how well it should be performed.

The assessment is predominantly by observation - the job-holder demonstrating how well he or she performs the activity. Feedback is given and assistance with corrective actions required where the performance does not match the standard set.

2.7 Techniques of appraisal

(a) Employee ranking - employees are ranked on the basis of their overall performance. This method is particularly prone to bias and its feedback value is practically nil. It does, however, have the advantage that it is simple to use.

(b) Rating scales - graphic rating scales consist of general personal characteristics and personality traits such as quantity of work, initiative, co-operation and judgement. The rate judges the employee on a scale whose ratings vary, for example from low to high or from poor to excellent. It is called 'graphic' because the scale visually graphs performance from one extreme to the other.

The main problem associated with rating scales is the 'clustering' of results around the 'average' or 'satisfactory' level with little use made of the extreme levels. This negates the whole purpose of an appraisal scheme. To overcome this, some specialists replace terms like 'poor', 'satisfactory' or a numbering system with a series of statements. Each statement is tested for the best match to the performance.

Despite their popularity there are problems with the use of rating scales. They provide little information to the individual as to how to improve his/her performance. There is no identification of training needs so it is difficult to design training programmes on the results of rating scales. Frequently rating scales will induce resistance on the part of superiors doing the rating because they are required to assess on factors where they do not feel they have adequate information. For the person being assessed, rating scales can readily provoke resistance, defensiveness and hostility. Telling someone that they lack initiative or that their personality is unsatisfactory can strike at the heart of their self-identity and self-esteem.

(c) Description/Report - this is a qualitative method of assessment where the manager writes a brief description of the employee under a number of headings.

3 THE PURPOSES AND BENEFITS OF STAFF APPRAISAL

3.1 Performance appraisal

The general purpose of any assessment or appraisal is to improve the efficiency of the organisation by ensuring that the individual employees are performing to the best of their ability and developing their potential for improvement. Performance appraisal may be defined as:

Definition   the regular and systematic review of performance and the assessment of potential with the aim of producing action programmes to develop both work and individuals.

Staff appraisal is a procedure where the managers or supervisors in an organisation discuss the work of their subordinates. They see each person individually and consider the progress they have been making in their job, their strengths and weaknesses and their future needs as regards training and development and the employee's potential for promotion.

3.2 Appraisal as a management tool

In a sense all individuals are constantly appraised but a systematic appraisal involves more than a casual assessment of individual performance. Systematic performance appraisal is a vital management tool for the following reasons:

(a) It enables a picture to be drawn up of the human 'stock' of an organisation - its strengths and weaknesses, enabling more effective personnel planning.

(b) By identifying weaknesses in an individual's performance it may identify training needs and once training has taken place, performance appraisal enables some evaluation of training effectiveness.

(c) It allows managers and subordinates to plan personnel and job objectives in the light of performance.

(d) In some circumstances it may be used to assess the level of reward payable for an individual's efforts, eg, in merit payment systems.

(e) By encouraging two-way communication it permits an evaluation of a subordinate's strengths and weaknesses and the reasons for them. Thus, for example, if a subordinate's failure to perform is due to some failure in the work system corrective action can be taken quickly.

(f) It is the ideal situation for assessing potential. At the organisational level this permits career and succession planning. At the individual level it permits superior and subordinate to assess the most effective development plans for the subordinate.

It is, however, important if the appraisal is to fulfil the last point that it is regular and systematic, based on objective criteria and permits a two-way flow of communication in a reasonably trusting atmosphere. No subordinate is likely to admit to weaknesses or training needs in a climate of distrust.

Conclusion Appraisal is used for personnel planning, identifying training needs, evaluating training effectiveness, planning personnel and job objectives, assessing the level of reward payable and assessing potential.

3.3 Categorising training needs

Training needs may be identified from the appraisal process, in which actual performance is compared with pre-defined objectives. Shortcomings or 'gaps' in performance are then used as indicators of the training required. At the same time, training based upon the appraisal process can be used to develop and build individual personal capacity and competence and to develop and build group/departmental capacity and competence.

The process of appraisal may also be used to review and develop departmental role objectives and job descriptions, from which further training needs analysis can be undertaken. Actual training needs may be categorised on the basis of:

(i) competencies associated with work quality, including:

- technical and task knowledge;
- accuracy and consistency;
- exercise of judgement and discretion;
- communication skills;
- cost consciousness.

(ii) competencies associated with work quantity, including:

- personal planning and time management;
- capacity to meet deadlines or work under pressure;
- capacity to cope with upward variations in work volume.

(iii) supervisory and managerial skills and competencies including:

- planning and organising;
- communication and interpersonal skills;
- directing, guiding and motivating;
- leadership and delegation;
- co-ordination and control;
- developing and retaining staff;
- developing teamwork.

3.4 The benefits of appraisal

(a) Effective appraisal is grounded in the belief that feedback on past performance influences future performance, and that the process of isolating and rewarding good performance is likely to repeat it.

(b) Agreement on challenging but achievable targets for performance motivates employees by clarifying goals and setting the value of incentives offered.

(c) Effective appraisal can allow employees to solve any workplace problems and apply creative thinking to their jobs.

3.5 The negative effects of appraisal

Sometimes the effects of appraisal show some negative effects where:

- criticism has a negative effect on goal achievement;
- subordinates react defensively to criticism during appraisal interviews;
- inferior performance results from defensive reactions to criticism;
- repeated criticism has the worst effect on subsequent performance of individuals who have little self confidence;

4 THE PROCESS OF STAFF APPRAISAL

4.1 Appraisal process methods

There are a number of staff appraisal process methods in use, these include the review and comparison method, management by objectives and the task-centred method.

Review and comparison - This consists of the individual being assessed and analysed in terms of objectives, tasks, workflows and results achieved. These are then compared with previously agreed statements of required results and performance levels.

Management by objectives - This is a system whereby managers agree certain objectives with their subordinates and then review the results achieved. It is a common-sense approach to staff appraisal based on the idea that if subordinates know their objectives they are more likely to reach them. Motivation will also be higher as they have more control over the setting of objectives and targets and also the methods by which those objectives and targets can be met.

The **task-centred method** - This relates to what the subordinate is doing and how he does it. It avoids the more formal approach to staff appraisal and adopts a continual assessment approach. After the completion of each task an assessment is carried out and performance monitored.

Whichever type of appraisal method is used the criteria must be clearly stated, understood and agreed by the subordinate. Subordinates must also be clear about the objectives and results required.

The objectives set, and statement of results required, must also relate to:

(a) job description;
(b) personnel specifications;
(c) salary grading.

4.2 The appraisal criteria

The appraisal criteria may include the following.

(a) Volume of work produced:

- within time period;
- evidence of work planning;
- personal time management;
- effectiveness of work under pressure.

(b) Knowledge of work:

- gained through experience;
- gained through training courses;
- gained prior to employment.

(c) Quality of work:

- level of analytical ability;
- level of technical knowledge;
- accuracy;
- judgements exercised;
- cost effectiveness.

(d) Supervisory or management skills:

- communication skills;
- motivation skills;
- training and development skills;
- delegation skills.

(e) Personal qualities:

- decision-making capabilities;
- flexibility;
- adaptability;
- assertiveness;
- team involvement;
- personal motivation;
- commitment to the organisational goals.

4.3 Measures of effective performance

A key issue in performance appraisal is determining what constitutes valid criteria or measures of effective performance. The problem is made more difficult because almost all jobs have many dimensions so that performance appraisal must employ multiple criteria or measures of effectiveness in order to accurately reflect the actual job performance of the employee.

Although it is impossible to identify any universal measures of performance that are applicable to all jobs, it is possible to specify a number of characteristics that a criterion of job performance should possess if it is to be useful for performance appraisal. It should be:

(a) capable of being measured reliably. The concept of reliability of measurement has two components. (i) stability - meaning that measures taken at different times should yield the same results. (ii) consistency -meaning that if different people use the criterion or a different form of measurement is used the results should still be more or less the same.

(b) capable of differentiating among individuals according to their performance. If everyone is rated the same the exercise rapidly becomes pointless.

(c) capable of being influenced by the job-holder. If a person is to improve performance after appraisal then it must be about matters over which the individual has discretionary control.

(d) acceptable to those individuals whose performance is being assessed. It is important that people feel that their performance is being measured against criteria that are fair and accurate.

A key issue that has to do with the criteria of effectiveness is the question of whether they should focus on the activities (tasks) of the job-holder or the results (objectives) achieved. For example, a salesman might be assessed in terms of activities - number of cold calls or speed of dealing with complaints or in terms of results - total sales volume or number of new customers. Measures of results pay no attention to how results were achieved.

There are advantages and disadvantages of using either results or activities as criteria. Appraisal based on results has the advantage of encouraging and rewarding the results desired by the organisation. However, it has the disadvantage that it might encourage people to break rules or go against company policy to get the desired results. It may lead to frustration if the failure to achieve results is due to factors beyond the control of the individual. Assessment in terms of results also has the shortcoming that it does not generate information about how the person is doing the job and hence has limited value in suggesting ways of improving performance.

A major advantage of appraising in terms of activities is that it helps in generating information that can help in the training and development of poor performers. However, it may only encourage people to concentrate on their activities at the expense of results achieved. This can result in excessive bureaucratic emphasis on the means and procedures employed rather than on the accomplishments and results. There are then problems in incorporating the successful non-conformist into the appraisal system.

An effective appraisal system needs to have a balance of both measures of results and measures of activities.

Conclusion Appraisals should be fair, consistent and disciplined in approach, relying more on objective than subjective input and aiming to help the person being appraised consider future planning

5 THE BENEFITS OF EFFECTIVE TRAINING AND DEVELOPMENT

5.1 Training in the organisation

It is important that any organisation should adopt a systematic approach to training. The increasing pace of technological change is perhaps the single biggest impetus for training programmes. In the first half of this century, workers acquired their skills through apprenticeships and college courses that equipped them with knowledge and skills sufficient for their working lives. Today, however, few people can expect to do the same work in the same way for more than a few years and the number of jobs for untrained workers has declined.

A systematic approach to training will involve:

- defining training needs.
- deciding what training is required to satisfy these needs.
- using experienced trainers to plan and implement training.
- following up and evaluating training to ensure that it is effective.

This approach can be illustrated diagrammatically:

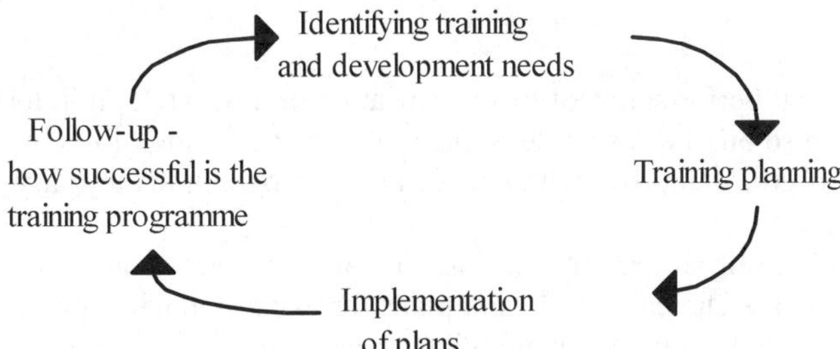

5.2 Benefits to the organisation

The benefits to the organisation of effective training and development are:

(a) provision of trained manpower;
(b) improvement of existing skills;
(c) increased employee knowledge;
(d) improved job performance;
(e) improved customer service;
(f) greater staff commitment;
(g) increased value of the organisation's human assets; and
(h) the personal development of employees.

5.3 Benefits to the individual

The benefits to the individual of effective training and development are:

(a) increased motivation;
(b) individual goals equating with those of the organisation;
(c) needs and aims to develop abilities and talents satisfied;
(d) newly acquired skills for future use.

Conclusion — The purpose of training in the work situation is to develop the abilities of the individual and to satisfy the current and future manpower needs of the organisation.

6 THE METHODS USED TO ANALYSE TRAINING NEEDS

6.1 Job training analysis

The training needs will be indicated by a job training analysis. This can be defined as:

Definition — the process of identifying the purpose of the job and its component parts, and specifying what must be learnt in order for there to be effective performance.

A job analysis will reveal the 'training gap' which is the difference between the knowledge and skill required for the effective performance of a specific job and the knowledge and skill already possessed by the employee.

Some of this training requirement will relate to the longer term, for example where a company has a strategy to enter a particular overseas market or move into a new industry. The knowledge and skill gap will be defined for the future needs of the organisation and expressed for each of the future time periods. It will then be detailed in the manpower plan and used to define training and development needs as well as the recruitment and promotion of staff.

6.2 Identifying training needs

There are a number of means that are used to assess training needs. These range from a very broad analysis of corporate strategy and organisational goals, which should be outlined in the manpower plan, to the details of individuals' performance appraisal.

(a) *Organisational analysis* - an analysis of the features of an organisation and a diagnosis of its problems may well indicate that training is necessary. Such an analysis may involve consideration of the following factors:

- The overall performance of the organisation or any part of it in terms of output, sales, profit, costs and so on. For example if materials wastage is high for a batch of new recruits it might show a need for improvement in the training programme they have been through.

- The policies of an organisation may involve training as a means of achieving future goals. Forecasts of technical change and plans for expansion have implications for training with the requirements to train for new skills or increase the supply of traditional skills. Similarly changes in personnel policies eg, a new promotion policy or a career development plan will create new training needs.

- There are various indicators of organisational health that may well suggest that training is necessary. Such indicators might include labour turnover, absenteeism or the level of grievances. For example, several studies have shown that inadequate training often leads to workers failing to achieve targets that affect their chances of gaining financial incentives. Many such employees experience frustration that manifests itself in grievances and labour turnover.

- Governmental influences and legislation in particular have caused and still do cause organisations to reconsider their position concerning the provision of training.

(b) *Performance appraisal* - individual training needs can be established by feedback on individual assessments

(c) *Job analysis* - There are a variety of approaches to job analysis which involve greater or lesser degrees of detail but the basic procedure is similar for all and covers the following stages:

- A broad analysis of the requirements of the job and any special problems surrounding it as seen by the job-holder, the superior and, possibly, colleagues.

- An analysis of the particular skills needed to do the job. This can be done by either a manual skills analysis where the analyst records hand, finger and body movements in great detail or a faults analysis where the analyst produces a specification showing what typically causes frequently occurring faults and how to identify and resolve them.

- A detailed study of the responsibilities, duties and tasks carried out. This forms the basis of the job description.

- An analysis of the knowledge and skills required by the job-holder that forms the basis of the person specification. This analysis might include a role analysis, which lists the behaviours and duties considered to be essential for effective performance, and an interpersonal skills analysis which analyses those skills that determine good performance in jobs involving a great deal of face-to-face contact.

- A description of the training requirements for the job ie, the training specification.

(d) *Other approaches* - though we have looked at the main ways of examining training needs there are other sources of information and methods of investigation that can be useful. Information may be gained from records of employee performance, feedback from customers or simply from observation of employees. Other methods available include surveys of staff with questionnaires or interviews of superiors and subordinates and customer surveys covering their satisfaction and dissatisfaction.

Conclusion

The means used to assess training needs include:

- organisational and departmental goals;
- overall performance of the organisation or any part of it in terms of output, sales, profit, costs;
- performance appraisal;
- job analysis;
- records of employee performance;
- feedback from customers;
- observation of employees;
- surveys of staff and customer surveys covering their satisfaction and dissatisfaction.

7 WAYS IN WHICH TRAINING NEEDS CAN BE MET

7.1 Training intervention

The organisation has to determine exactly what it hopes to achieve by the training and development intervention. There are five stages for the organisation to consider:

(a) Determination of the development and training objective - this will specify the task, procedures, techniques, skills and ability that employees should be able to perform/exhibit and the standards required.

(b) Determination of the appropriate strategy - the criteria used to determine the appropriate strategies are:

- compatibility with objectives;
- estimated likelihood of transfer of learning/development to the work situation;
- available resources;
- employee considerations.

(c) Planning and implementation - careful briefing of employees and their managers should take place, in order that they know what is happening, when and why.

(d) Evaluation of the programme - this is perhaps the most difficult stage of the process. The aim is to evaluate the effectiveness of the investment, in terms of resources, and find out whether it has achieved the stated objectives

(e) Reviewing the system on a regular basis to ensure that it is still satisfying the organisation's training and development needs

7.2 Training solutions

Once the training needs are collated, the training funds available and the priorities established in relation to the urgency of the training, the training decisions must be made. These include decisions on:

- the scale and type of training system needed, and whether it can best be provided by the organisation's own staff or by external consultants;
- training methods;
- timing and duration - specific training courses will need to be planned to ensure that they are properly timed to allow normal operations to continue;
- location; and
- the training provider.

Training may be carried out 'in-house' or externally. If any of the training is done in-house, decisions will need to be made on such things as:

- training workshops;
- location and equipping of classrooms;
- selection of training officers.

External courses are provided by colleges, universities, training organisations, or management consultants. There are also open and distance learning facilities via the Open University and other programmes.

To make sure that the training needs are being met, separate training and development co-ordinators may be allocated the responsibilities for training within the firm and for any external training. They may also be responsible for reviewing the system on a regular basis to ensure that it is still satisfying those needs.

7.3 Activity

What choices does the organisation have about the location of the training and development?

7.4 Activity solution

There are four possibilities:

All training and development done within the organisation, using the organisation's resources;
All training and development done outside the organisation;
All training and development done within the organisation, with courses run by outside bodies;
Some internal, some external to the organisation

8 METHODS OF STAFF EVALUATION AND FOLLOW-UP

8.1 The evaluation of training

Definition The evaluation of training is an attempt to obtain information (feedback) on the effects of a training programme and to assess the value of the training in the light of that information'.

Every organisation should ask itself at the end of any substantial training activity:

(a) Was the training effective? Did the employee acquire the knowledge and skills that the activity was intended to provide him or her with? Can the employee do the job which requires the knowledge and skills that he or she has acquired; and

(b) Was it worthwhile in terms of return on expenditure incurred in giving the training? Is there some other way that the organisation can secure a suitably skilled employee that is less expensive, eg, different training arrangements; buy-in the skills and so forth.

To evaluate the effectiveness of training, an organisation needs information about training arrangements; content, objectives, assessments, etc, and criteria by which to evaluate the training.

If the evaluation is to be used to improve training, then the organisation will also need machinery for feeding the evaluation into the training design activity so that courses and programmes can be adjusted as necessary. It has been suggested that evaluation can take place in relation to the trainee's subsequent behaviour.

(a) Trainee's behaviour

 (i) What was the trainee's reaction and response to the training? Did he or she enjoy it or feel that they had benefited from it?

 (ii) Has there been a transfer of learning to the job, ie, has the trainee's job behaviour been modified in the desired way?

(b) Organisation behaviour

(i) Has the training had a beneficial effect on quality, costs, output and employee morale?

(ii) Has the training improved the quality of the welfare and its commitment to the organisation?

Evaluation is not a simple, logical business; on the contrary it is a highly problematic affair; organisations cannot, however, afford not to do it.

8.2 The five levels of evaluation

Hamblin, a writer on training, suggests that there are five levels at which evaluation can take place:

(a) Reactions of the trainees to the training, their feelings about how enjoyable and useful it has been etc.

(b) Learning the new skills and knowledge that have been acquired or the changes in attitude that have taken place as a result of the training.

(c) Job behaviour - at this level evaluation tries to measure the extent to which trainees have applied their training on the job.

(d) Organisation - training may be assessed in terms of the ways in which changes in job behaviour affect the functioning of the organisation in which the trainees are employed in terms of measures such as output, productivity, quality etc.

(e) Ultimate value - this is a measure of the training in terms of how the organisation as a whole has benefited from the training in terms of greater profitability, survival or growth.

8.3 Sources of information for the assessment of training.

The potential sources of information that can provide data for the evaluation of training are:

(a) Observation - the trainers are able to see if and how people are gaining from their training. What is more, most training programmes will generate written reports and comments, and these can be used by the trainers for evaluation purposes.

(b) Informants - the judgements of people who have attended the training, qualified observers, the managers of trainees and senior management are sources of information based on their observation of the training. These judgements are likely to be rather subjective and should not be relied on too heavily.

(c) Data collection methods:

- Objective tests - an example is a personality test which might be used on a training course which seeks to develop some aspect of personality. By administering the test at the beginning and end of the course it is possible to evaluate the success of the course in developing personality.

- Attitude scales - these are particularly useful where training is geared to change people's attitudes and provide a valuable measure of attitudes before and after training.

- Rating scales - rating scales can be applied to the inputs to the course, the outputs, the processes, the impact, the overall effectiveness and the administration of the course.

- Questionnaires - a popular device that asks questions such as: What did you get out of the course? What improvements would you suggest? How has the course affected the way you do your job? The questionnaire does permit the collection of information cheaply and quickly but it can be subjective and partial.

- Interviews - though time consuming, the two-way interchange of the interview situation can provide useful information on which to judge the success of training.

Conclusion Evaluation sources include: testing, end of course questionnaires and the judgements of people based on their observation of the training.

9 SELF TEST QUESTIONS

9.1 Define a competence (2.1).

9.2 Describe the techniques of appraisal (2.7).

9.3 What is the purpose of appraisal? (3.1).

9.4 Give three good reasons for appraisal (3.2)

9.5 How can you categorise training needs? (3.3).

9.6 Outline the negative effects of appraisal (3.5).

9.7 Draw a diagram showing training as a system (5.1).

9.8 What are the benefits of training? (5.2/5.3)

9.9 What sort of information is needed to evaluate the effectiveness of training. (8.1)

Chapter 9

IMPROVING THE SYSTEM

PATHFINDER INTRODUCTION

This chapter covers the following performance criteria and knowledge and understanding

- Methods of measuring cost effectiveness and systems reliability. (Element 10.2)
- Quality management, quality circles. (Element 10.2)
- Understanding that the accounting systems of an organisation are affected by its organisational structure, its MIS, its administrative systems and procedures and the nature of its business transactions. (Elements 10.1, 10.2 & 10.3)
- Work activities are closely monitored in order to ensure quality standards are being met. (Element 10.1)
- Weaknesses and potential for improvements to the accounting system are identified and recommendations made to the appropriate specialists. (Element 10.2)
- Methods of operating are regularly reviewed in respect of their cost-effectiveness, reliability and speed. (Element 10.2)
- The system is updated as in accordance with changes in internal and external regulations, policies and procedures. (Element 10.2)

Putting the chapter in context – learning objectives.

This chapter should cover all of the areas within an organisation that you might investigate when looking for ways of improving the effectiveness of an accounting system.

At the end of this chapter you should have learned the following topics.

- the measurement of work performance;
- standards of work performance measurement;
- the importance of quality control;
- the purpose and nature of work study;
- the approaches used within work study.

1 IMPROVING THE EFFECTIVENESS OF AN ACCOUNTING SYSTEM

1.1 Introduction

This chapter is about improving the effectiveness of an accounting system. We have already looked at systems, with their inputs, processes and outputs and we have looked at typical accounting systems, including their subsystems, which may include the payroll, purchases, sales, stock and cash systems.

When we think about how we are going to improve the effectiveness of any system, the steps are to:

- analyse the feedback of actual versus budgeted results for the period;
- clarify any strengths and weaknesses, and
- suggest remedial action and amended plans to revise the whole process in order to achieve the objectives of the department more effectively and efficiently.

For example the continuous nature of corporate planning uses the feedback from budgetary control to revise the budgets. In this context it should be noted that the term 'budgets' means performance budgets (units sold, production, percentage of waste product, number of customer returns, etc) as well as financial budgets.

1.2 Culture

The effectiveness of an organisation is strongly influenced by the organisational culture, which dictates the way in which the management functions of planning, organising, controlling, staffing and leading are carried out.

Definition Culture can be defined as 'the way we do things around here'.

The essence of a culture is that the values, attitudes and beliefs within the company are shared and accepted. Some organisations, for example, IBM, Marks & Spencer, have deliberately set out to create a culture that is conducive to customer satisfaction and company growth.

The culture of an organisation is influenced by the style of management which, in turn, influences the management/staff relationships and helps to promote higher performance. If we consider three main management approaches, then we can recognise that each will give rise to different cultures.

Paternalistic management approach - typified by the Quaker companies eg, Cadbury -where the company sets out to be a caring employer and looks to staff to reciprocate in a similar, fair manner. This approach is based on the belief that a satisfied worker is an effective performer. The company establishes itself as the source of important rewards and staff can be induced to work harder out of a feeling of gratitude. This general style promotes a culture of people 'being comfortable and well regarded'. Staff tend to be loyal, good timekeepers and interested in their work but there is little real effort to raise productivity.

Scientific management approach - is encountered in some sales-based organisations and manufacturing companies. The approach is based on the belief that a person will be induced to work if rewards and penalties are tied directly to performance - all rewards follow, and are conditional upon personal performance. A culture stemming from this approach would tend to put practical results above people factors. Success and failure would be clearly measurable, and carry individual responsibility.

The human relations management approach - believes that man derives satisfaction and motivation from doing an effective job - ego, pride, etc, are involved. Such an approach works best in ideas and management areas where there is freedom in deciding how to do the work. It is also heavily dependent upon group pressures and norms. As you would expect, the culture here has a high regard for individuals. Staff tend to be treated as individuals and senior management are readily accessible.

However, companies rarely fall neatly into one category; for example, most large companies will have aspects of all three.

1.3 SWOT analysis

When an organisation wishes to improve its effectiveness, it carries out a SWOT analysis. SWOT stands for strengths, weaknesses, opportunities and threats. The analysis consists of the internal appraisal of the organisation's strengths and weaknesses, sometimes called a position audit and an external appraisal of the opportunities and threats open to organisations in competition within the industry. Therefore, strengths and weaknesses are peculiar to an individual organisation but opportunities and threats are open to all organisations within the market place. The analysis requires an understanding of both the environment and the resource capabilities of the organisation.

If we apply the same principle to the accounting system under scrutiny we must appraise the environment of the accounting system and the resource capabilities, processes, procedures and documentation within the department.

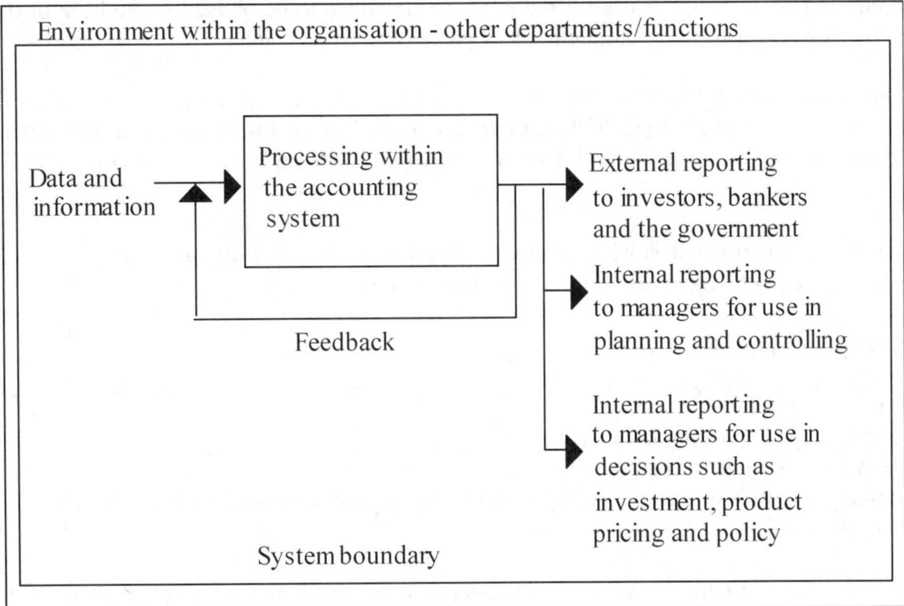

The analysis may highlight strengths or weaknesses in any of the following:

- Resources - both human and mechanical;
- Design of processes, procedures and controls;
- Systems eg, computer system;
- Location and layout of office;
- Relationships with other departments.

The environment may offer opportunities and/or threats:

- It may offer threats (to the well-being of the organisation, such as Government legislation, or, say, national action by trade unions) and opportunities (for exploitation, such as growth in market demand, or new technological possibilities). Technological improvements in computing could be seen as an opportunity for the accounting system if it led to faster processing.

- It is the source of organisational resources (human resources come from outside the organisation, as do funds and supplies generally). Difficulty in recruiting staff of the right calibre could be a threat to the accounting system.

2 APPRAISAL

2.1 Types of appraisal

As we have already seen, controlling is the measuring and correcting of activities to ensure that events conform to plans. Plans must be made but they will not be achieved unless activities are monitored and deviations from the plan identified and corrected as soon as they become apparent. It requires a control system, an inspection organisation to set standards, monitor performance and take corrective action if it is needed.

All of the systems and procedures in the organisation can be appraised - the procedures in the accounting department, the management information system and the appraisal of staff - are outlined below.

2.2 Appraisal of the clerical work procedures

As in any office it is important that the systems in the accounts department are based on sound principles. The procedures followed should be recorded in a manual and should be subject to periodic reviews to establish whether improvements in methods of working could be introduced. Reviews would also be necessary as and when new technology becomes available.

There is an old adage: 'Bookkeeping was made for business, not business for bookkeeping'. No procedure should be taken as sacrosanct. Also, no matter how loyal and long-serving an employee is, the time honoured methods of working they have been used to for many years may have to be revised in the light of the need to develop a procedure as work loads alter and methods of processing data change.

With the increasing complexity of business more and more adjustments may be made to systems until the time comes when there is a need to take a fresh look at the procedures. Before any necessary improvements can be formulated and implemented, an review of existing procedures must be undertaken. This may be divided into two parts:

- a general view of the office as a whole and the role it plays within the organisation;
- a more detailed step-by-step view of the procedures themselves.

The general overview will consider:

(a) the purpose of the office;
(b) what actually happens within the office;
(c) who does what within the office;
(d) the techniques and methods employed by staff in carrying out assigned responsibilities;
(e) the quality of performance.

The establishment of such information is vital as a first stage. After this a more detailed analysis of the day-to-day routine may be attempted. It will include:

- determining the purpose of the review exercise, eg it is likely that weaknesses may have already been highlighted (for instance, too much paperwork);

- examining the techniques and methods currently used within the procedure and inspecting and analysing existing forms and documentation, such items representing information;

- constructing, in written form, a record of the operations involved and revealed by examining the current techniques and methods.

- converting the steps in these operations into some form of chart description, eg flowchart;

- examining each individual step closely to ascertain its effectiveness or inefficiency;

- endeavouring to determine alternative methods and techniques;

- determining the most suitable of the alternatives on offer;

- altering the new chart to show the effect of the new methods and techniques upon the procedures;

- initiating trial runs for test purposes;

- developing new, re-designed job specifications for staff;

- implementing the new procedure; and

- ensuring that the new procedure is monitored and modified where necessary.

Initially the procedure should be examined in detail, probably using charts. The work being done should be analysed in depth. Of each operation, and the procedure as a whole, the following questions could be asked.

- Is this operation essential?
- Is the information used?
- What is the information used for?
- Is the information already provided elsewhere?
- Can the method of working be simplified?
- Would computerisation be appropriate?
- Are there any bottlenecks?
- Is work fairly divided between staff?
- Are the correct grades of staff employed for each stage?

- Does the work flow correctly?
- Would a change in office layout be helpful?
- Are the correct instructions given to staff?

From the above list of questions it would suggest that a fresh view from the outside could perform the task best. However the investigators should be willing to accept the views of staff in question as they will have intimate knowledge of the problem. Also, in many organisations, involvement of staff is actively encouraged through membership of groups such as 'quality circles' where questions such as those above are discussed and examined to give improved and simplified methods of working.

From such approaches great savings in clerical procedures costs have been achieved in many organisations.

2.3 Activity

Consider the procedures in your office and see how they compare with the guidelines given

2.4 Appraisal of the management information system

Some form of management information systems will exist whether they are planned or not. If they are not planned, managers will devise their own ways of finding the information they need. These are likely to be inefficient, as there will be duplication of effort and a tendency for managers to keep their information to themselves rather than communicate it widely. This will result in lost opportunities.

For many organisations, the management information system represents a significant investment. At the development stage of the system, management determine future information needs and desires, but over time the system procedures may need appraising to make sure that they are meeting the objectives set initially. When appraising the management information system, the real question of performance centres around what the user wants from the system, and what the user is getting. So there is a comparison between planned and actual system behaviour, assessment of the extent to which system objectives have been achieved, and a consideration of overall system behaviour.

The evaluation or appraisal process should:

- assess system operational performance;
- verify system objectives and how realistic they are;
- compare planned and actual performance;
- establish the extent to which the agreed objectives have been achieved.

The aspects that are assessed and measured are:

- error reports created by the system;
- performance characteristics;
- turnaround and response time;
- machine usage;
- data input volumes, paper handling;
- output reports: - accuracy, necessity, punctuality.

Reference to the costs and benefits, expected and achieved, is made during the evaluation.

Conclusion Just as in any other system, effectiveness can be improved in the accounting system by looking for weaknesses in the sub-systems (clerical work procedures and management information system) and finding solutions that achieve the agreed objectives.

2.5 Performance appraisal

The starting point of all appraisal schemes is that, by analysing past performance, an individual can be helped to improve future performance. You may remember the gist of the definition:

Definition Performance appraisal is the regular and systematic review of performance and the assessment of potential with the aim of producing action programmes to develop both work and individuals.

Staff appraisal is a procedure where an employee completes an appraisal form. This stage is followed by an interview, in which the employee will have a discussion with his or her manager to consider:

- progress in the job;
- strengths and weaknesses;
- future needs as regards training and development; and
- potential for promotion.

Appraisals are important for several reasons:

- they establish an individual's current level of performance;
- they identify strengths and weaknesses in an individual's performance;
- they identify training and development needs;
- they can motivate individuals;
- they provide a basis for rewarding staff in relation to their contribution to organisational goals;
- they assess potential;
- they provide information for succession planning.

The outcome of the appraisal procedure can be a job improvement plan, a salary increase or promotion.

2.6 Activity

Why is it important to appraise staff?

2.7 Activity solution

Appraisals may be regarded as important for the following reasons:

- they provide information for the organisation's inventory of people, therefore facilitating long-range personnel planning;
- they provide a rational basis for determining the performance of an individual so that he or she may be appropriately rewarded;
- they allow the organisation to make an evaluation of its general effectiveness;
- they allow managers and subordinates to plan personnel and job objectives;
- they provide employees with feedback on job performance and on individual strengths and weaknesses;
- they establish the quality of managers in an organisation; and
- they determine the requirements for development and selection programmes.

Conclusion In all organisations, each employee' performance is assessed by someone. Often this is a casual, subjective and infrequent activity but, increasingly, many organisations (particularly larger ones) have decided to formalise the assessment process and use it to improve performance, assess training needs and predict the potential of employees.

3 ACCOMMODATION AND EQUIPMENT

3.1 Introduction

When we are appraising the accommodation and equipment, we must remember that, as with all the procedures and processes, the aim of the appraisal is to highlight strengths or weaknesses. The aim is for a design that achieves the objectives of the department efficiently and effectively.

3.2 The accounts department

It is often the case that the reality of organisational structure is very different from that described in the organisation chart or operating manual. In particular, channels of communication are not always properly aligned to the authority structure, leading to waste and increased operating costs.

The central role of an accounts department and the service that it provides to all other functions would suggest that it should be sited as conveniently as possible to the areas it serves most. However, with the increasing availability of data-links, this aspect may not be so crucial.

Consideration must initially be given to the style of offices to be used by an accounts department. Amongst questions to be discussed would be the following.

- Would one large open office be suitable?
- Would all different sections of accounts be in the same room, or should there be different offices for financial and cost accounting staff and also for the wages section?
- What criteria should be adopted in the allocation of individual offices to senior staff?
- What security arrangements for the confidentiality of information and also for the cashier's department are required?
- Where would the computers be sited and how can security be safeguarded?

3.3 Layout of office

There are advantages to having an open office - economy in floor space and occupancy costs, flexibility of layouts, better supervision and minimisation of movement of staff and documents. However it must be recognised that with the confidential nature of much of the accounts work and the need for security and privacy, separate offices must be provided for certain categories of work. Many organisations would consider the private ledger section and the staff salaries section as falling in this category. In addition many organisations pay great attention to the security of the computer installation, even to the extent of restricting access to a very limited number of authorised personnel. Also, of course, the cashier's department would require special attention to security.

Certain higher levels of accounting staff might be entitled to individual offices, either because of the nature of their work and/or their status within the organisation. For senior staff privacy may be important when dealing with other members of staff, both in discussions with their superiors or when dealing with the confidential problems of subordinates, or disciplining them.

Whatever the type of office, furniture and equipment should be so arranged as to give the best possible use of the space allocated. The emphasis should be on a simple flow of work with documents going forward in a straight line through the office. Gangways should be free from obstruction and allow easy evacuation in case of emergencies. The best use should be made of the light from windows and the requirements for minimum working space should be allowed for. Particular attention should be paid to the physical conditions such as heating, lighting, ventilation and noise in order to ensure the best possible environment conducive to the most efficient performance of duties. With careful planning an office layout should help to increase the efficiency of work, should be economic in the use of floor space and yet give an attractive appearance and provide a comfortable environment to maintain staff morale.

3.4 Testing the layout

Once the design of the office is determined, the layout can be tested by the use of a string diagram. A scale plan of the office layout is prepared with pins inserted at the work-stations, cabinets and any other office furniture or equipment. Journeys made by office staff between the various fixtures are reproduced on the plan by means of cotton wound from one pin to another. Each time a journey is made the cotton is wound from pin to pin, so that a heavily traversed route very quickly emerges as such. Study of the diagram allows all the movements to be determined and any deficiencies in the layout will be shown and can be remedied by adjustments in the location of certain pieces of equipment, etc.

Apart from efficient and effective production, the advantages of good layout are to:

- achieve the optimal use of space;
- allow for the most efficient flow of work;
- facilitate effective control;
- reduce materials handling to a minimum;
- minimise waste;
- promote employee satisfaction and motivation;
- allow for change and development; and
- maximise productivity.

3.5 Office furniture

Because it can aid efficient working and maintain staff morale, care must be taken when choosing the type and quality of office furniture. It is obviously important that furniture should be appropriate for its function, but it should also look attractive and appeal to the workers who must use it. In addition, for senior categories of staff such as the chief accountant and his immediate assistants, it may be appropriate to equip their offices with 'executive-style' furniture to impress visitors with the prestige and importance of the person using it.

In choosing furniture, in addition to the points noted, consideration will be given to its demands on floor space, its ease of movement, the correctness of the height for comfortable working and its fire risk. Providing the price is within the capital expenditure budget of the organisation, the best possible furniture should be purchased and false economy in buying cheap stock furniture should be avoided for the sake of the health and comfort of staff.

3.6 Office equipment

Similar care should be taken when providing equipment for use in the office. Careful comparison should be made of the merits and performance of equipment such as files, calculators and even items such as pencil sharpeners. Again false economy might prove detrimental to the efficiency and effectiveness of the staff.

This is not to say that equipment should be lavished on the department. Each item of equipment obtained should be justified first, and of course, where major items of equipment are to be purchased, this would only be done after exhaustive surveys of the benefits that would be obtained and of cost and performance comparisons of the different models available.

4 WORK STUDY

4.1 Definitions

Work study, sometimes known as work simplification, is concerned with the examination of human work in its total context. It is essential, in order to achieve cost-effectiveness, to examine the way in which an activity is carried out to ensure that maximum effect is obtained with the minimum of effort.

Work study can be applied in manufacturing industries, commercial undertakings, municipalities, hospitals, agriculture, in fact in any situation where work is done or plant is operated by people. The emphasis may differ, but the main objective remains the same: to achieve the desired results with the most effective use of the resources available.

At the outset it will help you to understand if you look at these terms that are in use in work study since students frequently get them confused.

Definition Work study covers the techniques of method study and work measurement and examines human work, investigating the features that affect the efficiency and economy of the situations being reviewed in order to bring about improvements.

Definition Method study is the systematic recording and critical examination of existing or proposed ways of doing work, as a means of developing and applying easier and more effective methods and reducing cost.

Method study helps an organisation to find:

- ways to eliminate the unnecessary;
- the best way of doing something it has not done before;
- a better way of doing something it is already done.

In general, 'better' ways are ways which:

- involve less work;
- reduce waiting time;
- remove the need for special skills;
- produce better results;
- make greater use of resources.

Definition Work measurement is a group of techniques for determining how long a specified task should take given a stated set of circumstances (environment).

All tasks take time. Just how long depends on:

- the task itself and the length of time it requires;
- the physical conditions under which it is done;
- the machines, equipment and tools used;
- the method employed;
- the operator.

4.2 Basic divisions in work study

As we have seen there are two main aspects of work study; they are:

- method study, concerned with how work should be done;
- work measurement, concerned with how long work should take.

Each of these major aspects embraces a number of work study techniques. The relationship between these is set out in the figure below.

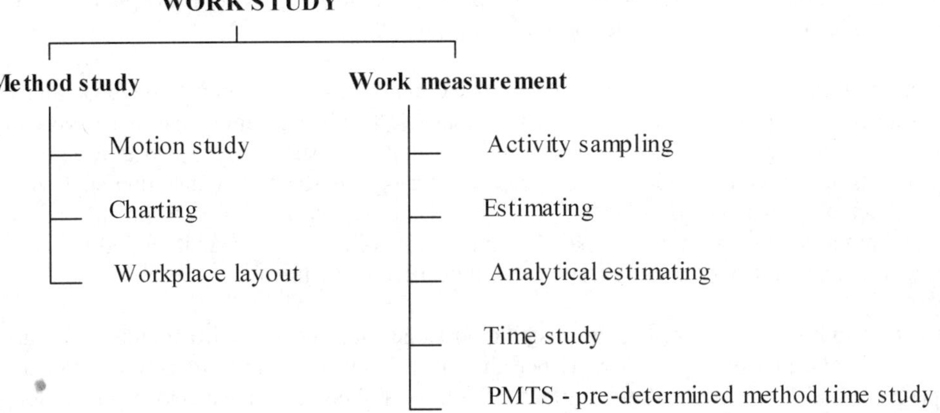

4.3 Method study

The aim of method study is to ensure that the work to be done makes the best use of the available resources. The procedure for doing this uses seven fundamental steps.

(a) *Select* the work to be studied;
(b) *collect* the facts;
(c) *record* the facts;
(d) *examine* the facts;
(e) *develop* a better method;
(f) *install* the better method;
(g) *check* the results achieved.

Select the work to be studied - this is largely dictated by the whole work study programme. Within that programme it is naturally best to start with activities where the need for improvement is most urgent or where the benefits are likely to be obtained are the greatest in relation to the time and effort expended.

Collect the facts - when the order of priorities has been determined, the next step is to decide what information is required. The relevance of some data will be evident, but other data which comes in the 'could be relevant' class should also be gathered. Everything relevant that can be measured should be measured whether it is time, distance, temperature, humidity or any other records of any trials undertaken should be kept. Direct observation is more reliable than opinions.

Record the facts - the three traditional techniques are observation, interview and questionnaire. The scope and the means for making improvements can be more easily seen if the information collected is depicted in charts or diagrams of the type described later. There are two other good reasons for constructing charts in method study:

- they force an observer to make a much more critical and detailed analysis of method (you must have the detail to draw the chart);

- it is easier to explain proposals for change to others if existing and proposed methods of working are expressed in pictorial form.

Examine the facts - the 'examine' step refers to the critical and systematic examination of each feature of existing methods, a process that is greatly facilitated by the charts and diagrams referred to in the previous paragraph. It is at this stage that the so-called critical examination procedure is used. Each operation is subjected to the following questions:

Why? What is achieved? Is it necessary? Can it be eliminated?

When? –Any advantage in changing the sequence of, or combining operations?

Where? –Is it being done in the best place?

Who? –Would it be better if someone else did it?

How? –Is it being done in the best way? Any scope for new techniques or equipment? What about the workplace layout and the principles of motion economy?

Develop a better method - the critical examination carried out during the 'examine' stage is almost certain to reveal opportunities for improvement. The old saying that two heads are better than one is very pertinent at the 'develop' stage and two people working together can usually get better results and in a quicker time than one person working in isolation. Opportunities also arise during this stage for consulting supervisors and the people who are actually involved in doing the job. There are human as well as technical reasons for such consultation and practitioners and managers have a joint responsibility to ensure that the individuals concerned understand the reasons for changes and the way they will be affected by them.

Install the better method - it is during the installation stage that unexpected difficulties can arise. Even where training is provided workers can experience difficulty in changing over to new methods of working. However, people usually overcome these initial difficulties if their assistance and co-operation has been sought at an earlier stage. Again, it can also happen that a new method fails to take absolutely everything into account; it may work well at first but run into trouble as soon as an infrequent or unexpected set of conditions arises. It may then take modifications and a few more trials to get things running smoothly again.

Check results - although it is the responsibility of the work study section to satisfy all concerned that a new method is a success, it is up to line management to take whatever steps are necessary to maintain it and to notify the work study section of any difficulties they meet.

The words 'check results' refer to the need for work study personnel to check and report the benefits that have been achieved as a result of improvements in method, also to the need for them to regard their work as unfinished until new methods have been proved successful.

4.4 Motion study

In the course of examining how a job is done it is sometimes necessary to consider method in great detail – down to the way in which a person uses his arms, hands and even fingers at the work place. The technique for making this type of examination is called motion study and, because it is concerned with methods, motion study comes under the general heading of method study. The use of a video camera and the analysis of the results is essential for this work.

4.5 Work charts

Representing a procedure on a chart is a useful aid in that it portrays the flow of work and also gives a simplified overall presentation. Study of charts by an experienced investigator will reveal where there are problems such as bottlenecks, duplication of work, etc. Dependent on the type of problem being considered, there may be a special type of chart, eg, a string diagram that examines movement in an office. Other approaches could be as follows:

(a) Bottlenecks can be identified by means of a critical path analysis chart. The paths taken and the timing of each operation are drawn and a study of the chart reveals which path is critical and demonstrates the areas where attention should be paid.

(b) The flow of each copy of office forms from section to section can be shown in a procedure flowchart.

(c) Distribution of work amongst employees can be shown on work distribution charts that show recorded details of the tasks performed in the office. Against the tasks are noted the time allowed and the members of staff involved.

(d) Daily usage of office machinery, particularly the more expensive items, could be recorded on an equipment usage chart to indicate under-/over-usage of the investment made.

5 WORK MEASUREMENT

5.1 Introduction

Work measurement is

Definition 'the application of techniques designed to establish the time for a qualified worker to carry out a specified job at a defined level of performance'.

A 'qualified worker' is assumed to have the necessary physical attributes, to possess the required intelligence and education, and to have acquired the necessary skill and knowledge to carry out the work in hand to satisfactory standards of safety, quantity and quality.

The 'specified job' is one in which the method and sequence of its performance have been determined and recorded.

A 'defined level of performance' is stated as being 'the rate of output that gratified workers will naturally achieve without over-exertion as an average over the working day or shift provided they know and adhere to the specified method and that they are motivated to apply themselves to their work'

The information derived from work measurement is necessary for the setting of cost and time standards and hence the evaluation of budgets.

5.2 Methods of measuring work performance

Work or performance measurement methods are generally concerned with quantity and quality. The term 'measurement' implies that a particular performance, be it in terms of quantity or quality, is to be measured against some form of required standard. The methods of measurement therefore involve the setting of standards to provide a yardstick for comparison. The main problem is that some methods are less precise than others.

5.3 Standards

Before the quality or quantity of work can be measured, a standard must not only be available but that standard must be set. The main ways in which those responsible for setting standards can obtain the necessary information are:

- personal observation and timings;
- estimates from managers and supervisors, and/or employees actively engaged in the task;
- activity sampling;
- time/diary sheets of individuals.

Personal observation - a trained observer should record the time taken to complete a particular task. Reliance should not be placed on one observation, rather repeated observations should be made over a period of time. It should be remembered that employees may not work at their normal rate when observed - some may increase their performance whilst some may resent being observed and deliberately lower their performance. The partial solution to this problem is to observe a number of different individuals on a number of occasions thus producing a reasonably reliable average for the task under observation.

Estimates - may be from supervisors or from employees. Estimates from supervisors may be relied upon if the work is of a repetitive nature and the supervisor is experienced. Such estimates would not be suitable where duties are varied. There is of course the problem of employees resenting standards set by immediate supervisors. An estimate from an honest employee may be realistic. However, it may be that the individual may not be totally honest, with an unrealistic standard resulting.

Activity sampling - is a technique designed to establish the proportion of a work period spent by an employee on each of a number of different activities. Random observations are made over a period of time and the activity being performed at each observation is recorded.

Time/diary sheets - are daily or weekly records of which tasks have been accomplished and how long each task took. Over a period of time a reliable picture will be compiled by the determination of average times for particular types of tasks. This approach is well suited to measuring work that is by its nature hard to measure. It is also well suited to measuring the usage of machines thus establishing idle time or breakdown time.

As mentioned above, it is perhaps unrealistic to expect a perfect performance from all employees all the time. For this reason it is the usual practice in setting standards to incorporate a time allowance to take account of:

- breaks for refreshment;
- natural breaks required to renew vigour and concentration.

It should be remembered that the performance of individuals is subject to peaks and troughs. These high points and low points vary not only throughout the day but also from one day to another.

5.4 The measurement of performance

Once standards have been set it is necessary to employ them as yardsticks against which the performance of an individual, section or department can be measured. There are several methods currently available, each having advantages and disadvantages giving appropriate suitability for particular types of task. Methods commonly employed include:

- PMTS - pre-determined method time study;
- the BMDF system - the British Management Data Foundation system;
- task inspection;
- activity sampling;
- diary sheets and time logging.

PMTS - the task to be measured is broken down into its essential components. A standard is set by timing each constituent activity of the task using a stop-watch. To ensure that a realistic average time is set as the standard, several different employees should be timed at different times. Having set the standard, employees are timed periodically to ensure that the standard is being kept. Because the complete task is broken down into individual component activities it is possible to determine at which stage of the task an employee may need to improve his/her performance. The main disadvantage of this measurement method is that employees may resent being timed; others may just be incapable of performing normally whilst being observed and timed.

The BMDF system - is the result of the study of the skills and time involved in carrying out tasks that are common to many organisations. It involves the timing of tasks and comparison with the predetermined standards. It is really an extension of PMTS but does not require the organisation to spend time and money on setting the standards, the process being undertaken by a central organisation - the BMDF.

Task inspection - a departmental or sectional supervisor is required to maintain accurate records of the time work is handed out to individual employees with agreed time limits for completion. Although in essence it is a good idea it is fraught with practical difficulties in that it is time-consuming and causes employee resentment. It is, perhaps, useful for longer-term tasks such as projects that need to be completed over a period of several days or weeks.

Diary sheets and time logging - as with activity sampling, these were discussed earlier regarding the setting of standards. One problem is that employees may resent the time spent on collating information and, indeed, where many tasks are involved valuable time may be spent recording the required information.

5.5 Related techniques

During recent years, a number of techniques have been developed which in some respects overlap work study. They are:

- O & M (organisation and methods) - corresponds to method study applied to clerical and administration functions as a whole. For all practical purposes the approach is the same as in work study but with more emphasis on the organisation of the clerical function as a whole, on the design of information systems and of routines and form design. It is less concerned with detailed methods at the individual workplace.

- OR (operational research) - work study gives way to operational research where the problem is so complex as to require the construction of a mathematical model of the real situation. It is mainly the mathematical characteristics of OR that distinguishes it from work study.

- Value analysis - otherwise known as 'cost engineering' and 'value engineering' is a technique in which a firm's products are subjected to a critical and systematic examination by a small group of specialists representing various functions such as design, production, sales and finance. To the extent that value analysis teams review the design, production, finish and packing of a company's products, the technique of value analysis overlaps that of method study.

- Ergonomics - is the name for the scientific study of workers and their immediate environment. It first became known during the Second World War when a group of specialists with knowledge of functional anatomy, physiology and applied psychology were asked to study the design of aircraft cockpits with particular reference to the design and positioning of indicators and controls. Ergonomics are employed for example, in the design of machine tools and other kinds of industrial equipment. Ergonomics overlaps method study when it is used for the detailed study of workplace design.

Conclusion Work study is a technique for developing better ways of doing physical work and for determining how long that work should take.

6 DISPLAY DESIGN

6.1 Use of forms

An important part of the work in the accounting function is the completion of forms. Many of the procedures discussed depend on the practicability of the forms used and it is evident that the better the form, the greater the aid to achieving efficiency within the systems.

Many of the questions we asked of procedures could equally be asked of forms, and in fact this approach should be an integral feature of any clerical work procedure review. Typical questions might be as follows.

- Is the form really necessary?
- Could an existing form serve the same purpose?
- Could existing forms be combined to reduce paperwork?
- Are all the copies in a set necessary?
- Are there sufficient copies in a set?

6.2 Principles of good form design

When a new form is being designed or an old one being revised the following factors should be considered:

- Who will complete the form?
- Under what type of conditions will the form be completed?
- Who requires the information and for what purpose?
- Are additional copies required?
- How long will the form be kept?

All these factors need to be considered to ensure that the right person receives the right information.

Wherever possible a standardised approach should be taken throughout the organisation. This may lead to economies in printing and filing procedures and efficiency of staff completing forms throughout the organisation may also be improved. On designing a form, the following principles should apply:

- It must contribute to the objectives of the procedure and the content and layout must take account of any other stages in a procedure;
- It should have a title for its purpose and, where appropriate, a code reference;
- The name of the organisation should appear on forms that go outside the undertaking;
- Items should appear in a logical sequence;
- As much information as possible should be pre-printed and, where required for control purposes, forms should be consecutively numbered;
- Adequate space should be allowed for entering information, including signatures;
- Wherever possible, answers should be in the form of marking, eg, tick against one of several conditions;
- The quality of the paper used will be determined by the amount and style of handling and the type of entries, ie, handwriting, stamp impression. Top-quality paper should only be used for prestige documents;
- A pleasing appearance should be aimed for with a minimum variety of fonts used;
- If required, instructions for completing the form should be incorporated;
- Where forms are prepared in sets the distribution should be marked on each copy and different colours used to aid identification;
- Form size should be standard eg, A4 wherever possible, to assist filing.

6.3 Activity

You should take the opportunity to study several of the many forms that you encounter and ask yourself if you consider them well or badly designed

Conclusion A useful way of improving systems and procedures, with beneficial effects upon efficiency, is to ensure that forms are sensibly designed - that they record all the information required and are easy to understand and complete.

6.4 User/computer interface design

The user interface design covers screen layout and dialogue design. The types of dialogue to choose from are:

- menu selection;
- questions and answers;
- form filling;
- natural language;
- command languages.

Dialogue design considerations include:

- user needs consistent and logical messages;
- user should receive rapid responses;
- user problems and dialogue effectiveness should be logged by the system;
- user should be encouraged, not discouraged, by dialogue which is simple to comprehend;
- dialogue must be user- (not analyst-) oriented;
- system must be able to validate and edit;
- user should be monitored and guided (perhaps by menu-driven progress);
- errors must be clearly indicated;
- dialogue must be able to adapt to user speed and awareness;
- user must be able to question in order to seek guidance.

If the user is a specialist a more coded dialogue may be adopted, whereas a casual user requires simple dialogue.

The dialogue must be devised so as to satisfy special needs (the keyboard may require special keys, such as 'debit entry'). Various graphics-oriented displays provide differing aspects of the same item (eg, 3-D).

6.5 Visual display design

This can be either text or graphic display. Graphics displays are a feature of most business applications and offer these advantages:

- the emphasis on relationships;
- disclosing previously unobserved facts;
- focusing interest.

Graphics may be used in three ways:

- information graphics (presenting to the user);
- report graphics (in printed page format);
- presentation graphics (printing out directly to a transparency for projection).

The design of visual displays is linked to the dialogue adopted. When the VDU is activated for data entry, the user is shown a menu presenting various options that prompt him or her to select the next keyboard operation. So, the visual display has to be clear, unambiguous and free of distractions, such as unnecessary details.

Some visual displays appear as forms that have to be completed; fields needing completion are highlighted by adoption of colour, and so on. The designer specifies the display required in the form of a layout sheet, and the programmer is then responsible for providing it. The beneficial results when users participate in system design may be:

- it is ego-enhancing and builds users' self-esteem;
- it is challenging and intrinsically satisfying;
- the user becomes more knowledgeable and is better trained in the use of the system;
- the solution to the problem is better because participants know more about the system than the computer department staff members;
- the user retains much of the control over operations.

7 QUALITY CONTROL

7.1 Controlling quality of output

The aspects considered above are concerned with the quantity of output. Earlier studies indicated that work measurement is concerned with both quantity and quality. Here some consideration will be afforded to quality control.

Quality control is essential because people are prone to errors and mistakes. Errors need to be corrected - this takes time and therefore costs money. For example a document with lots of mistakes will need to be re-keyed or altered and this will take time - productivity effectively decreases and costs per unit, given that it has taken more time than it should have, will also increase. Sometimes errors are not spotted until it is too late - the document containing the error may have been sent to a third party and might well involve additional correspondence and/or telephone calls to resolve the problem.

The benefits of quality control include:

- reductions in costs of scrap or re-working;
- reductions in complaints;
- enhanced reputation for products/services;
- feedback to designers and engineers about the performance of products and the machines required to produce them;

7.2 Quality control methods

There are three main methods to ensure that quality of output is controlled, each being a logical extension of the other. They are:

- 100% checking;
- random sampling;
- partial checking.

100% checking is probably the most foolproof of all methods but at the same time the most expensive in terms of time and money. It involves a variation on the theme of proof-reading and involves checking words and figures on a one-for-one basis. It should only be used for work of the greatest importance.

Random sampling is a modification of the 100% checking method. Here samples of work are selected at periodic intervals and usually checked completely from start to finish. The problem of determining the optimum cost/benefit relationship is important under this method. If sampling is undertaken too frequently then the cost/benefit relationship will deteriorate. If sampling occurs only rarely then no reliance of any value will be placed upon the results.

Partial checking is a compromise between 100% checking and random sampling. It involves checking only the most important portion of the work and assuming that if such vital sections are accurate then the remainder of the work is likely to be of the required standard. Partial checking is the most commonly employed method and is easily operated by supervisors.

7.3 Causes of errors

Another aspect of quality control is the identification of why errors occur - once the cause is known steps can be taken to eliminate the causes of errors.

The most sensible approach to the elimination of errors involves the implementation of a system that will necessitate the identification of the causes as soon as the errors have been made. If the causes are not identified then errors will continue and may indeed increase in frequency.

Errors can be due to either the fault of the worker or the fault of management or the working conditions.

There are many causes that may be attributed to the worker himself/herself. The most common are:

- haste;
- carelessness;
- lack of the correct attitude;
- lack of method in working;
- lack of back-up/associated knowledge;
- inexperience;
- general standard of education.

Management faults include:

- defective or lack of training;
- poor recruitment policies;
- lack of organisation;
- lack of supervision and control;
- wrong attitude towards workforce.

Working conditions at fault may be due to:

- poor ventilation, heating etc;
- bad lighting;
- too much noise/too many distractions;
- poor furniture, decor and general surroundings.

7.4 Error tolerance

In an ideal world it would be possible to identify all causes of errors and to take action to prevent them. Unfortunately, an error-free world does not exist and most organisations are content to set a pre-determined level of error tolerance. Each group of tasks will have different levels of error tolerance and account must be taken of this. It may well be possible to eliminate nearly all errors by 100% checking but this is often not cost-effective. It is this aspect of cost-effectiveness that is the key to the determination of an acceptable level of error tolerance.

Conclusion The introduction of quality control could mean reductions in costs of scrap or re-working, reductions in complaints, enhanced reputation for products/services and feedback to designers and engineers about the performance of products and the machines required to produce them.

8 SELF TEST QUESTIONS

8.1 What is a SWOT analysis? (1.3)

8.2 How would you assess the management information system? (2.4)

8.3 Why is there a debate about siting the accounts department? (3.2)

8.4 What is a string diagram used for? (3.4)

8.5 Compare and contrast work study and method study. (4.1)

8.6 List some work study techniques. (4.2)

8.7 Outline the 7 steps to method study. (4.3)

8.8 What are the assumptions about a 'qualified worker' when measuring work? (5.1)

8.9 What is ergonomics? (5.5)

8.10 Why is A4 the suggested size for a form? (6.2)

8.11 Describe the benefits of Quality Control. (7.1)

8.12 In Quality Control, what is random sampling? (7.2)

Chapter 10

EFFECTIVENESS OF CONTROL SYSTEMS

PATHFINDER INTRODUCTION

This chapter covers the following performance criteria and knowledge and understanding

- Methods of measuring cost effectiveness and systems reliability (Element 10.2)
- Understanding that the accounting systems of an organisation are affected by its organistional structure, its MIS, its administrative systems and procedures and the nature of its business transactions (Elements 10.1, 10.2 & 10.3)
- Weaknesses and potential for improvements to the accounting system are identified and considered for their impact on the operation of the organisation (Element 10.2)
- Past examples of control avoidance are analysed and used to inform evaluations of the controls within the system (Element 10.3)
- Areas of potential fraud within the control avoidance accounting system are identified and the risk graded (Element 10.3)
- Possible methods of avoiding the risks and safeguarding the system are identified (Element 10.3).

Putting the chapter in context – learning objectives.

We studied in earlier chapters the general principles governing the organisation and management of systems. In chapter seven we looked in some detail at the theory and practice of control systems.

Before moving on to fraud management, we shall now look in detail at how accounting controls can be established for the various areas of the accounting system with particular emphasis on the proper internal controls that should be in place.

This is an essential part of improving the effectiveness of the accounting system, because in addition to the matters discussed in the earlier chapters, it is essential that the accounting systems comply with good practice and are secure. A key part of improving them is to identify any weaknesses and take the appropriate action to correct these.

At the end of this chapter you should have learned the following topics.

- Identify specific control procedures.
- Evaluate the control system by means of internal control questionnaires and evaluation checklists.

1 WHY DO COMPANIES NEED INTERNAL CONTROLS?

At its simplest, companies need internal controls to stop things going missing and to make some sense of how the business is doing. Documents get lost and assets go home with the staff even where there are controls in place to record everything. Managers have a gut feeling for how the business is doing, but when all they have to prove it is three large boxes stuffed full of invoices and two large boxes full of expenses (and neither of these are *quite* complete), they may find it difficult to prove their ideas to the Inland Revenue, and of course they may well be very wrong.

2 SPECIFIC CONTROL PROCEDURES

These include:

(a) Approval and control of documents

In a purchases system for example, there should be authority limits. An order up to the value of £1,000 could be approved by a department head, up to £5,000 by any one director, and beyond this by the Board as a whole.

(b) Controls over computerised applications and the IT environment

These are dealt with later in the text.

(c) Checking the arithmetical accuracy of the records

Such controls include checking the casts on a purchase invoice, and recalculating the VAT on sales invoices.

(d) Maintaining and reviewing control accounts and trial balances

Control accounts include sales and purchase ledger control accounts, bank reconciliations and fixed asset registers.

(e) Comparing the results of cash, security and stock counts with the accounting records

(f) Comparing internal data with external sources of information

This might include supplier statement reconciliations.

(g) Limiting direct physical access to assets and records

An important general principle with respect to assets and records is that of *segregation.*

In particular there should be a division of responsibilities for:

(i) *authorising* or initiating the transaction;
(ii) the physical *custody* and control of assets involved;
(iii) *recording* the transaction.

No one person should be in a position both to misappropriate an asset and to conceal his act by falsifying the records. For example, in a sales system the duties of receiving money from debtors and writing up the sales ledger should be separated. If not, money could be misappropriated and the records falsified to cover this.

3 EVALUATING THE CONTROL SYSTEM

3.1 Internal control questionnaires (ICQs)

(a) **Introduction**

In the large company, it is usual to place reliance on internal controls to gain confidence in the security of a system. This is because of the volume of many different types of transaction which will be processed and the impossibility of checking each one individually for correctness. Management will be interested in key controls which are relevant, namely the internal accounting controls. These can afford reasonable assurance of the completeness and accuracy of the accounting records and the validity of entries therein and thus of the financial statements which will be prepared.

Underlying their construction, internal control questionnaires have a number of objectives:

(i) *to ascertain* the systems of accounting and internal control;

(ii) *to evaluate* the control system thus recorded; and hence

(iii) *to identify* those controls which indicate strengths in the system upon which the management can rely; and

(iv) *to identify* those areas over which there are weak or no controls and which therefore must be subjected to more extensive testing and which will require changes to the system.

(b) **Construction rules for an ICQ**

(i) It is good practice when designing ICQs to state, as a brief foreword to the standard questions:

- a list of *control objectives* which each sub-system under consideration should seek to achieve.

- accompanied by *any business considerations* specific to the enterprise under review which should be taken into account.

The reason for such inclusions is essentially to highlight key areas for consideration in the exercise of ascertaining, evaluating and testing systems so that a sense of perspective is maintained and encouragement is given to individuals to exercise initiative.

(ii) The questions in an ICQ should be designed to ascertain whether the control objectives are being achieved and should therefore cover:

(1) instructions;
(2) authorisations;
(3) originating documents;
(4) initiating procedures;
(5) recording procedures;
(6) sequence of procedures;
(7) custody procedures;
(8) controls;
(9) relative independence of the persons involved at each stage of a transaction.

(iii) The questions should be framed in a manner which observes *exception principles*. Not all questions can be framed to get a *Yes/No* answer but those which can should be so worded. Throughout the questionnaire there should be consistency of either a *Yes* or *No* answer being indicative of a weakness. The most common practice is for *No* to indicate a weakness.

(iv) An ICQ is a formal, usually standardised document and hence should observe certain basic conventions, such as:

(1) the name of the document (ICQ);

(2) the system to which it relates (eg, purchasing cycle);

(3) the accounting period under review;

(4) evidence of who has prepared and reviewed the document;

(5) the provision of columns for:

- *Yes* and *No* answers;
- comments where neither *Yes* or *No* are applicable;
- indicating the significance or otherwise of apparent weaknesses;

3.2 Example of part of an ICQ

INTERNAL CONTROL QUESTIONNAIRE THE PURCHASING CYCLE COMPANY:	Prepared by: Date:
PERIOD:	Reviewed by: Date:

(a) Control objectives.
(b) Business considerations.
(c) The questionnaire.

(a) **Control objectives**

To ensure that:

(i) purchased goods/services are ordered under proper authorities and procedures;

(ii) purchased goods/services are only ordered as necessary for the proper conduct of the business operations and are ordered from suitable suppliers;

(iii) goods/services received are effectively inspected for quality, quantity and condition;

(iv) invoices and related documentation are properly checked and approved as being valid before being entered as trade creditors;

(v) all valid transactions relating to trade creditors (suppliers' invoices, credit notes and adjustments), and only those transactions, should be accurately recorded in the accounting records.

(b) **Business considerations**

	Points	**Effect on audit procedures and on financial statements**
(i)	Nature of the company's purchases.	Auditor must be aware of the varying nature of goods purchased.
(ii)	The existence of a purchasing department.	As far as possible ordering should be centralised.
(iii)	The company's purchasing policy.	The fixing of minimum/maximum stock and re-order levels should ensure efficient control. However, buying in bulk, with resulting higher inventory levels, may be part of a company policy to reduce unit costs, in which case stock obsolescence problems may arise.
(iv)	The selection of suppliers.	The purchasing department should maintain a suppliers' register to record past purchases, prices, satisfaction received etc. The constant seeking of alternative sources of supply at keener prices is an indication of efficient management.

(c)

Questionnaire	Yes	No	Comments	References
Initiation and authorisation				
1 Are standard order forms (SOFs) issued showing names of suppliers, quantities ordered and prices?				
2 Are copies of SOFs retained on file?				
3 Who authorises orders and what are their authority limits?				
4 Are the persons in 3 above independent of those who issue requisitions?				
5 Is a record kept of orders placed but not executed? (If yes, specify type of record kept and filing sequence).				
Custody				
6 Are goods from suppliers inspected on arrival as to quantity and quality?				
7 How is the receipt of supplies recorded (eg, by Goods Received Notes)?				
8 Are these records prepared by a person independent of those responsible for: - ordering functions? - processing and recording?				
Recording				
9 Are all invoices received - compared with copy orders? - compared with goods received notes? - checked for prices? - checked for calculations, extensions and additions?				
10 Are the functions in 9 above performed by a person independent of those responsible for: - ordering? - receipt, control and custody of goods?				
11 Are bought ledger personnel independent of those responsible for: - approving invoices and credit notes? - cheque payments?				
12 Is the person maintaining the control account independent of bought ledger personnel?				

Notes

(i) The items in this reproduced questionnaire have been edited in the interests of clarity.

(ii) The style of question asked (eg, *Are SOFs issued etc?, who authorises order?)* is geared to ascertaining both the system in force and the effectiveness of the controls imposed.

3.3 Internal Control Evaluation Checklists (ICEs)

ICQs represent an attempt at a formalised, more systematic, approach to large complex organisations. It is however increasingly apparent that such questionnaires can become too complex and detailed for meaningful evaluation. There is a danger that ICQs can provoke too stylised an approach to an assignment, concentrating as they do *on the controls* themselves *rather than upon the fraud or irregularity that the controls are designed to prevent.* To overcome these possible shortcomings, most internal audit departments have amended their approach to internal control evaluation by the adoption of *Internal Control Evaluation Checklists* (ICE).

The ICE is designed to determine if desirable internal controls are present, using key control questions to ascertain where specific frauds or errors are possible. It is normally employed where systems information has *already* been recorded (usually in the form of flowcharts).

Note that virtually all the rules applicable to the construction of an ICQ apply to the construction of an ICE. In fact the format itself is very similar - as may be seen from the example below. The structure of the questions, however, differentiates between the two techniques.

Key questions are asked in an ICE, the answers to which prompt further supplementary questions. Reference is made to a supporting flowchart which is the means of ascertaining the existing systems.

3.4 Example of part of an ICE

INTERNAL CONTROL EVALUATION CHECKLIST
PURCHASES - CREDITORS - PAYMENTS
COMPANY:

PERIOD:

Prepared by:
Date:

Reviewed by:
Date:

(a) Control objectives.
(b) Business considerations.
(c) The checklist.

(a) **Control objectives**
As ICQ

(b) **Business considerations**
As ICQ

(c) **The checklist**

---

1 **Purchases**

		Comments	Reference
1.1	**Can goods be purchased without authority?**		
	(a) purchase requisitions and order approvals?		
	(b) limit of buyers' authority to order?		
	(c) purchasing segregated from receiving, accounts payable and inventory records?		
	(d) unissued orders safeguarded against loss?		
1.2	**Can liabilities be incurred although goods not received?**		
	(a) receiving segregated from purchasing, accounts payable and inventory records?		
	(b) are all goods passed directly to stores?		
	(c) GRNs or equivalent prepared independently?		
	(d) adequate comparison with order, claims for short shipment etc?		
	(e) invoices, GRNs, direct to accounts payable not purchasing?		
	(f) invoices checked to order and GRNs, prices checked?		
	(g) check of extensions, additions, discounts?		
	(h) documents cancelled to prevent re-use?		
	(i) unmatched documents investigated regularly?		
	(j) freight checked, bills matched to consignments?		
	(k) purchase returns and allowances controlled - follow-up?		
	(l) forward purchases controlled?		
1.3	**Can cut-off errors occur?**		
	(a) time lapse from receipt of goods to invoice processing?		
	(b) valuation of unmatched GRNs?		
	(c) adequate control and recording of receipts?		

1.4 Can invoices be wrongly allocated?

(a) nominal ledger analysis?
(b) analysis independently checked?
(c) staff purchases controlled?
(d) independent and regular review?

1.5 Can liabilities be recorded for goods or services not ordered?

(a) goods received without authority?

---

2 Creditors

2.1 Can liabilities be incurred but not recorded?

(a) creditors agreed periodically?

(b) supplier's statements independently reconciled?

(c) invoice register?

(d) forward contracts?

(e) order backlog follow up?

(f) debit balances controlled?

---

3 Payments

3.1 Can payments be made if not properly supported?

(a) discounts taken?

(b) control over invoices before validating complete?

(c) cheque signatories independent of purchasing, receiving, accounts payable and cheque preparation?

(d) signatories examine support for payment, check completeness, cancel support?

(e) control over signature plates or presigned cheques?

(f) control where one signature?

(g) frequency with which cheques mailed?

(h) independent regular bank reconciliation, with cheques directly from bank and review reconciliation?

(i) cheques crossed *account payee only*, continuity accounted for, control over unused cheques?

(j) bank transfers controlled - standing orders?

(k) issue of bearer or 'cash' cheques?

(l) advances and loans controlled?

(m) giro payments, traders credits, direct debits?

3.2 **Can payments for non-routine purchases be made if not authorised or properly supported?**

(a) services, expense accounts, taxation payments in advance, staff purchases and goods on consignment?

3.3 **Can fixed assets be acquired or removed without proper authorisation and recording?**

(a) approved work orders for fixed assets and major repairs?

(b) approval of cost over-runs?

(c) reporting of scrapping or disposals?

(d) detailed fixed asset register, regular physical inspection and review of values?

(e) periodic insurance appraisals, adequate coverage?

(f) control over loose tools?

Chapter 11

EFFECTIVENESS OF SALES AND PURCHASES SYSTEMS

PATHFINDER INTRODUCTION

This chapter covers the following knowledge and understanding

- Understanding that the accounting systems of an organisation are affected by its organisational structure, its MIS, its administrative systems and procedures and the nature of its business transactions (Elements 10.1, 10.2 & 10.3)
- Overview of the organisation's business and the critical external relationships (customer/clients, suppliers, etc.) (Elements 10.2 & 10.3)
- Organisation of the accounting function; relationship between the accounting function and other departments; structure of the accounting function (Elements 10.2 & 10.3)

Putting the chapter in context – learning objectives.

This is the first of two chapters which set out the objectives and procedures involved in the practical organisation of the accounting systems, outlining the sorts of procedures which should be in place if the systems are to operate successfully.

At the end of this chapter you should have learned the following topics.

- understand the typical control objectives for the sales cycle
- list the controls which may be appropriate for the sales system
- understand the typical control objectives for the purchases cycle
- list the controls which may be appropriate for the purchases system.

1 GENERAL

1.1 Control objectives, procedures, and tests of control

Why do we need internal controls in the sales and purchases systems? Because of what would happen if they were not there! If sales orders are not prenumbered, and if they are not cancelled after they have been filled they may well be lost and not filled at all, or filled twice. This would not please our customers who will not pay us for orders that have been delivered to them twice and will go to other suppliers if we do not fill orders at all. If despatches are not matched with invoices, we might not be invoicing our customers and we would effectively be giving our goods and services away! If invoices are not matched with despatch notes, we may be invoicing for goods that our customers have not received, or invoicing them wrongly which will damage goodwill and we will incur unnecessary administrative costs in sorting the problem out.

If we do not batch our invoices and check the totals, invoices may go missing and never be recorded at all, our customers would pay us and we will show credit balances on the sales ledger because there are no invoices processed to cancel them out, or we will just show large amounts of unallocated cash. And either way, our records will show creditors that are simply not real! The financial information will not make sense.

2 SALES SYSTEM

2.1 Control objectives

How do the control objectives noted above translate into 'real life' objectives for sales?

For many businesses, sales are made on credit and thus the sales cycle includes control objectives for debtors. These control objectives include:

(a) Customers' orders should be authorised, controlled and recorded in order to execute them promptly and determine any provision required for losses arising from unfulfilled commitments.

(b) Goods shipped and work completed should be controlled to ensure that invoices are issued and revenue recorded for all sales.

(c) Goods returned and claims by customers should be controlled in order to determine the liability for goods returned and claims received but not entered in the debtors' records.

(d) Invoices and credits should be appropriately checked as being accurate and authorised before being entered in the debtors' records.

(e) Validated debtors' transactions, and only those transactions, should be accurately entered in the accounting records.

(f) There should be procedures to ensure that sales invoices are subsequently paid and that doubtful amounts are identified in order to determine any provisions required.

2.2 Achievement of objectives

In order to achieve these objectives there should be good *segregation of duties*. There are three distinct processes in the sales system which should be segregated and performed by different staff in order to establish effective internal controls. They are:

(a) **Accepting customers' orders.** Sequence-controlled documents should be used to acknowledge all orders received. Any uncompleted orders should be regularly reviewed.

Credit limits should be checked by the credit control department. Selling prices, special discounts and delivery dates should be fixed by senior members of the sales department - never by the accounts staff.

(b) **Despatch department.** Sequence-controlled documents should be used (goods outwards or despatch notes) for all goods leaving the premises. These should be completed by the gatekeeper or the despatch department - never by the accounts staff.

(c) **Invoicing the goods.** Sequence-controlled invoices should be raised by the sales department and then passed to the accounts department for recording. Independent checks should be made to ensure that invoices have been raised for all goods outwards notes.

In addition strict control of credit notes is essential to ensure that they are raised by proper authority in the sales department against goods received notes. It is not uncommon for credit notes to be raised to 'hide' what are in fact bad debts. Credit notes can also be used to cancel out fictitious sales invoices which have been raised in order to boost sales figures artificially.

2.3 Control procedures over sales and debtors

There are a large number of controls that may be required in the sales cycle due to the importance of this area in any business and the possible opportunities that exist for diverting sales away from the business and other persons benefiting.

(a) Orders

(i) The orders should be checked against the customer's account; this should be evidenced by initialing. Any new customer should be referred to the credit control department before the order is accepted.

(ii) Existing customers should be allocated a credit limit and it should be ascertained whether this limit is to be exceeded if the new order is accepted. If so the matter should be referred to credit control.

(iii) All orders received should be recorded on pre-numbered sales order documents.

(iv) All orders should be authorised before any goods are despatched.

(v) The sales order should be used to produce a despatch note for the goods outwards department. No goods may be despatched without a despatch note.

(b) Despatch

(i) Despatch notes should be pre-numbered and a register kept of them to relate to sales invoices and orders.

(ii) Goods despatch notes should be authorised as goods leave and checked periodically to ensure they are complete and that all have been invoiced.

(c) Invoicing and credit notes

(i) Sales invoices should be authorised by a responsible official and referenced to the original authorised order and despatch note.

(ii) All invoices and credit notes should be entered in sales day book records, the sales ledger, and sales ledger control account. Batch totals should be maintained for this purpose.

(iii) Sales invoices and credit notes should be checked for prices, casts and calculations by a person other than the one preparing the invoice.

(iv) All invoices and credit notes should be serially pre-numbered and regular sequence checks should be carried out.

(v) Credit notes should be authorised by someone unconnected with despatch or sales ledger functions.

(vi) Copies of cancelled invoices should be retained.

(vii) Any invoice cancellation should lead to a cancellation of the appropriate despatch note.

(viii) Cancelled and free of charge invoices should be signed by a responsible official.

(ix) Each invoice should distinguish between different types of sales and VAT. Any coding of invoices should be periodically checked independently.

(d) Returns

(i) Any goods returned by the customer should be checked for obvious damage and, when accepted, a document should be raised.

(ii) All goods returned should be used to prepare appropriate credit notes.

(e) Debtors

(i) A sales ledger control account should be prepared regularly and checked to individual sales ledger balances by an independent official.

(ii) Sales ledger personnel should be independent of despatch and cash receipt functions.

(iii) Statements should be sent regularly to customers.

(iv) Formal procedures should exist for following up overdue debts which should be highlighted either by the preparation of an aged list of balances or in the preparation of statements to customers.

(v) Letters should be sent to customers for collection of overdue debts.

(f) Bad debts

(i) The authority to write off a bad debt should be given in writing and adjustments made to the sales ledger.

(ii) The use of court action or the writing-off of a bad debt should be authorised by an official independent of the cash receipt function.

2.4 Assessing the effectiveness of the controls

Assessments of controls should be designed to check that the control procedures are being applied and that objectives are being achieved. Tests may be appropriate under the following broad headings and you can usefully produce documents and evidence for your project by looking at your own company's systems (with the appropriate authorty and clearance of course) to see how things are working.

(a) Carry out *sequence test checks* on invoices, credit notes, despatch notes and orders. Ensure that all items are included and that there are no omissions or duplications.

(b) Check the *authorisation* for the

- acceptance of the order (the creditworthiness check),
- despatch of goods,
- raising of the invoice or credit note,
- pricing and discounts,
- write-off of bad debts.

Check both that the relevant signature exists and that the control has been applied eg, check pricing for accuracy and credit limits to ensure that they have not been exceeded. This last test will also serve as a substantive procedure.

(c) Seek evidence of *checking of the arithmetical accuracy* of

- invoices,
- credit notes,
- VAT.

This is often done by means of a ‘grid stamp’ containing several signatures on the face of the invoice. Ensure that the control has in fact been applied by checking the accuracy of such invoices and credit notes. This last test will also serve as a substantive procedure.

(d) Check *despatch notes* and goods returned notes to ensure that they are *referenced* to *invoices* and credit notes and vice versa.

(e) Check that *control account reconciliations* have been *performed and reviewed.* Reperform the control by checking the reconciliation to source documentation.

(f) Ensure that *batch total controls* have been *applied* by seeking signatures and tracing batches from input to output.

In all cases, tests should be performed on a *sample* basis. The auditor should investigate errors and consider the need for further testing to obtain comfort on the proper application of the control procedure.

3 PURCHASES SYSTEM

3.1 Control objectives

For all businesses, purchases can be made on credit and thus the purchases cycle includes control objectives for creditors. You also need to bear in mind that 'purchases' has a wide meaning in terms of the purchases cycle as purchases will include all types of expense and the purchase of fixed assets. The ultimate destination of the purchases is therefore not confined to cost of sales and stock.

In detail, the control objectives are as follows.

To ensure that:

(a) purchased goods/services are ordered under proper authorities and procedures;

(b) purchased goods/services are only ordered as necessary for the proper conduct of the business operations and are ordered from suitable suppliers;

(c) goods/services received are effectively inspected for quality, quantity and conditions;

(d) invoices and related documentation are properly checked and approved as being valid before being entered as trade creditors;

(e) all valid transactions relating to trade creditors (suppliers' invoices, credit notes and adjustments), and only those transactions, should be accurately recorded in the accounting records.

3.2 Control procedures over purchases and creditors

As with the sales system, there are a large number of controls that may be required in the purchases cycle due to the importance of this area in any business and once again, the following list is classified by type of control.

(a) Orders

(i) Requisition notes for purchases should be authorised.

(ii) All orders should be authorised by a responsible official whose authority limits should be pre-defined.

(iii) Major items eg, capital expenditure, should be authorised by the board.

(iv) All orders should be recorded on official documents showing suppliers' names, quantities ordered and price.

(v) Copies of orders should be retained as a method of following up late deliveries by suppliers.

(vi) Re-order levels and quantities should be pre-set and preferably recorded in advance on the requisition note.

(b) Receipt of goods

(i) Goods inwards centres should be identified to deal with the receipt of all goods.

(ii) All goods should be checked for quantity and quality. Goods received notes should be raised for all goods accepted. The GRN should be signed by a responsible official.

(iii) GRNs should be checked against purchase orders and procedures should exist to notify the supplier of under or over-deliveries. GRNs should be sequentially numbered and checked periodically for completeness.

(c) Invoicing and returns

(i) Purchase invoices received should be stamped with an approval grid and given a unique serial number to ensure purchase invoices do not go astray.

(ii) Purchase invoices should be matched with goods received notes and should not be processed until this is done.

(iii) The invoice should be checked against the order and the GRN, and casts and extensions should also be checked.

(iv) The invoices should be signed as approved for payment by a responsible official independent of the ordering and receipt of goods functions.

(v) Invoice sequential numbers should be checked against purchase day book details.

(vi) Input VAT should be separated from the expense.

(vii) Invoices should be properly allocated to the nominal ledger accounts, perhaps by allocating expenditure codes. A portion of such coding should be checked independently.

(viii) Batch controls should be maintained over the posting of invoices to the purchases day book, nominal ledger and purchase ledger.

(ix) A record of goods returned should be kept and checked to the credit notes received from suppliers.

(d) Purchase ledger and suppliers

(i) A purchase ledger control account should be maintained and regularly checked against balances in the ledger by an independent official.

(ii) Purchase ledger records should be kept by persons independent of the receiving of goods, invoice authorisation and payment routines.

(iii) Statements from suppliers should be checked against the purchase ledger account.

3.3 Assessing the effectiveness of controls

As already noted, tests of control should be drawn up so as to check that control procedures are being applied and to achieve control objectives. One suggested way to design tests of control for a particular situation is to list the documents in a transaction cycle and generate appropriate tests of control for each document.

Document	Tests
Purchase Order	Test for: (i) Evidence of a sequence check. (ii) Evidence of approval. (iii) Adherence to authority limits.
Goods Received Note	Test for evidence of a sequence check.
Goods Returned Note	Test for evidence of a sequence check.

Purchase Invoice	Test for: (i) Serial numbering. (ii) Evidence of sequence check. (iii) Evidence of matching purchase invoices with goods received notes and purchase orders. (iv) Evidence of checking casts, extensions and VAT treatment. (v) Evidence of account coding. (vi) Initialing of invoice grid for work done. (vii) Approval of purchase invoice for further processing.
Credit Note	Test for evidence of matching credit notes to goods returned notes.
Purchase ledger	Test for evidence of authorisation of adjustments to purchase ledger.
Purchase Ledger Control	Test for: (i) Evidence of review of reconciliation of purchase ledger listing. (ii) Evidence of authorisation of adjustments to purchase ledger control account.

4 SELF TEST QUESTIONS

4.1 What are the control objectives for the return of goods by a customer? (2.1)

4.2 What are the control objectives for valid debtors' transactions? (2.1)

4.3 What are the three distinct processes in the sales system where there should be good segregation of duties? (2.2)

4.4 What are the substantive tests to be applied on sales invoices? (2.3)

4.5 What are the control objectives for the purchase of goods by the business? (3.1)

4.6 What are the substantive tests to be applied on purchase invoices? (3.2)

Chapter 12

EFFECTIVENESS OF WAGES AND CASH SYSTEMS

PATHFINDER INTRODUCTION

This chapter covers the following knowledge and understanding.

- Understanding that the accounting systems of an organisation are affected by its organisational structure, its MIS, its administrative systems and procedures and the nature of its business transactions (Elements 10.1, 10.2 & 10.3)
- Organisation of the accounting function; relationship between the accounting function and other departments; structure of the accounting function (Elements 10.2 & 10.3)

Putting the chapter in context – learning objectives.

The wages and cash systems can be among the most vulnerable to fraud or manipulation of the system and it is vital that a business maintains effective control over these areas.

At the end of this chapter you should have learned the following topics.

- Understand the typical control objectives for the wages cycle.
- List tests of control and substantive procedures which may be appropriate for the wages system and wages total.
- Understand the typical control objectives for the cash cycle and list appropriate tests of control.
- Understand the typical control objectives for the other accounting systems which will exist.

1 CONTROL OBJECTIVES

1.1 Introduction

Why do we need internal controls for payroll, cash, fixed assets and stocks? With cash, fixed assets and stocks, one objective is clear, we need to safeguard them as assets. With payroll, we need to be sure that we are paying only for work that has been done, at the correct rates and that our liabilities to the tax authorities are accurate, to avoid fines and penalties. It is very easy for payroll records to be falsified such that the company pays for work that has not been done. Overtime needs to be authorised because if it is not, employees can put in fictional claims and whilst the accounting may be correct, the business suffers. Payroll calculations need to be checked, especially where produced manually and also when produced by a computer because if tax or social security rates are too high, employee relations suffer and we incur administrative costs in sorting the problem out; if they are too low, we are still liable to the tax authorities, but we cannot reclaim the amounts that are due from employees.

Most cash transactions involve checking by at least two people, one of whom deals with the cash, and the other who deals with the records (segregation of duties). For example, when cash comes in from customers, if only one person opens the mail and updates the cash book and the sales ledger, that person could steal the cash (or part of it) and then claim that no cash was received. This applies to cheques as well as notes and coins because it is not so difficult to pay a cheque made out to a company into ones own bank account (although it is more difficult than it used to be because the 'A/C payee' crossing means that the paying bank takes the risk of error if the cheque is paid into any account other than the account of the named person). If there are two people opening the mail, there is a reduced chance of this happening. If two individuals supervise the opening, there is of course the possibility that they will collude to steal the cash, falsify the records and split the proceeds between them. This is an example of an inherent limitation in a control system; no system is perfect as people can always 'get around' it.

Stock and fixed assets are often more easily stolen than cash. The bulk of theft in shops in the UK is believed to be not theft by 'customers', but theft by employees. It is not possible to have two people present every time stock is dealt with; stock has to be controlled by means of counting it regularly, reconciling it to stock, sales and purchases records and trying to establish reasons for differences. If there are always large discrepancies in the food section of a department store, and many of those discrepancies often relate to cheese, it may be appropriate to move staff around. Fixed assets are less portable than stock but it is surprising how often companies do not know what fixed assets they have or where they are. A fixed assets register that shows names, numbers and descriptions of fixed assets which is regularly checked to the assets themselves, helps here, and discourages the assets from 'walking'.

1.2 Control objectives

The control objectives of a sound system of internal control for wages and salaries are as follows:

(a) The computation of wages and salaries should be only in respect of the client's employees and at authorised rates of pay.

(b) Wages and salaries should be in accordance with records of work performed, eg time, output, commissions on sales.

(c) Payrolls should be calculated accurately.

(d) Payment should be made to the correct employees.

(e) Liabilities to the tax authorities for PAYE and NI should be properly recorded.

2 WAGES SYSTEMS

2.1 Introduction

Systems in force with regard to wages and salaries vary considerably with the size and nature of the business but the procedures involved generally fall into the following broad categories:

(a) Engagements, promotions, transfers and discharges of employees.
(b) Time attendance and job recording.
(c) Preparation of payroll and analysis of wages and salaries.
(d) Make up and payments of wages and salaries.

2.2 Control procedures - wages

(a) **Approval and control of documents**

(i) There should be written authorisation to employ or dismiss any employee.

(ii) Changes in rates of pay should be authorised in writing by an official outside the wages department.

(iii) Overtime worked should be authorised by the works manager/supervisor.

(iv) An independent official should check the payroll and sign it.

(v) The wages cheque should be signed by two signatories evidenced against the signed payroll.

(vi) Where weekly pay relates to hours at work, clock cards should be used. There should be supervision of the cards and the timing devices, particularly when employees are clocking-on or off.

(vii) Personnel records should be kept for each employee giving details of engagement, retirement, dismissal or resignation, rates of pay, holidays etc, with a specimen signature of the employee.

(viii) A wages supervisor should be appointed who could perform some of the authorisation duties listed above.

(b) **Arithmetical accuracy**

(i) Payroll should be prepared from clock cards, job cards etc, and a sample checked for accuracy against current rates of pay.

(ii) Payroll details should provide for the accurate calculation of deductions eg, PAYE, NI, pensions, trade union subscriptions etc, which should be checked periodically.

(c) **Control accounts**

(i) Control accounts should be maintained in respect of each of the deductions showing amounts paid periodically to the Revenue, trade unions etc.

(ii) Overall checks should be carried out to highlight major discrepancies eg, check against budgets, changes in amounts paid over a period of time, check against personnel records.

(iii) Management should exercise overall control.

(d) **Access to assets and records**

(i) An employee should sign for his wages.

(ii) No employee should be allowed to take the wages of another employee.

(iii) When wages are claimed late, the employee should sign for the wage packet and the release of the packet should be authorised.

(iv) The system should preferably allow the wages to be checked by the employee before the packet is opened, by using specially designed wage packets.

(v) The wages department should preferably be a separate department with their personnel not involved with receipts or payments functions.

(vi) The duties of the wages staff should preferably be rotated during the year, and ensure that no employee is responsible for all the functions in respect of any particular department.

(vii) The employee making up the pay packets should not be the employee who prepares the payroll.

(viii) A surprise attendance at the pay-out should be made periodically by an independent official.

(ix) Unclaimed wages should be recorded in a register and held by someone outside the wages department until claimed or until a predefined period after which the money should be rebanked. An official should investigate the reason for unclaimed wages as soon as possible.

The above categorisation is taken from the list of types of controls listed in SAS 300 *Accounting and internal control systems and audit risk assessments* noted in an earlier chapter. It may help you to come up with ideas for a system with which you are not familiar. The following parts of this section illustrate controls expected in other major areas. These are not classified by type.

Try generating a couple of these areas yourself then review the controls suggested. There is no *necessity* to learn these lists but you should practise the technique to generate them, and use the rest of the section for reference.

2.3 Control procedures - salaries

(a) Personnel records should be kept similar to those for hourly paid employees.

(b) Written authority should be required to employ or dismiss an employee or change salary rate.

(c) Overtime should be authorised by someone outside the payroll department.

(d) The usual checks on deductions are required.

(e) When an employee has been absent for a significant period his entitlement to salary should be checked against personnel details.

(f) Cheques should have two signatories and should be checked against an approved payroll entry.

(g) Direct bank transfers should also be signed and checked regularly against details on personnel files.

2.4 Assessing the effectiveness of the systems

The programme of tests should ensure that the following key controls are in existence and working efficiently:

(a) Employees can be paid only for work done.
(b) Employees are paid at the correct rate.
(c) Errors cannot occur in the calculation of the payroll or the deductions from gross pay.

A suggested programme of tests of control is:

(a) Test sample of time sheets, clock cards or other records, for approval by responsible official. Pay particular attention to the approval of overtime.

(b) Test authority for payment of casual labour, particularly if in cash.

(c) Observe wages distribution for adherence to procedures ensuring employees sign for wages, that unclaimed wages are rebanked etc.

(d) Test authorisation for payroll amendments by reference to personnel records.

(e) Test control over payroll amendments.

(f) Examine evidence of checking of payroll calculations (eg, a signature of the financial controller).

(g) Examine evidence of approval of payrolls by a responsible official.

(h) Examine evidence of independent checks of payrolls (eg, by internal audit).

(i) Inspect payroll reconciliations.

(j) Examine explanations for payroll expense variances.

(k) Test authorities for payroll deductions.

(l) Test controls over unclaimed wages.

3 CASH SYSTEM

3.1 Control objectives

The control of cash is clearly of prime importance in any business. The central objectives are that:

(a) all sums are received and subsequently accounted for
(b) no payments are made which should not be made
(c) all receipts and payments are promptly and accurately recorded.

Beyond this, it is better to consider detailed controls for each area of the business dealing with cash. In reality there is not one 'cash system' in the same way as there is a sales cycle for example; there are a number of systems which have their own considerations as to control due to the specific circumstances of that part of the business.

You should also appreciate that the cash system also refers to cheque receipts and payments. Businesses should try as much as possible to conduct all their cash transactions by means of cheques or other forms of bank transfers as controls over cheque transactions are easier to establish and maintain.

Controls are set out below for various cash systems.

3.2 Controls over cash receipts by post

(a) The company should safeguard against possible interceptions between the receipt and opening of the post eg, by using a locked mail box and restricting access to the keys.

(b) The opening of the post should be supervised by a responsible official and where the volume of mail is significant, at least two persons should be present when the mail is opened.

(c) All cheques and postal orders should be restrictively crossed 'Account payee only, not negotiable' as soon as the mail is opened.

(d) A record should be made at the time of the opening of the post of:

   (i) cheques and postal orders received;
   (ii) cash received.

   This record may be in the form of a rough cash book, adding machine list or copies of remittance advices. It provides control over the eventual sums banked and entered into the cash book.

(e) The cashier and sales ledger personnel should not have access to the receipts before this record is made.

(f) Post should be date stamped. It provides evidence of when remittances are received and can periodically be checked against the date of banking. This helps to prevent cash received one day being banked as representing different receipts on a later day (a process known as 'teeming and lading').

3.3 Controls over cash collected by salesmen and travellers

(a) Authority to collect cash should be clearly defined.

(b) Salesmen and travellers should be required to remit cash and report sales at regular intervals which should be formally notified to such employees.

(c) A responsible official should quickly follow up salesmen who do not submit returns as required.

(d) Collections should be recorded when received eg, in a rough cash book or copies of receipts which should be given to the salesmen or travellers.

(e) The collector's cash receipts should be reconciled to the eventual banking.

(f) Periodically a responsible official should check the salesmen's own receipt books with cash book entries.

(g) If salesmen hold stocks of goods, an independent reconciliation of stock with sales and cash received should be made.

3.4 Controls over cash sales

(a) Cash sales should be recorded when the sale is made normally by means of a cash till or the use of cash sale invoices.

(b) If cash sale invoices are used they should be pre-numbered, a register should be maintained of cash sale invoice books and copies should be retained.

(c) Cash received should be reconciled daily with either the till roll or the invoice totals.

(d) This reconciliation should be carried out by someone independent of those receiving the cash and recording the sale.

(e) Daily banking should be checked against the till roll or invoice total and differences investigated.

(f) A responsible official should sign cancelled cash sale invoices at the time of cancellation. All such invoices should be checked periodically for sequential numbering.

3.5 Controls over banking

(a) Receipts should be banked intact daily.

(b) Each day's receipts should be recorded promptly in the cash book.

(c) Sales ledger personnel should have no access to the cash or the preparation of the paying-in slip.

(d) Periodically a comparison should be made between the split of cash and cheques

(i) received (and recorded in rough cash book);
(ii) banked (and recorded on paying-in slip).

3.6 Controls over cheque payments

(a) Unused cheques should be held in a secure place.

(b) The person who prepares cheques should have no responsibility over purchase ledger or sales ledger.

(c) Cheques should be signed only when evidence of a properly approved transaction is available. Such evidence may take the form of invoices, payroll, petty cash book etc.

(d) This check should be evidenced by signing the supporting documentation.

(e) In a large concern those approving the original document should be independent of those signing cheques.

(f) Cheque signatories should be restricted to the minimum practical number.

(g) Two signatories at least should be required except perhaps for cheques of small amounts.

(h) The signing of blank cheques and cheques in favour of the signatory should be prohibited.

(i) Cheques should be crossed before being signed.

(j) Supporting documents should be cancelled as paid to prevent their use to support further cheque payments. This cancellation could be done by the cashier before the cheque is signed (provided the cancellation identifies the cheque number) or by the cheque signatory at the time of signing the cheque.

(k) Cheques should preferably be despatched immediately. If not, they should be held in a safe place.

(l) Returned cheques may be obtained from the bank and a sample checked against cash book entries and supporting documentation.

3.7 Bank reconciliations

(a) Bank reconciliations should be prepared at least monthly.

(b) The person responsible for preparation should be independent of the receipts and payments function or, alternatively, an independent person should check the reconciliation.

(c) If the reconciliation is prepared by an independent person he should obtain bank statements directly from the bank and hold them until the reconciliation is completed.

(d) The preparation should preferably include a check of at least a sample of receipts and payments against items on the bank statement.

3.8 Controls over petty cash

(a) The level and location of cash floats should be laid down formally.

(b) There should be restricted access to the floats.

(c) Cash should be securely held eg, in a locked drawer, with restricted access to keys.

(d) All expenditure should require a voucher signed by a responsible official, not the petty cashier.

(e) The imprest system should be used to reimburse the float ie, at any time the total cash and value of vouchers not reimbursed equals a set amount.

(f) Vouchers should be produced before the cheque is signed for reimbursement.

(g) Vouchers should be cancelled once reimbursement has taken place.

(h) A maximum amount should be placed on a petty cash payment to discourage normal purchase procedures being by-passed.

(i) Periodically the petty cash should be reconciled by an independent person.

(j) Rules should exist preferably preventing the issue of IOU's or the cashing of cheques.

3.9 Assessing the effectiveness of controls

(a) **Cash receipts**

(i) Attend mail opening and ensure procedures are adhered to.
(ii) Test independent check of cash receipts to bank lodgements.
(iii) Test for evidence of a sequence check on any pre-numbered receipts for cash.
(iv) Test authorisation of cash receipts.
(v) Test for evidence of arithmetical check on cash received records.

(b) **Cash payments**

(i) Inspect current cheque books for:

- sequential use of cheques;
- controlled custody of unused cheques;
- any signatures on blank cheques.

(ii) Test (to avoid double payment) to ensure that paid invoices are marked 'paid'.

(iii) Test for evidence of arithmetical check on cash payments records, including cashbook.

(iv) Examine evidence of authority for current standing orders and direct debits.

(c) **Bank reconciliations**

(i) Examine evidence of regular bank reconciliations (usually one per month).

(ii) Examine evidence of independent check of bank reconciliations (eg, a signature).

(iii) Examine evidence of follow-up of outstanding items on bank reconciliations. Pay particular attention to old outstanding reconciling items that should be written back such as old, unpresented cheques.

(d) **Petty cash**

(i) Test petty cash vouchers for approval.
(ii) Test cancellation of paid petty cash vouchers.
(iii) Test for evidence of arithmetical check on petty cash records.
(iv) Examine evidence of independent check of petty cash balance.

4 OTHER SYSTEMS

4.1 Introduction

The type and range of other systems will depend upon the nature of the business but, as a general rule, most other systems you may encounter will be primarily concerned with the safe custody of an asset of the business. Thus there will be a system for stock in a manufacturing company and a system for fixed assets in many businesses. Some businesses may have significant investments and thus will have a system to maintain control of this type of asset.

In this section, we will consider two systems: fixed assets and stock.

4.2 Stock

(a) **Control objectives**

Although stock records may vary considerably from client to client, the control objectives of a sound system of internal control over inventories are the same in all cases, namely:

(i) Authorisation and purchase procedures.

(ii) Control over goods inwards.

(iii) Stock records substantiated by physical counts.

(iv) Control over despatches and goods outwards.

(v) Adequate steps should be taken to identify all stock for which provisions may be required.

(vi) Stock levels should be controlled so that materials are available when required but that stock is not unnecessarily large.

(b) **Control procedures over stock**

(i) **Approval and control of documents**

- Issues from stocks should be made only on properly authorised requisitions.

- Reviews of damaged, obsolete and slow moving stock should be carried out. Any write-offs should be authorised.

(ii) **Arithmetical accuracy**

- All receipts and issues should be recorded on stock cards, cross-referenced to the appropriate GRN or requisition document.

- The costing department should allocate direct and overhead costs to the value of work-in-progress according to the stage of completion reached.

- To do this standard costs are normally used. Such standards must be regularly reviewed to ensure that they relate to actual costs being incurred.

- If the value of work-in-progress is directly comparable with the number of units produced, checks should periodically be made of actual units against work-in-progress records.

(iii) **Control accounts**

- Total stock records may be maintained and integrated with the main accounting system; if so they should be reconciled to detailed stock records and discrepancies investigated.

(iv) **Comparison of assets to records**

- Stock levels should be periodically checked against the records by a person independent of the stores personnel, and material differences investigated.

- Where continuous stock records are not kept adequately a full stocktake should be held at least once a year.

- Maximum and minimum stock levels should be pre-determined and regularly reviewed for adequacy.

- Re-order quantities should be pre-determined and regularly reviewed for adequacy.

(v) **Access to assets and records**

- Separate centres should be identified at which goods are held.

- Deliveries of goods from suppliers should pass through a goods inwards section to the stores. All goods should pass through stores and hence be recorded and checked as received.

- Stocks should be held in their locations so that they are safe from damage or theft.

- All stock lines should be identified and held together eg, in bins which are marked with all relevant information as to size, grade, origin, title for identification.

- Access to the stores should be restricted.

(c) **Tests of controls**

(i) Observe physical security of stocks and environment in which they are held.

(ii) Test procedures for recording of stock movements in and out of stock.

(iii) Test authorisation for adjustments to stock records.

(iv) Test authorisation for write-off or scrapping of stocks.

(v) Test controls over recording of stock movements belonging to third parties.

(vi) Test procedures for authorisation for stock movements ie, the use made of authorised goods received and despatch notes.

(vii) Inspect reconciliations of stock counts to stock records (this gives overall comfort on the adequacy of controls over the recording of stock).

(viii) Check sequences of despatch and goods received notes for completeness.

(ix) Assess adequacy of stocktaking procedures and attend count to ensure they are carried out.

4.3 Fixed assets

(a) Control objectives

The control objectives are to ensure that:

(i) fixed assets are correctly recorded, adequately secured and properly maintained;

(ii) acquisitions and disposals of fixed assets are properly authorised;

(iii) acquisitions and disposals of fixed assets are for the most favourable price possible;

(iv) fixed assets are properly recorded, appropriately depreciated, and written down where necessary.

(b) Control procedures over fixed assets

(i) Annual capital expenditure budgets should be prepared by someone directly responsible to the board of directors.

(ii) Such budgets should, if acceptable, be agreed by the board and minuted.

(iii) Applications for authority to incur capital expenditure should be submitted to the board for approval and should contain reasons for the expenditure, estimated cost, and any fixed assets replaced.

(iv) A document should show what is to be acquired and be signed as authorised by the board or an authorised official.

(v) Capital projects made by the company itself should be separately identifiable in the company's costing records and should reflect direct costs plus relevant overhead but not include any profit.

(vi) Disposal of fixed assets should be authorised and any proceeds from sale should be related to the authority.

(vii) A register of fixed assets should be maintained for each major group of assets. The register should identify each item within that group and contain details of cost and depreciation.

(viii) A physical inspection of fixed assets should be carried out periodically and checked to the fixed asset register. Any discrepancies should be noted and investigated.

(ix) Assets should be properly maintained and adequately insured.

(x) Depreciation rates should be authorised and a written statement of policy produced.

(xi) Depreciation should be reviewed annually to assess the need for changes in the light of profits or losses on disposal, new technology etc.

(xii) The calculation of depreciation should be checked for accuracy.

(xiii) Fixed assets should be reviewed for the need for any write-down.

(c) Tests of controls

(i) Check authorisation of purchase to board minutes, capital expenditure budgets and capital expenditure form.

(ii) Check authorisation for disposals of significant assets.

(iii) Confirm existence of fixed asset register which adequately identifies assets and comments on their current condition. Ensure register reconciles to nominal ledger.

(iv) Test evidence of reconciliation of register to physical checks of existence and condition of assets.

(v) Check authorisation of depreciation rates, and particularly changes in rates.

(vi) Examine evidence of checking of correct calculations of depreciation.

4.4 Typical report on findings following review of an accounting system

REVIEW OF CONTROLS IN SYSTEMS

UPPER PLC - YEAR ENDED 31 DECEMBER 20X0

(a) **Computer processing**

Weakness:

Lack of control exercised over computer processing.

Implications:

The completeness, accuracy and validity of the accounting records may be undermined.

Recommendations:

(i) Authorisation of input especially journals not arising from books of prime entry.

(ii) Batch controls using registers over all input in terms of value and number of documents/transactions processed.

(iii) Use of hash totals.

(iv) Management control over master file amendments.

(v) Reconciliation to control accounts.

(vi) Clear audit trail for the correction and resubmission of any rejected transactions.

(vii) All financial information processed at one location.

(viii) A back-up system should be available if the bureau is unable to process the input.

(b) **Payroll**

Weakness:

No evidence of approval.

Implications:

Unauthorised changes may occur.

Recommendations:

Management should evidence their approval of the payroll, changes in rates of pay and the employment of new staff.

(c) **Stock**

Weakness:

Lack of physical and financial control over stocks.

Cut-off errors were discovered for widgets despatched prior to the year end but uninvoiced.
Overhead allocation in valuation of widgets lacked support.

Implications:

Stock could be misappropriated.
The year end stock figure could be misstated.

Recommendations:

(i) A simple system of perpetual inventory should be implemented at each location. This should be used to check for the despatch and receipt of stock and would provide good overall control to enable a comparison of:

- expected use to actual by comparison with orders; and
- book stock to actual after regular stock checks.

(ii) Improvements should be made to the system of control to facilitate a review of the despatches at the year end to ensure that a proper cut-off is achieved.

(iii) The valuation of widgets depends on the estimated throughput during the year. It is important that the number of widgets produced is properly recorded and that consideration is given to normal production levels to allow compliance with SSAP 9.

(d) **Fixed assets**

Weakness:

Lack of physical control.
Lack of clear capitalisation policy.
Assets with nil net book value were subject to a depreciation charge.

Implications:

Portable assets could be misappropriated.
Items could be incorrectly capitalised.
The depreciation figures in the accounts could be overstated.

Recommendations:

(i) A register should be introduced to record all assets at cost together with associated depreciation.

(ii) In previous years capital additions, notably the improvements to the leasehold premises, have been written off. Also, assets scrapped have not been written off. The effect of these cancel out and therefore we have not proposed an adjustment to opening figures. A capitalisation policy should be laid down and adhered to.

(iii) A register would enable the identification of fully depreciated assets and allow them to be excluded from the depreciation calculations.

(e) **Purchases payments**

Weakness:

Lack of proper allocation of costs.
Lack of supporting documents.
Lack of control over cheque books.
Unauthorised charges.
Poor control over unrecorded liabilities.

Implications:

Purchases in the accounts may be misstated.
Creditors may be understated if unrecorded liabilities are not controlled.

Recommendations:

(i) All charges incurred should be allocated to the relevant cost centre to promote accountability of these centres.

(ii) Proper supporting documents for all payments must be retained and properly filed for easy retrieval.

(iii) Control over payments would be improved if only one cheque book was in use at any one time.

(iv) Documents supporting charges should be authorised by an appropriate level of management.

(v) A purchase day book should be introduced. Payments should be marked off. This would provide control over unpaid invoices and a means for regular control account reconciliation.

Prepared by: .

Date:

5 SELF TEST QUESTIONS

5.1 What are the control objectives for the payroll? (1.2)

5.2 What are the substantive procedures to be applied on personnel records? (2.2)

5.3 What are the central control objectives for any cash system? (3.1)

5.4 What controls should exist over cash sales? (3.4)

5.5 What controls should exist over petty cash? (3.8)

5.6 What are appropriate tests of control for current cheque books? (3.9)

5.7 What are the control objectives for stock? (4.2)

5.8 What are the control objectives for fixed assets? (4.3)

Chapter 13
FRAUD MANAGEMENT

PATHFINDER INTRODUCTION

This chapter covers the following performance criteria and knowledge and understanding

- Common types of fraud (Element 10.3)
- Implications of fraud (Element 10.3)
- Methods of detecting fraud (Element 10.3)
- Existing systems for preventing fraud are evaluated and compared with examples of best practice (Element 10.3)
- Past examples of control avoidance are analysed and used to inform evaluations of the controls within the system (Element 10.3)
- Areas of potential fraud within the control avoidance accounting system are identified and the risk graded (Element 10.3)
- Areas of concern and weakness within the system are reported to management (Element 10.3)
- Possible methods of avoiding the risks and safeguarding the system are identified (Element 10.3)
- Recommendations for the prevention of fraud are made to the appropriate people. (Element 10.3)

Putting the chapter in context – learning objectives.

The management of the risk of fraud is a matter for all levels of an organisation. Senior management should strive to create an anti-fraud culture, which should permeate the entire organisation. For example, the culture will result in personnel managers considering the security elements of different posts, assessing what backgrounds are not appropriate for potential post holders. The IT department will keep up to date with the techniques of computer hackers, and the measures that can be taken against them.

An important consideration in the implementation of fraud management strategies and policies is the concept of communication. Effective lines of communication, when built in to the organisational structure, allow staff at all levels to pass on their local knowledge of procedures, processes and activities to decision-making senior staff, providing them with insights into possible areas of fraud that they would not have otherwise understood.

At the end of this chapter you should have learned the following topics.

- The types of fraud
- Implications of fraud.
- Methods of detecting and preventing fraud

1 FRAUD

1.1 What is fraud?

Definition: Fraud may be defined as: the use of deception with the intention of obtaining an advantage, avoiding an obligation or causing loss of another party

The context of this definition of fraud relates to theft, false accounting, and bribery and corruption.

- **Theft:** - dishonestly appropriating the property of another with the intention of permanently depriving them of it (Theft Act 1968)

- **False accounting**:- dishonestly destroying defacing concealing or falsifying any account, record or document required for any accounting purpose, with a view to personal gain or gain for another, or with intent to cause loss to another or furnishing information which is or may be misleading, false or deceptive (Theft Act 1968)

- **Bribery and corruption-** - offering a bribe to any public officer to influence behaviour and similarly accepting such a bribe (Prevention of Corruption Acts 1889-1916).

Fraud has not been defined in law, but is seen instead as a collection of offences, many of which are covered by the Theft Acts of 1968 and 1978. When talking of fraud, the areas of criminal activity that could be involved include the following:

- Embezzlement
- Corruption
- Conspiracy
- Theft
- Extortion
- Forgery
- Deception
- Bribery
- Misappropriation of funds
- False representation
- The concealment of material facts
- Collusion.

Conclusion Fraud is deviant behaviour that is intended to gain a dishonest advantage by reducing the net worth of the victim in circumstances where guilt can be best concealed.

2 TYPES OF FRAUD

2.1 Introduction

There is a whole portfolio of fraud available ranging from theft from petty cash through to the type reported by an officer from the serious fraud squad. He went to a house that was stunning, with furniture and ornaments worth hundreds of thousands of pounds. It turned out that the house was owned by a company that was owned by a trust which was administered by a solicitor who, coincidentally, was the solicitor for the suspect's company - and he rented the house for five pence a year.

We can cover the common types of fraud in this section but some people will always be looking for new ways to gain at someone else's expense.

2.2 Theft

There are incidences of theft that will go unnoticed because of the scale of the crime. Small amounts of cash taken from the till of a retailer or the petty cash box in an office might not be noticed because the sums involved are not significant enough to have any impact on the organisation. Many employees think nothing of taking pens and paper from the stationery cupboard to stock up their home supply. We can all laugh at the Far Side cartoon of a huge counter assistant in a doughnut shop with the owner despairing at his lack of profit.

There are thefts that are for significant amounts. The last cheques in the company's cheque book can be taken out with a razor and the thief can do a passable imitation of a couple of authorised signatures, clear the funds, withdraw and disappear. No one realises until the bank statement comes, so it may be weeks, or months before they realise they are missing a quarter of a million pounds.

Examples of other types of theft are where:

- employees can claim to have purchased supplies in excess of the actual amount;

- employees can fiddle their time sheets and claim for overtime hours they did not work or claim a higher rate for the job;

- staff make private telephone calls (to friends in Australia);

- takings are remitted at irregular intervals, and the rate that they are remitted could be kept permanently behind the rate at which they are actually received (teeming and lading). It could mean that substantial sums are available to the employee;

- expenses are deducted from takings without prior authorisation and could thus be inflated.
- there is no control on prices charged and the employee could be keeping a percentage of the takings.
- money is transferred abroad to a numbered bank account by an employee giving the computer an instruction;

2.3 False accounting

Modification of data could include the fraudulent manipulation of important accounting or other financial information or, mistakes that could cause loss of business and be costly to rectify. Fraudulent manipulation includes:

- situations where a fictitious customer can be created. Orders can be sent, goods despatched on credit and the 'customer' can neglect to pay their bill. The debt is written off.
- corruption and bribery;
- misappropriation of incoming cheques;
- the creation of fictitious supplier accounts;
- giving unauthorised discounts to customers;
- stock losses, including short deliveries by driver;
- fictitious staff on the payroll - a dummy name can be added to the payroll and the fraudster could open an account in that name and have wages paid into the account;

The owners or managers of the company could cook the books by:

- a misuse of pension funds;
- overvaluing assets;
- not writing off bad debts and avoiding the effects on profits and assets;
- understating depreciation;
- understating expenses; or
- illegally supporting their own company by purchasing shares to force up their value.

Management may occasionally wish to 'window dress' their balance sheet (ie, present either a better or worse picture than that which can be fairly presented) by a variety of devices.

- Keeping the cash book open for some days after the year end so that money received after the year end is included in the cash book balance.
- Cheques paid are entered before the year end but are not sent to creditors until after the year end. This will give an incorrect impression of the company's credit worthiness to a reader of the accounts.

The manipulation of computer systems for financial gain must result in the creation of false accounting records. This can be achieved at input by entering additional data, failing to enter valid data or by simply altering the data. Computer output can be destroyed or withheld to conceal the impact of the fraud - (to reduce liabilities or improve performance).

2.4 Activity

Can you think of three ways that stock can be used to show a false increase in the value of the assets in the company.

2.5 Activity solution

The ways of artificially inflating the value of stock include the following.

(a) Instead of being written off, obsolete or damaged stock may be shown at cost on the balance sheet.

(b) Records can be falsified at the stock count.

(c) Returns to suppliers may not be recorded or suppressed until after the year end stock count.

(d) Similarly with deliveries to customers - the reduction in stock may not be recorded or suppressed until after the year end stock count

2.6 Collusion

Definition Collusion is a common element in frauds whereby individuals pool their resources to achieve their aims - specialist skills might not be available to the individual acting independently.

Employees can collude with customers, with other employees or with friends. Some examples follow:

- The price, quantity or quality of goods sold to a customer can be manipulated to defraud the company.
- An employee could write off a debt or issue a credit note and get something in return.
- An employee could arrange for a supplier to falsify their invoice and show more goods or services than were received.
- Fictitious supply of goods or services.

Conclusion There are many types of fraud including theft, collusion and false accounting. They all amount to the victim being deprived of funds or assets or the financial position of the organisation being misrepresented.

2.7 Activity

To be in a position to combat fraud, you need to think like a fraudster. Make a list of the ways expenses can be fiddled.

2.8 Activity solution

This list could be really long, but here are a few to start you off:

- You can claim for a meal that you did not have;
- You could take someone with you on business and both stay at the hotel at the company's expense.
- You could use the free 'park and ride' service but charge for parking the car in the city centre.
- You could travel in a group and share petrol costs but claim individually for mileage allowance.
- You could claim for tips that you did not give.

3 IMPLICATIONS OF FRAUD

3.1 Fraud for different reasons

Fraudulent activity is not always for personal monetary gain. People may do it for power, prestige and status. An employee may give a friend or relative more, or better, goods that other customers would have because he or she feels obliged or feels that it is expected of them.

3.2 Computer fraud

As organisations have grown to depend more and more on systems and the data stored on them, in parallel, individuals and other organisations have become increasingly interested in gaining access to those systems and/or the data.

Individuals within the organisation can manipulate the accounts during data processing, destroy data and/or access personal or confidential data. Malicious damage can occur when disaffected employees plant a 'logic bomb' (where a specific date makes the system crash) or include a 'trap door' in their software which allows future penetration into a program. Disclosure of information could damage the company if it fell foul of the data protection legislation and caused embarrassing publicity or helped a competitor by allowing sensitive information to be accessed by outsiders or non-related employees.

There has been a growth of an underclass of highly intelligent individuals who, using their knowledge of systems in general or of particular systems with which they have been directly involved in their development and/or maintenance, have gained unauthorised access to systems for their own purposes. This form of activity is called 'hacking' and the perpetrators 'hackers'. Unauthorised access to systems by hackers can:

- provide the basis for fraudulent activity;
- cause data corruption by the introduction of a virus;
- alter or destroy files.

Conclusion Computer systems allow individuals within the organisation to behave fraudulently by manipulating the accounts during data processing, destroying data and/or accessing personal or confidential data.

3.3 Activity

Why might an employee be motivated to act against their company's interest?

3.4 Activity solution

There may be a variety of reasons, including:

- envy and resentment of the success of other employees;
- frustrations that their own high expectations of rewards or recognition have not been achieved;
- greed and selfishness (some employees consider this form of extra earning capacity as a perk);
- the intellectual challenge of beating the system or of having fun.

3.5 Targets of fraud

In systematic frauds, the precise extent of the losses may be concealed. Frauds concealed in income or expense accounts are closed to the profit and loss account. They result in reduced profit and a reduced tax liability for the victim. Because they directly affect profitability they are easily detected. Frauds concealed in assets or liability accounts are not closed to profit and loss, do not reduce profits and do not produce tax offsets for the amount defrauded. This type of fraud is more difficult to detect.

The deceptive loss-making properties of fraud can be aimed at a wide variety of possible targets including shareholders, customers, suppliers, bankers and external auditors.

Frauds against shareholders and people outside of the organisation may include:

- producing false accounts simply to conceal losses or to pull in more investment money/loans/credit where the quality of the investment does not justify it.

Frauds against employers may include:

- bribery;
- extortion (threats to poison products or destroy computer files);
- pirating copyright or patented information or commercial espionage;
- manipulation of electronic funds transfer systems or in-house data, or
- the more crude theft of goods or cheques etc.

When funds or assets are taken from the organisation, the immediate effect is that the net asset position is lower. If the fraud continues, or is more substantial than petty cash theft and modest pilfering, the long-term effects can be serious and may lead to the collapse of the organisation.

3.6 How much fraud is being committed?

It is not clear how much fraud is being committed. The rewards of successful fraud are so great that the temptations are irresistible to quite a number of people. The statistics based upon reported and prosecuted crime are unreliable. Estimates suggest that less than 15% of discovered cases are reported to the police. The failure to report crime may arise for a number of reasons:

- Not all those involved may recognise that a criminal offence has been committed.
- The employer (or victim) may not want to involve the offender in the consequences of prosecution.
- The employer may regard the offence as too trivial to justify reporting it to the police.
- The employer may be too pessimistic about the chances of gaining a successful prosecution.
- There may be embarrassment and loss of public confidence if the fraud was reported.
- The offender may have disappeared.

Even if the offence is reported and the offender is traced, a prosecution may still not happen because:

- The evidence may not be considered sufficiently convincing to justify the expense of a trial.
- The law may be unclear and consequently the risk of acquittal high.
- The offence is committed across national boundaries.
- The police may feel that a warning is sufficient.

3.7 Attitude towards fraud

In some areas of organisational life, fraud is not only tolerated, but it has become institutionalised as a perk. The problem is that fraud has either a contagious or a cumulative quality. Hence, if small offences are not dealt with, they are likely to spread and grow. Some excuses for not taking action to control fraud include the following:

- Many managers make no serious attempt to quantify the nature of the risks being run, and live in the hope that most of the employees are honest.
- Some managers are of the opinion (which may only be subjective guesswork) that bringing fraud down to negligible levels would not be cost effective.
- The management have already tried controls but they have proved to be ineffective - (it is easier to design ineffective controls).

- Some managers find the imposition and enforcement of security systems to be socially unpleasant and demoralising.

- Many managers are incompetent and believe that the auditors will detect all criminal activity.

Conclusion The impact of fraud is wide reaching with the target aimed at employers, shareholders, customers, suppliers, bankers and external auditors.

4 DETECTING FRAUD

4.1 Warning signs

Warning signs should be understood, and watched for at all times. The warning signs that fraud is a possibility, or actually taking place, are as follows:

- Staff showing signs of stress, where the workload or individual responsibility does not seem to be the blame. The presence of stress could be a function of their reaction to the seriousness of the act they are about to commit, or are actually committing.

- Late working, again where the workload does not seem to be to blame. This may be quite innocent, but it also could be due to the member of staff wishing to be alone in the office to provide the opportunity of, say, accessing documentation or assets which are not usually within their own sphere of work.

- Reluctance to take annual or other leave is not a normal trait. This could be a cover up attempt, where the staff member concerned fears being discovered when another member of staff has the opportunity to inspect their work. An innocent member of staff would not mind having their work laid open to others.

- Refusals to accept a change of post, especially promotion, may be a sign of a staff member wishing to remain in their existing post in order to continue or complete fraudulent activity.

- Fraudulent activity will normally be committed for financial gain, though there are cases where the activity is designed to damage an organisation against which a staff member has a grudge. In many occasions the staff member becomes accustomed to the increase in wealth due to their criminal activity, and display indications of an expensive lifestyle without realising it.

This presents a difficult position, as the manager must attempt to investigate what might be considered as unexplained wealth or changes in lifestyle which are not normally associated with that person's post. The fraudster may be receiving gifts from a third party in lieu of payment for their part in a fraud; therefore lifestyle change may be present in the absence of increased wealth.

There may be a perfectly good reason for additional wealth or lifestyle change, and so the manager must execute his duty fully but tactfully, to avoid unnecessary offence, embarrassment, or slander to a perfectly respectable staff member.

Although a manager should not want to offend staff, it does no harm at all for all members of staff to understand that investigations will take place should there be indications of unexpected increased wealth. This is a valid deterrent.

- New staff suddenly resign - it is the manager's responsibility to investigate the reason for the sudden resignation, and satisfy him or herself that the reason is legitimate. A member of staff who has gained employment as part of a criminal plan may leave suddenly because they feel they are in danger of being 'found out', or may simply have achieved what they joined the organisation for.

- Intimacy with suppliers and contractors - Good relationships should be cultivated, so that the best terms are obtained from suppliers, and so that contractors are as obliging as possible. However, there is a danger that, where an employee becomes friendly with a member of an outside organisation, collusion could result.

Guarding against the adverse aspects of the relationships existing between staff and outside bodies can be logically seen as not only a protection for the organisation, but also protection for the staff concerned.

- Employee morale low - this may be due to poor pay or lack of promotion possibilities but resentment towards the organisation can cause fraudulent behaviour.

4.2 Odd results

Managers often get a feeling that there is something amiss. Suspicions can be raised where:

- The demand for a certain products increases unusually.
- Turnover goes up without a similar increase in costs.
- The organisation starts under or over performing relative to the competition.
- There is increased activity in investment.

4.3 Activity

What were the signs in the Barings Bank fraud? Can you remember what Nick Leeson did?

5 FRAUD POLICY

5.1 Policy statement

An organisation may choose to communicate its chosen fraud control culture through what is known as a fraud policy statement.

The areas covered in such a policy statement could include the following:

- an allocation of responsibilities for the overall management of fraud, such that all those concerned are fully aware of their individual responsibilities, and so that accountability can be ensured;

- a manual of formal procedures to which staff must adhere if a fraud is discovered. This is required so that continuity of action results, and so that the actions of staff in such a situation are planned and well thought out, rather than ad hoc and ill-conceived

It necessarily follows that where a manual of formal procedures exists, staff must be adequately trained to identify fraud, or better still, work to prevent it. Part of the communication process would include briefing sessions and written material, designed to facilitate an awareness amongst staff that plans have been devised to respond to fraud in such a way that damage is minimised.

As part of the organisation's policy statement on fraud, there should be a section to guide staff away from finding themselves in compromising situations. Areas that could be covered might relate to the acceptance of gifts, or other rewards in kind. It is not enough for the organisation to point out these tricky positions, rather it should go further and instruct staff how to handle any conflict of interest.

5.2 Activity

Check whether your company has a fraud policy statement. There may be opportunities for improvement in the system relating to the policy.

5.3 Managing the risk

Managing the risk of fraud is no different in principle to managing the occurrence of any other kind of risk. A planned approach is required at the organisational level and the operational level, relying upon the determination and effective implementation of fraud policy statements. The steps are to:

- Identify areas that are the most likely fraud targets. This can be achieved by examining any pattern of suspected criminal loss, allowing those areas most likely to experience loss to be identified and categorised as being vulnerable to risk. This is an ideal opportunity to involve all relevant members of staff, by requesting their contribution of local knowledge to the risk identification process.

- Determine the likely scale of the risk - the scale of the risk is not what it may first appear because it will not be the total risk level, but rather the residual risk remaining after the implementation of fraud prevention policies. It is therefore not possible to accurately determined the scale of the risk, as we cannot be certain as to how successful the fraud prevention policies will be, as they depend on the human factor in their implementation.

- Allocate responsibility - as in any management operation, it is essential to identify those who are responsible for specific procedures.

- Consider what additional controls may be required to reduce the risk to the point of elimination. It will probably be impossible to totally eliminate risk, but it must still be a goal.

5.4 Creating the right conditions - an anti-fraud culture

Of all the resources in an organisation, the personnel are the only category that can commit a fraud. However, an organisation cannot exist and operate without staff members, even when heavily mechanised or computerised. Therefore it is the duty of managers and supervisors to create conditions that are hostile to fraudulent activity.

Managers and supervisors must be clear in their own minds that fraud is fraud no matter how small the amount involved, and this must be conveyed to all staff as a cultural element of the daily running of the organisation.

An important measure is to involve staff themselves in the fight against fraud. Staff can make an excellent deterrent, therefore the right conditions must be created under which: a) staff are dissuaded from committing fraudulent activities; and b) staff act to limit fraudulent activities by their colleagues.

Conclusion — It is better for an organisation to be prepared for fraud and to have a policy to cope with it. Because the employees play an important part in preventing and detecting fraud the conditions and culture that prevails will help in controlling fraudulent activities.

5.5 Activity

Someone in your organisation should be aware of the 'latest' fraud scams so that precautions taken can be as up-to-date as possible. Did you know that it is possible to park your van near a building, pick up radio waves from the air and read what is on the MD's computer screen. It is also easy to buy a machine that reads and writes the magnetic strips on credit cards. What could you do with a fax card plugged into the computer?

5.6 Activity solution

If you plug a fax card into your personal computer so that you can send faxes, you could prepare a document, scan someone else's signature in, scan in their company's letterhead, programme the little ID that a fax machine normally sends at the top of each fax and send off a completely bogus fax giving whatever instructions you want.

6 METHODS OF FRAUD PREVENTION AND DETECTION

6.1 Introduction

The detection of fraud is a difficult process and organisations may employ what are known as detective controls, that is controls to detect problems after events have occurred. It is worth restating here that fraud should be deterred as far as possible, and that it is better to prevent fraud happening in the first place than it is to detect it during or after the event. We now consider a range of control methods that are available.

6.2 Physical security

This is a basic but effective method of prevention, controlling access to physical documentation and IT systems, ensuring there is no unauthorised use, theft, or tampering. Examples of assets range from computer equipment to petty cash, but we must remember to keep up to date with criminal trends, for example appreciating that thieves often steal computer chips from desk top computers, leaving the main apparatus behind.

As a general rule, anything that is critical to the organisation's operations should be physically protected, and there may be justification in some instances to restrict the knowledge of the existence of some items.

6.3 Access

With so much critical information being held on computer, access to computerised systems must be closely policed and controlled, to ensure that all access is justified and authorised, and to further ensure that those accessing data are sufficiently trained to manipulate files without damaging or losing them inadvertently. The methods used include:

- physical safeguards to control access to computers (location, locks etc) and, where dial-in communication links are in place, a call-back facility is used;
- passwords to authorised personnel with a list of files and data within files that the user is allowed to inspect;
- data encryption where files are unintelligible unless a decoding password is used;
- hardware checks to limit update functions;
- software checks to establish control totals of updates;
- random checks on the system to ensure authorised activities;
- attempts to access unauthorised files or data prohibited by the operating system and a computer log of attempted violations kept.

Access to sensitive data should only be allowed to those who really need it and, where a password system is used, staff must be trained to use it correctly and:

- not log on in front of people who are denied access;
- log off even if only for short interruptions (natural breaks);
- not use a password that could be guessed;
- not write the password down by the side of the screen (for forgetful employees).

Note - The Data protection Act requires computer and data owners to secure information held on their systems, where this information concerns third parties.

Incidences of computer hacking have increased along with the growth of computer use in the office. Those who hack into computer systems may not necessarily want to take information, rather it may be part of their plan to corrupt the organisation's information so as to cause maximum disruption.

6.4 Activity

Lots of passwords are very basic. There are top ten password charts published in magazines. Can you guess what the most popular one are?

6.5 Activity solution

The top ones include - FRED, (because it is easy to type in), SECRET, PASSWORD, naughty words and people's names.

6.6 The application of organisation

We have expressed the need to allocate responsibilities to individuals, in the name of accountability. We can go further and state that allocation should include all necessary resources to enable these members of staff or management to meet their responsibilities. New levels of authority may have to be determined or defined, which do not equate fully to the standard organisational hierarchy.

In the case of a suspected or actual fraud, staff must be prepared to act quickly. Clear and effective communication channels must be established that will allow necessary information to be shared between different levels of the organisation, with the speed that the seriousness of a fraud situation demands.

Regarding span of control, the only way to get effective control is to ensure that those managing people and processes are not over burdened and spread too thinly. The span of control should be manageable even under pressure.

6.7 Dual control

Dual control is a method of separating duties, so as to avoid the opportunity to commit an offence, or rather an action which will be classed as offence. This is a preventative measure, however it is not fool proof, as it is not unknown for staff to collude for the purposes of committing a crime.

Certain preventative measures should take place in respect of choosing staff to be paired together. For example, staff who are in a relationship should not be paired, nor staff who cannot be relied upon to enforce the dual control mechanism.

6.8 Supervision

One of the many functions of supervision is assessing the work performance of staff. Before performance can be monitored, performance standards must be set, against which their performance can be measured. Measures and indicators of performance should concentrate on the areas of efficiency, effectiveness, economy, and service quality.

The action of measuring and monitoring performance also acts as a preventive measure and a detective measure, and such controls are essential where staff deal with cash, and the accounting for cash and other assets.

The processes and activities that are monitored should also be evaluated. The evaluation can be performed by the management of the organisation, or by an outside team. Internal evaluation is probably cheaper, and nobody knows the organisation's policies and activities better than its own people. Outside teams, however, are more objective, and bring a fresh approach to the process of evaluation.

The supervisor has to strike a balance between the value of the checking procedures and their cost. It is not necessary to check every staff member and every operation all of the time. If a method of random spot-checking is carried out, then this should be enough to dissuade staff members from committing fraudulent activity.

6.9 Audit trails

The audit trail is present to facilitate detection, but again its existence will act as a deterrent against fraud and so has a preventative element. The inclusion of the word 'trail' is very appropriate, as an audit trail allows the tracing of all transactions through a system from start to finish.

An additional benefit arising from the use of the audit trail is that it clarifies all of the stages through which a transaction passes, thus allowing analysis of these stages to determine, through a review process, the best way to maintain security at each stage

6.10 Budgetary and other financial controls

Expenditure must be approved and properly accounted for at all times, and this can be facilitated by the use of budgetary controls, and delegated limits and controls, in respect of certain categories of expenditure. This will make fraud more difficult, and will show up some types of fraud.

The most simple of frauds can be seen where members of staff falsely claim for reimbursement from a petty cash system. The low value of these transactions, in the minds of some, re- clarifies the false claim as a perk or acceptable dodge.

Conclusion

It is a manager's duty to successfully defend his or her organisation against the threat of fraudulent activity. This requires careful planning, and the creation of an anti-fraud environment.

Action should be planned, timely and thorough, impacting on any level or member of staff as appropriate, minimising loss of assets and reputation, whilst actively deterring future fraudulent activity.

7 OPERATIONAL RISK MANAGEMENT - A CHECKLIST

7.1 Activity

In your report you can use what follows as a checklist for effective operational risk management, using this to help you assess how successfully your organisation is countering risk.

7.2 The controls checklist

Cash handling controls:

- cash should be kept in a secure place at all times;
- cash balances should be kept at minimum levels, i.e. the minimum in respect of daily operational needs;
- cash is vulnerable when it is paid in on the premises, right up until the time it is banked. The issue of numbered receipts will allow tracking to take place, and all cash should be duly signed for and recorded. Cash should be banked as soon as possible;
- all accounting records and petty cash should be reconciled regularly. The reconciliation details should be kept and filed, with details of who performed the reconciliation. Any discrepancy that cannot be resolved, and losses that are uncovered, should be reported via a formal reporting system;
- all key holders should be properly vetted to ensure they are suitable staff members to be trusted.

The post desk - managers must control the opening of post if there is a likelihood of cash being sent via this method. Controls could include having the recipient's signature or dual control may be required.

The Bankers Automated Clearing System (BACS) is used to make cleared payments, for example when salaries are paid from companies to their employees bank accounts. It is essential to control those who can make changes or additions to the details, and all data should be independently checked and authorised. Dual control may be advisable.

Invoice-based control - a fraudster can generate a false payment by falsifying or duplicating an invoice. There should be role segregation, such that the process of ordering is kept separate from the process of paying invoices. Even so, checks for duplicate invoices should be regularly carried out. Invoices should be checked to ensure they are in fact bona fide invoices.

Cheque handling controls:

- Cheque books received must be recorded by serial number, and locked away securely until required. To provide legal protection and guard against fraudulent activity, such as interception of the post, cheques should be crossed 'not negotiable'.

- Before cheques and payable orders are issued, reference must be made to source documentation to ensure that the payment is accurate in terms of amount and recipient.

- Care should be taken when completing cheques. Use a pen so that words and figures cannot be changed or removed. Where there are blank spaces on the check, a single line should be drawn across to denote that there are no further amounts to be included.

- Make sure that the cheques is sent to the correct address, consider using recorded mail to track its progress, and reconcile the recorded amount of the cheque with the amount appearing on the company bank statement to ensure that the correct amount has been taken.

Payroll controls:

- Whenever the payroll system is updated, the entries must be properly authorised and validated. Only authorised personnel should be able to amend data on the payroll system, and then the additional safeguard of dual control may be prudent.

- Claims should be carefully policed to ensure false claims for subsistence, travel and other allowances are properly submitted in writing, checked for supporting documentation, and subject to a proper authorisation procedure that limits claims to only those necessary.

Purchasing systems controls:

- Any system that allows for the payment of goods should be arranged such that those who authorised the payment are separate from those receiving the item. Authorisation levels and frequency of checks, including spot checks, would be a function of the degree of risk prevailing and the amounts involved.

- It is possible to counteract spurious purchases by using sequentially numbered purchase order forms, making it easy to detect if one of the forms had been removed from the pad.

- All invoices for payment must be properly authorised, and matched to orders to ensure payment is actually due.

- Effective stock control should allow stock records to be kept up to date, so that orders and stock usage can be monitored to confirm correct usage. There needs to be a separation of duties between those ordering, receiving, approving, and paying for goods and services, to reduce the opportunity of one person obtaining goods fraudulently for their own use.

- In the supplier records there will be standing data, for example details of trade discounts awarded, or term periods which must be adhered to in respect of receiving cash discounts. This can amount to a significant sum, so it is necessary to allow only authorised access.

Controls over contractors:

- Formalised procedures that are clear and unambiguous must be set out in respect of tendering, and these procedures must be monitored closely to ensure they are being followed.

- Tenders must be delivered to those who are authorised for selection without any interference or barrier of any kind. Frequently tenders are opened in locked rooms, and there may only the in attendance the authorised sector of the tender and a secretary to type up appropriate replies.

- Deadlines relating to tenders must be strictly adhered to. Late tenders should not be accepted because there is an employee might see the details of tenders received, and then pass these to a potential contractor.

- Suppliers should only be selected from an approved suppliers' list. This list must be regularly updated, and additions must only take place if properly validated and authorised.

- The firm should maintain a register of contracts in progress, and further contracts should only be added when properly approved and authorised.

- Sometimes it is necessary to vary contracts and, where this happens, there should be a sequentially numbered variation raised, and the variations documented. Checks should be made against budget and planned expenditure before approval for payment is given.

Control of assets:

- an asset register should be maintained and kept up to date.

- there should be an adequate description of all assets on the asset register, and even a photograph if the asset is difficult to describe.

- Assets should be security marked where possible with, for example, the name of the organisation and the department where the asset is kept.

- There should be spot checks to confirm the continuing existence of assets.

8 FRAUD RESPONSE

8.1 The plan

If there were to be a fire you would expect managers to know how to respond. In the same way, a manager must know how to respond to fraudulent activity and draw up a fraud response plan. The plan will cover the following:

- Required evidence;

- To whom an actual or potential fraud should be reported;

- Who should not be informed, so as to avoid tipping off a fraudster;

- Methods for investigating fraudulent activity;

- Which members of staff should be involved in the investigation;

- Required action to ensure a planned fraud does not have the chance to come to fruition while the investigation takes place;

- At what point the police should be informed;

- What lessons can be learned from the experience, and what steps should be taken in the light of this experience with respect to the implications for the entire organisation.

8.2 Note

You should note that - if you complete a cheque in such a way that a fraud is committed, which cannot be detected by a banker examining the face of the cheque, then you are liable for the amount of the fraud. It would then be up to you to face the very difficult task of trying to track down the fraudster to obtain legal redress

9 SELF TEST QUESTIONS

9.1 What is 'teeming and lading'? (2.2).

9.2 Explain the term 'window dressing' (2.3).

9.3 Give an example of collusion (2.6).

9.4 What can hackers do? (3.2)

9.5 Outline one or two reasons why fraud is not reported to the police (3.6).

9.6 Describe a situation at work that might be a warning sign that fraud is taking place (4.1).

9.7 What areas would be covered in a fraud policy statement? (5.1).

9.8 What sort of access controls should be used on the computer system? (6.3).

9.9 List some cheque handling controls (7.2).

◈ FOULKS*lynch* **AAT**

FOULKS LYNCH
4 The Griffin Centre
Staines Road
Feltham
Middlesex, TW14 0Hs
United Kingdom

HOTLINES: Telephone: +44 (0) 20 8831 9990
Fax: +44 (0) 20 8831 9991
E-mail: info@foulkslynch.com

For information and online ordering, please visit our website at:
WWW. Foulkslynch.com

PRODUCT RANGE

Our publications cover all assessments for the AAT both current standards and revised of competence to be assessed from December 2000.

Our CIMA product range consists of:

Textbooks	£9.95	Workbooks	£9.95
Combined Textbooks/Workbooks	£9.95	Lynchpin	£5.95

OTHER PUBLICATIONS FROM FOULKS LYNCH

We publish a wide range of study material in the accountancy field and specialize in texts for the following professional qualifications:

- **Chartered Institute of Management Accountants (CIMA)**
- **Association of Accounting Technicians (AAT)**
- **Certified Accounting Technicians (CAT)**

FOR FURTHER INFORMATION ON OUR PUBLICATIONS:

I would like information on publications for: ACCA ❑ AAT ❑ CAT ❑ CIMA ❑

Please keep me updated on new publications: ❑ By E-mail ❑ By Post ❑

Your Name…………………………………….. Your email address……………………………
Your address:…………………………………………….
…………………………………………………………
…………………………………………………………
…………………………………………………………

Prices are correct at time of going to press and are subject to change